A GUIDE TO ONTARIO SCHOOL LAW

Benjamin Kutsyuruba, David Burgess,
Keith Walker, & J. Kent Donlevy

Turning Point Global
Kingston • Saskatoon • Calgary, Canada
Wellington, New Zealand

Turning Point
GLOBAL

First Paperback Edition (Revised) – December 2013

Cover Photos — iStockphoto

Table of Contents

Acknowledgements

There have been numerous guides to school legislation published throughout Canada over the years. We were first inspired by the mid-1990s work of British Columbia's Alan Nicholls, with the British Columbia School Trustees Association. Judith A. Clark has continued to update and revise editions in an extremely able fashion. We felt that other provinces needed similar guides. In conversation, Judith saw no reason that would prevent us from using many of the same format ideas that their publisher, EDUSERV in B.C. had used. Our desire was to provide a non-partisan, fair-reading of provincial educational statutes and regulations that will be a first-aid and reference to the lay reader. To date, members of our team have been involved in developing several editions of a *Guide to Saskatchewan School Law* and a *Guide to Alberta School Law*. This Guide details the educational statutes, regulations, and relevant educational policies in the province of Ontario. It has been developed with teacher candidates in mind, aiming to enhance their understanding of key aspects of Ontario's school legislation and policy and, ultimately, to assist them in transition from teacher education programs into teaching careers.

Second, we wish to acknowledge the work of many individuals and organizations who kindly vetted the first edition of this document. We would like to give particular thanks for invaluable feedback to our reviewers: Michael Schmitt (Catholic Principals' Council of Ontario), Alan Wilkinson (Faculty of Education, Queen's University), and James Murray (St. Martha Catholic School, Kingston, Ontario). We are grateful for the ongoing encouragement from undergraduate and graduate students, educators, central and school-based administrators, provincial policy makers, members of professional associations, parents, and others who have told us that they would find this Guide useful. These kind comments and expressions of support have motivated us to develop the first edition of the Ontario Guide.

Third, education in Ontario is based on a collaborative effort of many congenial and sensible partnerships. It was important for us to have the educational policy and law community of Ontario make comments they might wish to suggest before the first edition of this document was finally published. With their feedback incorporated into this edition, we continue to encourage further input from various educational partners and individuals for subsequent editions of these guidelines.

Fourth, we wish to acknowledge the kind support a number of individuals in the Faculty of Education at Queen's University. We would like to thank Dr. Steve Elliott (Dean of Education), Dr. Rebecca Luce-Kapler (Associate Dean of Graduate Studies and Research), and Dr. Peter Chin (Associate Dean of Undergraduate Studies) for providing advice and funding through the TEACH grant for this project. The support of Dr. John Freeman (Director of Social Program Evaluation Group (SPEG)) and Dr. Rosa Bruno-

Jofre (former Dean of Education) and encouragement of Dr. Nancy Hutchinson (Professor of Education) and Dr. Ruth Rees (Professor Emerita) are gratefully acknowledged. We wish to thank graduate and undergraduate student assistants for their work at various stages of this project, specifically Shireen VanBuskirk, Christina Kwiczala, Alicia Hussain, Anita Gopal, and Corina Starbuck.

Finally, we wish to acknowledge the ongoing support and encouragement of our families.

Benjamin, David, Keith, and Kent

Fall 2013

Preface

There are a number of Statutes (Acts), Regulations and Orders that directly relate to the provision and delivery of educational services in Ontario. These legal documents outline how "schooling" is to be governed and operated in the province and elaborate on a variety of salient and mundane topics. Sometimes we have found these documents difficult to access and insufficiently consolidated for practical use.

It is our goal to provide an accessible, user-friendly guide to these legal parameters for teachers, aspiring teachers, trustees, school administrators, central office administration, parents and interested community members.

Obviously, this is not a legal text but rather a non-legal interpretation of the *Education Act* and of a variety of other legal texts for the general informational use of laypersons.

WHEN A PARTICULAR LEGAL OPINION IS SOUGHT, A LAWYER OUGHT TO BE CONSULTED.

It is also important to note that the information and content found in this and other guides to school law is subject to change. The 14 Parts of this guide are provided as a starting place for questions and curiosities that parents, trustees, new and veteran teachers, school administrators, school support staff, district school board personnel, and others may have about the formal elements of school law in Ontario.

In this guide, we have placed the content of Ontario school legislation and policy under the following themes and headings:

Introduction: *Why Law Matters—or Should Matter—to Educators.* This part introduces the readers to the need for understanding the importance of legal and policy matters by educators.

PART 1.0: *The Student and the School.* This part provides the reader with general interpretation of legislation with respect to students and schools. This section covers the topics of school attendance, operation of schools, and provision of education. Of course, students are the core participants in schooling so the subsequent sections of the Guide will elaborate on people, structures and systems that surround the students in the delivery of learning services.

PART 2.0: *Parents and the Community.* This part provides an overview of the rights and obligations of parents, and the opportunities for community involvement in the educational affairs of individual schools and of school districts.

PART 3.0: *The School Teacher.* This part deals with topics such as teacher qualification and certification, professional status of teachers, teacher hiring, contracts, and conditions of employment will be briefly described. The guide also outlines the duties and responsibilities of teachers, professional and ethical codes of conduct, professional misconduct, and disciplinary actions against teachers. The section concludes with the discussion of a teacher's role in copyright protection and use of technology in classrooms. Attention is also given to the role and duties of teachers' assistants.

PART 4.0: *The School Principal.* This part of the Guide reviews the qualifications and appointment of principals, their employment status, duties and functions and describes the roles and functions of vice-principals and assistant principals.

PART 5.0: *Collective Bargaining.* Provincial collective bargaining, local collective bargaining, and the settlement of disputes are briefly described in this part of the Guide.

PART 6.0: *Ontario's Provincial School System.* This part presents background information on the major components of the public school system. (The roles and contributions of these components to school activities are dealt with in Part 1.0 of this Guide).

PART 7.0: *School Districts, Boards, and Authorities.* This part of the Guide deals with school districts, school boards, and school authorities and how they are established.

PART 8.0: *Administration and District School Boards.* This part outlines duties and responsibilities of key roles within Boards of Education as they govern school districts and the schools in these districts.

PART 9.0: *The Basics of School District Budgets.* This part of the Guide provides an overview of how education is financed in the Province of Ontario by giving a brief description of annual operating budgets, revenues and expenditures, capital budgets, and auditing and reporting to the Minister.

PART 10.0: *Francophone Education in Ontario.* This part of the Guide provides information regarding the history of French Language Education, the structure of Francophone education in Ontario, French instruction within English - Language schools, and describes the current state of Ontario's Francophone system of education.

PART 11.0: *Aboriginal (First Nations, Métis, Inuit) Education in Ontario.* This part describes key documents, trends and organizational patterns for provision of educational services to First Nations, Métis, and Inuit persons in Ontario.

PART 12.0: *Private Schools.* This part provides an overview of the provisions for the registration, types, funding, staffing, administration, and inspection of private schools in Ontario.

PART 13.0: *Home Schooling.* This part details home schooling provision, registration obligations, parental rights and responsibilities, school boards' responsibilities, and monitoring authority in Ontario.

PART 14.0: *Student Safety, Health, and Welfare*. This part presents an overview of the topics on student safety, positive and accepting school climate, student health and wellbeing, and protection of students against negligence and abuse.

Further Caveats

The practice of education in Ontario is a dynamic phenomenon. Sometimes changes occur in practice before the formal legal, policy, or professional structures are adjusted. The reverse also occurs. In a more general sense, the law is constantly evolving. This is most evident when one encounters the sections of the *Education Act* where certain text has been repealed or replaced. Of course this requires periodic updating of a Guide such as this and some diligence on the part of reader to appreciate the evergreen nature of education laws, regulations, and policies.

Between the time website information is gathered and then published, some sites may have closed. In addition, the transcription of URLs can sometimes result in typographical errors. We would appreciate notification where these occur so that they may be corrected in subsequent editions.

Also, we would like to comment on the use of the cover images in this Guide. Although we are fully aware that the iconic gavel does not figure into Canadian court use, we have none-the-less chosen the scales of justice and gavel because these symbols are deeply associated in our minds with justice, decision making, and order.

When citing this book…

do so as follows:

Kutsyuruba, B., Burgess, D., Walker, K., & Donlevy, J. K. (2013). *A guide to Ontario school law*. Kingston, ON: Turning Point Global.

How to use this book

This guide book has been designed to provide access to the legal aspects of education in Ontario. For this reason, particular attention has been paid to the layout of the text. The diagram below highlights the key features of the page design.

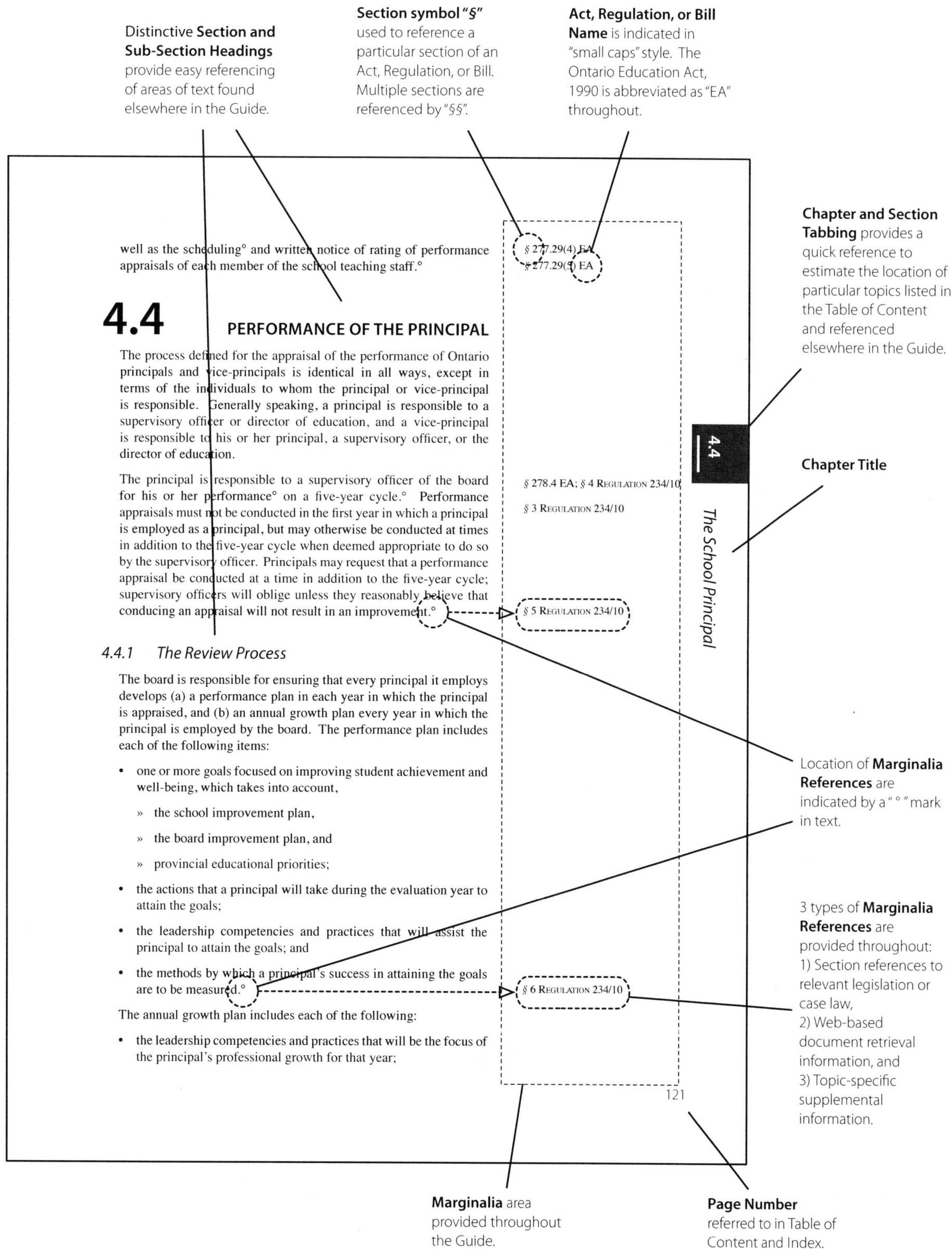

Distinctive **Section and Sub-Section Headings** provide easy referencing of areas of text found elsewhere in the Guide.
Section symbol "§" used to reference a particular section of an Act, Regulation, or Bill. Multiple sections are referenced by "§§".
Act, Regulation, or Bill Name is indicated in "small caps" style. The Ontario Education Act, 1990 is abbreviated as "EA" throughout.
Chapter and Section Tabbing provides a quick reference to estimate the location of particular topics listed in the Table of Content and referenced elsewhere in the Guide.
Chapter Title
Location of **Marginalia References** are indicated by a "°" mark in text.
3 types of **Marginalia References** are provided throughout: 1) Section references to relevant legislation or case law, 2) Web-based document retrieval information, and 3) Topic-specific supplemental information.
Marginalia area provided throughout the Guide.
Page Number referred to in Table of Content and Index.
well as the scheduling° and written notice of rating of performance appraisals of each member of the school teaching staff.°
§ 277.29(4) EA
§ 277.29(5) EA
4.4 PERFORMANCE OF THE PRINCIPAL
The process defined for the appraisal of the performance of Ontario principals and vice-principals is identical in all ways, except in terms of the individuals to whom the principal or vice-principal is responsible. Generally speaking, a principal is responsible to a supervisory officer or director of education, and a vice-principal is responsible to his or her principal, a supervisory officer, or the director of education.
The principal is responsible to a supervisory officer of the board for his or her performance° on a five-year cycle.° Performance appraisals must not be conducted in the first year in which a principal is employed as a principal, but may otherwise be conducted at times in addition to the five-year cycle when deemed appropriate to do so by the supervisory officer. Principals may request that a performance appraisal be conducted at a time in addition to the five-year cycle; supervisory officers will oblige unless they reasonably believe that conducing an appraisal will not result in an improvement.°
§ 278.4 EA; § 4 Regulation 234/10
§ 3 Regulation 234/10
§ 5 Regulation 234/10
4.4.1 The Review Process
The board is responsible for ensuring that every principal it employs develops (a) a performance plan in each year in which the principal is appraised, and (b) an annual growth plan every year in which the principal is employed by the board. The performance plan includes each of the following items:
• one or more goals focused on improving student achievement and well-being, which takes into account,
» the school improvement plan,
» the board improvement plan, and
» provincial educational priorities;
• the actions that a principal will take during the evaluation year to attain the goals;
• the leadership competencies and practices that will assist the principal to attain the goals; and
• the methods by which a principal's success in attaining the goals are to be measured.°
§ 6 Regulation 234/10
The annual growth plan includes each of the following:
• the leadership competencies and practices that will be the focus of the principal's professional growth for that year;
4.4
The School Principal
121

A GUIDE TO ONTARIO SCHOOL LAW

INTRODUCTION

Why Law Matters—or Ought to Matter—to Educators

Almost everything we do has a set of rules. There are rules for games, for sports, for the workplace, and for the society that tell us what we should and should not do. The law is often understood by the laity as a complex system of rules that a particular authority (country, jurisdiction, or community) recognizes as having the binding force to regulate, control, and change the actions of its members and may be enforced by various institutions through the imposition of penalties. Each of these rules, it could be argued, is connected with a particular consequence when broken. The police have the duty to investigate when a claim is made that a rule has been broken, and in the course of an investigation may need to question and even detain certain citizens whom they strongly believe to be involved in the wrongdoing. If detained, a citizen may consult a lawyer who is knowledgeable in the details of law and acts as that individual's advocate. The accused citizen may appear before a judge, who will consider the evidence and arguments provided on behalf of the police and those provided on behalf of the citizen. If the citizen is found to have broken the law, a consequence—which may be a fine, community service, or time in jail—is meted out.

And yet, the lay observer may remark, sometimes citizens, groups, companies, and other organizations may seek a judge's decision on a particular disagreement. Here, it would seem, the police need not be involved, but lawyers are; and the consequences do not seem to lead to jail. However, rules remain in law for these disputes, despite the myriad possible circumstances that might bring a disagreement into a courtroom.

While all of the above may be roughly true, like all other sectors of society—including education—there is often more to the story than the general impression held by the public. Just as teachers would argue that their fellow citizens do not fully grasp the details of teaching and school-life from their participation within schools as students, those involved in the justice system would suggest that years of observing crime-dramas on television offers an inadequate depiction of the legal system. For teachers, often the more a parent understands the education system, the teacher's aims and goals, and supportive techniques for school-based interactions, the better the ultimate result for the student and, by extension, society. Similarly, the more citizens understand their obligations under the law, the nature of the justice system, and supportive techniques for justice-based interactions, the better, it could be argued, the ultimate result for society. These analogues alone might provide a modest rationale for increased understanding of social-support endeavours like education and justice. But there are in fact more substantive reasons why educators, in particular, ought to develop their understandings of the law and the legal system. To do so, it is helpful to understand a singular and fundamental fact about modern education: the education system, its structures, operations, interactions, and finance are all governed by a complex and extensive collection of laws.

That most people do not appreciate this fact, is at least partially due to the bulwark of teachers, administrators, and other school officials who are often afforded professional latitude to deal with some matters as they see fit. But the professional latitude engaged by teachers, administration, and school officials is authorized in law and can carry the force of law—and its use is, ultimately, a legal act. At times, teachers and administrators can be unaware of the details underlying these legal powers as they are more commonly understood to simply be the *practice* of a teacher or principal. With all legal powers, however, come legal responsibilities; it seems rightly the work of a professional to understand the nature of the responsibilities they hold, and the consequences they too may suffer if neglected, inaccurately employed, or over-extended. Indeed, this is but one of the burdens entrusted to a teacher.

Defining the Law

The law is often difficult for the novice to contemplate given its technical vocabulary, assumed familiarity with traditional and historical practice, and anachronistic use of Latin terms and phrases. Before more deeply contemplating the law as it applies to education (and even daily life, for that matter), it seems prudent to offer a brief overview of legal vocabulary assumed by this *Guide to Ontario School Law*. Though the specifics and details may be unknown, many commonplace words will be familiar: lawyer, judge, police officer, court, offence, and incarceration. Unless we intend to discuss a specific use that might be uncommon, we will assume the definition generally known will suffice. Other words, however, one has heard but may struggle to pin down sufficiently for an educated discussion for the purposes embedded in this Guide. Consider statute, torts, the common law, and quasi-judicial body. Below, we endeavour to briefly explore these and other terms, in the context of their use within the Canadian legal system.

The law is a system, not a thing. In Canada and most current and former British Commonwealth countries (including England, Australia, New Zealand, and even the United States), it is a collection of interrelated ideas offering statements of how individuals and groups ought or must behave, many of which are written down—others of which are not. Most written-law is written by politicians whom we have elected to the House of Commons in Ottawa, or the Provincial Legislature at Queen's Park in Toronto. This type of law is known as *statute* and reads like a collection of rules. When you encounter documents referred to as *legislation*, *an Act*, or *acts*, these are all statutory law.

Some statutes are more important than others. In Canada, the most important of these are a collection of statutes and conventions collectively known as *the constitution*. They include the *Constitution Act*, 1867 (UK; which was formerly known as the *British North America Act*, 1867 [UK]), the *Constitution Act*, 1982 (being Schedule B of the *Canada Act*, 1982 [UK] and of which Part 1 is more commonly known as the *Charter of Rights and Freedoms*, or simply the *Charter*), and other conventions and documents not discussed in this Guide that include statutes of the Imperial Parliament at Westminster (a city within greater London) that pre-date Canada's confederation in 1867.° No law in Canada may be contrary to the constitution—and the *Constitution Act*, 1867 defines the type of law that may be created (or *enacted*) in statutes by the federal parliament in Ottawa for all of Canada, and which may be enacted in statutes by the legislatures of the provinces in their respective capitals.° With only one or two exceptions, laws governing education are only to be found in provincial statute,° but some statutes governing the actions of all individuals (whether involved at the time in the education system of a province or not) still apply. *Criminal law*, only to be found in federal statute,° provides an example. The most important statute in Ontario that deals with education is the *Education Act*—but there are others.

Hogg, P. (2007). *Constitutional Law of Canada*. Toronto, ON: Thomson Carswell.

§§ 91-95 CONSTITUTION ACT, 1867

§ 93 CONSTITUTION ACT, 1867

§ 91 CONSTITUTION ACT, 1867

Some documents elevated to law by statutes are known as *regulations*. These often outline technical details that more clearly define particular actions or processes to be followed as a consequence of a statement made in a statute. As an example, in Ontario, *Regulation 298* offers clarifications to the *Education Act* on the general operation of schools. Regulations are in place at both federal and provincial levels.

The historically unwritten type of law mentioned above is ancient in origin, and has evolved over at least the last eight centuries. Originally, society was governed by particular obligations one held to others in the community. Precisely as one might expect, many of these obligations were foundational to peaceful and prosperous community-life—e.g., one ought not to steal or trespass upon another's property; at a certain age, a man is entitled to his inheritance and may also consent to participate in a contract. The problem was that each community had its own customs for dealing with those who behaved contrary to these common obligations. That is, until the unifying reign of Henry II of England (r. 1154 – 1189 CE) who sought to ensure a consistent and effective implementation of these obligations as *common laws* to all in the realm. Over time, many common laws have been codified in criminal and other statutory law, but the sense of unwritten and customary *common law obligations* that one individual owes to another has not disappeared in both the legal system and discussions of it. We now refer to many of these obligations, written or otherwise, as *tort* law. Seeking a remedy in court by way of tort law—for a breach of an obligation by one citizen against another that results in a damage to an injured party—is called a *civil action*. Only the provinces may make laws in civil matters.

Criminal law is law written within the *Criminal Code of Canada*. Statutes may define particular offences that, while not criminal, are punishable through fines to the wrongdoer. In Canada, one does not normally attract a sentence in prison or in a provincial correction centre unless there is a breach of the *Criminal Code*. Hence, statuary breaches, such as speeding offences, are normally addressed through fines. The same is the case of breaches of the *Education Act*. While the remedy on a successful common law tort is left to the plaintiff to enforce, criminal and regulatory offences are enforceable by the police.

In Canada, despite the division of statutory law into federal or provincial jurisdictions, each of the RCMP, provincial, and local police services enforce all statutory laws. Along with provincial statutes, provincial courts adjudicate matters of federal criminal law.

Underlying Theories of Law

More theoretically speaking than is provided in the lay description at the outset of this chapter, the law may further be defined in many different ways. One theory sees the law as a system of rules that enforces agreements between the parties and, among other things, prohibits actions deemed to be contrary to the interests of the state. In such a system, rules are determined to be valid if they have the required legislative pedigree and where, in some cases, the interpretation of the legislated laws is subject to the broad discretion of judges who may include in their interpretations the consideration of government policy and the common values held by the people.°

Hart, HLA. (1961). *The concept of law*. Oxford, UK: Oxford University.

A second theory accepts the above system in part, but suggests that where the rules appear to be silent or unreasonable, a judge has the duty to interpret the words of the rules according to unwritten legal principles that already exist expressly within the body of law—or further principles that may reasonably be deduced from these unwritten principles. In accord with this second system, the judge's work is considered to be an exercise of *weak* discretion. Here the judge's discretion is weak because the judge may only refer to the law as it stands in context and may not decide on another basis—such as public policy, which is properly a legislative function.°

Dworkin, R. (1998). *Law's empire*. Oxford, UK: Hart.

A third view accepts that the law is indeed comprised of rules created by legislatures but that the validity of such rules is to be judged not by their legal pedigree as in the first theory, nor by—at least in the instance of hard cases—express or implied legal principles, but by their consonance with divine law as in the philosophy of Thomas Aquinas° or a select desiderata,° or by being in accord with specific criteria that define law as an efficacious project.°

Finnis, J. (2005). Aquinas' Moral, Political, and legal philosophy. *Stanford Encyclopedia of Philosophy.*;
Fuller, LL. (1964). *The morality of law*. New Haven, CT: Yale University.

Finnis, J. (2007). Natural law theories. *Stanford Encyclopedia of Philosophy*.

There are other theories of law, but whichever view of the law one takes it is clear that it provides the framework for those who work within the institution of education. School board trustees, superintendents, principals, and teachers all derive their authority from provincial statute. During their term of office or careers their actions will be judged not only by students, parents, electors, governmental officials, and their professional organizations, but also—when litigation arises—by the courts. In Canada, as it is undoubtedly the case in other jurisdictions, there seems to be a need for at least some more broadly offered legal instruction.

Law and Policy

Everyday activities of teaching and learning in schools are greatly affected by various policies. The term policy is usually defined as a general guideline that shapes decisions or actions; or a general approach to things, intended to guide behaviour.° Some people think of policies as an overall plan of authoritative statements (rules) that provide guidance or structure for a group to achieve its goals or objectives. These rules apply to individuals within a group, although different groups may have different rules (i.e., different school boards may have different policies for induction of new teachers. This is no different that different insurance companies having different regulations for their clients).

Young, J., Levin, B., & Wallin, D. (2007). *Understanding Canadian schools: An introduction to educational administration* (4th ed.). Toronto, ON: Nelson-Thomson.

The term policy denotes a complex, multi-layered phenomenon; therefore, there are different ways to understand and describe policy and related concepts. These disagreements arise from philosophical conflicts over the nature of society, the meaning of power, and the proper role of government. Therefore, there are probably as many definitions of policy as people who engage in policy analysis. An overview of policy literature produced a number of definitions that describe policy as:

- courses of purposive action directed towards accomplishment of some intended or desired set of goals;
- a vision of where we want to go and guidelines for getting there;
- principles that govern action directed towards given ends;
- a matter of authoritative allocation of values - policy projects images of an ideal society;
- a historical or contemporary statement or series of statements which describe, prescribe and/or proscribe a course of action. These statements are usually written, but they could be oral. They may or may not imply contractual legal obligations. Additionally,

Delaney, JG. (2002). *Educational policy studies: A practical approach*. Calgary, AB: Detselig.; Downey, LW. (1988). *Policy analysis in education*. Calgary, AB: Detselig.; Fowler, F. (2009). *Policy studies for educational leaders: An introduction* (3rd ed.). Boston: Allyn and Bacon.; Giles, T. E., & Proudfoot, A. J. (1990). *Educational administration in Canada* (4th ed.). Calgary, AB: Detselig.; Howlett, M., Ramesh, M. & Perl, A. (2009). *Studying public policy: Policy cycles and policy subsystems* (3rd ed.). Don Mills, ON: Oxford University Press.; Young, J., Levin, B., & Wallin, D. (2007). *Understanding Canadian schools: An introduction to educational administration* (4th ed.). Toronto, ON: Nelson-Thomson.

a policy may he developed at different organizational levels and may be binding for only that level or for other levels as well;

- what governments choose to do or not do;
- a course of action or inaction chosen by public authorities to address a given problem or interrelated set of problems;
- any authoritative communication about how individuals in certain positions should behave under specified conditions;
- a set of interrelated decisions taken by a political actor or group of actors concerning the selection of goals and the means of achieving them within a specified situation where those decisions should, in principle, be within the power of those actors to achieve;
- a set of values expressed in words, issued with authority, and reinforced with power (often money or penalties) in order to induce a shift toward those values; etc.°

(Delaney, 2002)

Policy definitions have several common elements to them; they all agree that policy is a formalized act; has pre-agreed objective; approved and sanctioned by a government, community, institutional body or authority; and, provides some kind of standard for measuring performance.°

Policy differs from rules or law. As Fowler (2009) noted, when people use the term law, they actually mean statutes - laws enacted by legislatures. In order to determine what the policy really is, one of the first sources to consult is written law. The difference between the law and policy is this: while law can compel or prohibit behaviors (e.g. a law requiring the payment of taxes on income), policy merely guides actions toward those behaviours that are most likely to achieve a desired outcome. Many outdated laws may still be "on the books," but never enforced; some laws are purely symbolic and were passed to help citizens feel better about a problem but were never really intended to address it. Moreover, not every policy appears in statutes (law). Policies serve as general guidelines, and the specifics of policy, sometimes referred to as the "nuts and bolts" of the policy are covered in regulations. Most statutes are worded in general terms, and many of the details needed to put them into practice are not written in the statute itself. These details are usually provided by rules and regulations that government agencies develop. As with statutes, these rules, and regulations provide clues as to what the policy really is.

A policy decision in education is one that has broad implications within a particular setting, be it a country, province, or school. Policies shape the structure of schools, the resources available in schools, the curriculum, the teaching staff, and the round of daily activities. Policies also determine how much money is spent, by whom and on what, how teachers are paid, how students are evaluated, and most other aspects of school as we know then. In other words, policies outline what is taught, who can teach, how students are treated, how teaching occurs, how schools operate, and where teaching occurs.° Some examples of important education policy areas that are presented in this Guide are equity and inclusive education policy, language policy, Aboriginal education policy, safe schools policy, etc.

(Young, Levin, & Wallin, 2007)

Current Research on Teacher Knowledge of Law

A Canadian study by Peters and Montgomerie found that in some provinces, educators

> revealed an extremely high level of uncertainty, already referred to as self-confessed ignorance, concerning rights in educational matters based in the *Charter* and found in the provincial statutes. (p. 45 °)

Peters, F., & Montgomerie, C. (1998). Educators' Knowledge of Rights. *Canadian Journal of Education, 23*(1), 29–46.

This should not come as a surprise. Moreover, beyond what may be found in the *Education Act* of Ontario there is an ocean of other law which applies to those in education: the common law or case law. For example, it may be counter-intuitive to suggest that when not at school or involved with students, teachers are still responsible to their school boards for their actions—yet it is clear that is the British Columbia case known as *Kempling*.° It seems contrary to the Canadian *Charter of Rights and Freedoms* to suggest that a public school teacher's failure to abide by certain moral beliefs might provide the grounds for discipline, but again, such is the case in *Shewan* from 1987.° It also seems contrary to a teacher's *Charter* rights to be terminated for failing to act in accord with certain religious beliefs yet in Catholic school districts this has happened and been supported in case law.° Other areas of law, such as negligence in tort law, also affect teachers, school administrators, and trustees. Indeed, common law is replete with cases where teachers have been sued—their school districts being held vicariously liable—for alleged acts of negligence in the performance of their teaching duties. The courts have made clear that students have substantive legal rights such as to be free from unreasonable search and seizure but it is also clear that students have procedural rights, such as procedural fairness.° Litigation in the United States has tended to target teachers and one can expect a similar phenomenon in an increasingly litigious society.°

KEMPLING *v* BRITISH COLUMBIA COLLEGE OF TEACHERS (BCCT) 2005 BCCA 327

ABBOTSFORD SCHOOL DISTRICT 34 *v* SHEWAN (1987) 21 BCLR (2D) 93

CASAGRANDE *v* HINTON ROMAN CATHOLIC SEPARATE SCHOOL DISTRICT NO. 155, 51 ALR (2D) 349, [1987] ABQB

R *v* M(MR), [1998] 3 SCR 393; JO *v* STRATHCONA-TWEEDSMUIR SCHOOL, 2010 ABQB 559

Gullatt, DE, Tollett, JR. (1997). Educational law: A requisite course for pre-service and in-service teacher education programs. *Journal of Teacher Education, 48*(2), 129–135.

Novices to the law see many judicial decisions as often nothing more than common sense. However, that determination are after the fact with full knowledge of the circumstances and with calm, rational deliberation, generally unrestricted by the pressure of time. For busy teachers, school administrators, and board members, decisions must be made during the course of unfolding of events. Moreover, things which appear innocuous at the time of decision making may appear foolish and negligent in hindsight. Keeping this in mind, to whom do those in schools turn for legal advice in difficult situations? Clearly for teachers, school administrators are the first source of information. In that regard, a recent study indicates that school administrators failed 50% of the time to correctly answer legal questions.°

Findlay, NM. (2007). In-school administrators' knowledge of education law. *Education and Law Journal, 17*(2), 177-202.

What might be the impact expected upon schools and educators if they were to study education law? In a small study, Delaney found four main themes which describe the everyday impact of such instruction.

1. the heightening of awareness, understanding, and sensitivity with respect to the various legal issues confronted by educators in today's schools;
2. the facilitation of sound and responsible decision-making when dealing with various legal issues in schools;
3. the fostering of a certain degree of professionalism; and lastly,
4. the raising of teachers' self-confidence levels.° (p. 123)

Delaney, JG. (2009). The value of educational law to practicing educators. *Education and Law Journal, 19*, 119–137.

Possessing a strong knowledge and understanding of the education law and policy is crucial for educators at any level, particularly in a society where legal issues can arise unexpectedly and at virtually any moment. "Traditionally, teachers have been largely immune from examination under the microscope of the law. However, as the law becomes increasingly involved in education, so too are teachers swept into the legal process" (p. xvii).° Educators must understand the legal parameters within which they work in order to guide their professional actions and to protect themselves from legal concerns. Understanding the laws surrounding professional conduct and interactions with students is of particular importance for educators, as ignorance of such laws may lead to legal complications and ultimately may provide employers with grounds for dismissal.

MacKay, AW., & Sutherland, LI. (2006). *Teachers and the law* (2nd. ed.). Toronto, ON: Emond Montgomery.

Knowledge of the law not only guides teachers' actions in terms of prevention of negative behaviours, but also informs them of actions which are deemed to be legal necessities; in other words, the law dictates what teachers must do, and not only what they must not do. For example, teachers are required by law to report suspicions of child abuse. Teachers have a legal responsibility to act *in loco parentis* (i.e., in the place of a reasonable, prudent, caring, and judicious parent). Any person in a position of authority over students must understand their legal duty to provide a high standard of care and appropriate protection for the physical, mental, and emotional wellbeing of the students for whom they are responsible.

Moreover, the role of the teacher has changed over the years. In the past, the teacher relied on the traditional *in loco parentis* model of teaching, when it was possible to simply rest on your judgment as a parent. However, in today's schools, the teacher is required to act not only as a parent, but also as a police officer, social worker, and professional educator. As a result of this change in role from 'in the place of a parent' to that of police officer, social worker, and professional educator, teachers must be aware of the laws that effect their behaviour.°

(MacKay & Sutherland, 2006)

The law affects educators in every area of study, at every level of education. As professionals, educators must be aware of the law as it relates to confidentiality of information, treatment of pupils, and educational policies, among other areas. As employees, teachers must be aware of issues relating to collective agreements and collective bargaining, union membership, and teaching contracts.° The law determines conditions of teaching and guides teaching practices in virtually every aspect, from the treatment of students with exceptionalities to issues pertaining to curriculum. In short, the law touches virtually every aspect of a teacher's professional life, and as such, it is crucial that educators have a working knowledge and understanding of the legal parameters within which they function.

Bezeau, LM. (2007). *Educational administration for Canadian teachers* (7th Ed.) [Electronic version]. *retrieved April 1, 2008 from http://www.unb.ca/education/bezeau/eact/*

Considerations

In summation, although one can argue about what the law is, we can at least agree that those in education are empowered by statute and that their duties and responsibilities are to a large degree iterated in those statutes and interpreted by common law which shape, or should guide, school board policies.° Clearly, knowledge of the law better informs those entrusted with the care of students and the institution of education.° That being the case the law matters, or at least should matter, to those in education and should be incorporated as an area of study in BEd programs, MEd programs, and seminars and workshops for teachers, school administrators, and school trustees across Canada.

Sergiovanni, TJ, Burlingame, M, Coombs, FS, & Thurston, PW. (1992). *Educational governance and administration*, (3rd ed.). Needham Heights, CA: Allyn and Bacon.

Paige, MA. (2009, October 26). The Case for School Law in Teacher Preparation Programs. *Teachers College Record.*

To quote Leschied, Dickinson, and Lewis:

> Given the principals' prominence as purveyors of legal information and advice, important questions are raised about the adequacy of their preparation for playing such a role. At [this particular time], these findings would seem to have even greater significance. [A]s ... College[s] and ... provincial government[s] threaten to winch-up teacher accountability, it would seem only fair that adequate programming be provided in order to permit teachers to attain and sustain the expected levels of professional knowledge and practice in this particular area. (p. 43 °)

Leschied, A. Dickinson, G., & Lewis, W. (2000). Assessing educators' self-reported levels of legal knowledge, law-related areas of concern, and patters of accessing legal information: Implications for training and practice. *Journal of Educational Administration and Foundations*, 15(1), 38–44.

Our effort in this book is to offer a resource not only focused upon teachers, principals, and central office officials in training, but also as an at-arms-length support during times when legal questions arise in the course of daily school-based practice.

1.0 THE STUDENT AND THE SCHOOL

Part 1.0 provides the reader with general interpretation of legislation with respect to students and schools. This section covers the topics of school attendance, operation of schools, and provision of education. Of course, students are the core participants in schooling so the subsequent sections of this Guide will elaborate on people, structures and systems that surround the students in the delivery of learning services.

1.1 ATTENDANCE AT PUBLICLY FUNDED SCHOOL

The right and requirement for children and youth to attend school are the focus of this section of the guide. In addition, this section outlines obligations and exceptions regarding attendance, enforcement of compulsory attendance, tuition and fees for attendance, and student records.

1.1.1 The Right to Attend

In Ontario, *Education Act* establishes basic rights and responsibilities regarding school attendance. Every person has the right to attend school, without payment of a fee, within the jurisdiction of the school board in which the person is qualified to be a resident pupil.° § 32.1 EA

The resident pupil qualifications are divided into elementary and secondary.

A person, between the age of 6 and 21 who resides in the district, is qualified to be a resident pupil for elementary school purposes. Based on the person's parent or guardian residence and tax support, the person may qualify to be a resident pupil either in a public district school board (English-language or French-language) or in a separate district school board (English-language or French-language).° §§ 33(1)–33(4) EA It is the responsibility of the parent or guardian to submit evidence and proof of age that the child has a right to attend an elementary school.° § 33(5) EA

With the requirement to offer optional kindergarten classes in all school boards, a person may become a resident pupil and enter kindergarten at the age of 5 or enter junior kindergarten at the age of 4.° Starting in 2010, the Ontario government has been phasing in the early learning plan to allow every four- and five-year-old child to go to full-day kindergarten by September, 2014. Similar to existing kindergarten programs, parents continue to have the choice about whether to enrol their children who have not attained the age of six years into full-day kindergarten.

§§ 34(1)–34(2) EA

The requirements for a person to qualify to be a resident pupil for secondary school purposes are primarily dependent on the age of a person. If the person is under the age of 16, a person and person's parent or guardian must reside in the secondary school district and be a tax supporter of the board. If a person is 16 or 17 years of age and has withdrawn from parental control, or is at least 18 years of age, a person must reside in the secondary school district in order to qualify as a resident pupil. Similarly, based on the residence and tax support, the person may qualify for a public district school board (English-language or French-language) or in a separate district school board (English-language or French-language). Despite the fact that there is no age limit for secondary school qualification, students who are promoted from elementary school must be admitted to secondary school.

In addition, a person who is otherwise entitled to be admitted to a school and who is less than eighteen years of age has the right to attend school even if the person or the person's parent or guardian is unlawfully in Canada.

1.1.2 The Requirement to Attend—Compulsory School Age

§ 21(1) EA

§ 21(1)(b) EA

Compulsory school age in Ontario is age 6 to 18 years inclusive.° Every child of compulsory school age must attend an elementary or secondary school on every school day.° Schools must ensure that students and their parents are informed about the school's policy on attendance. Where, in the principal's judgement, a student's frequent absences from school are jeopardizing his or her success, school staff should meet with the student and the parents to explain the potential consequences of the absences and discuss steps to be taken to improve attendance.

§ 30(1) EA ► § 7(2) Education Amendment Act (Learning to 18), 2006 (*section yet to be proclaimed*)

§ 30(2) EA ► § 7(2) Education Amendment Act (Learning to 18), 2006 (*section yet to be proclaimed*)

Although there are many complex and detailed provisions relating to school attendance, several aspects are of major importance. Persons in charge of a student (e.g., parent or guardian) must ensure the student's regular attendance in school if the student is of compulsory school age.° If a parent or guardian neglects or refuses to cause the child to attend school, unless the person is at least 16 years old and has withdrawn from parental control, that individual is guilty of an offence and on conviction is liable to a fine of not more than $1,000.° Furthermore, it is an offence to employ children of compulsory school age during school hours; anyone who employs a child is guilty of an offence and on conviction is liable to a fine of not more than $1,000.

A child who is required by law to attend school and who refuses to attend or who is habitually absent is guilty of an offence and on conviction is liable to the penalties under Part VI of the Provincial *Offenses Act*. In addition, the person's driver's licence may be suspended for a specific period extending no later than the date on which the person is no longer required to attend school.°

§ 30(5.1) EA ► § 7(4) EDUCATION AMENDMENT ACT (LEARNING TO 18), 2006 (*section yet to be proclaimed*)

1.1.3 Exceptions to Attendance Requirements

The requirement to attend school, as above, does not apply to a student who is receiving satisfactory instruction at home or elsewhere.° If students are educated at home or attend a private or independent school, parents are required to notify school board officials of their decision. A failure to ensure satisfactory instruction by parents can be the ground for legal prosecution. Non-attendance is also permitted where a sickness or other unavoidable cause are the reasons for the student's absence. Physical or developmental disabilities are not deemed an avoidable cause to be considered sufficient reason for non-attendance.° In cases where a student needs to be educated at home for medical reasons or a student lacks proper immunization documentation, the principal may arrange for home instruction by the school board teacher.°

§ 21(2) EA

§ 21(3) EA

§ 11(11) REGULATION 298

As well, attendance is excused where transportation is not provided by the board and the distance to the nearest school from a place of residence is not accessible; where a student has been suspended, expelled or excluded from attendance at school; and, where a student has completed all requirements to obtain a secondary school graduation diploma or equivalent. In addition, there may be instances where a student's absence is excused for the purposes of receiving instruction in music (for up to one-half day in a week) and on a day regarded as a holy day by the church or religious denominations to which student belongs. A student who has significant difficulties with regular attendance may be excused from attending school for the purpose of participating in the school board's supervised alternative learning program.° Part-time study for up to a year is allowed for sixteen- and seventeen-year-old students for compassionate reasons, with the principal's approval.°

§ 7 REGULATION 374/10

§ 26 REGULATION 374/10

1.1.4 Attendance Counsellors

The Provincial School Attendance Counsellor is appointed to superintend and direct the enforcement of compulsory school attendance in Ontario.° The Provincial School Attendance Counsellor has all the powers of a school attendance counsellor and may exercise such powers anywhere in Ontario. Where the parent or guardian of a child and the appropriate school attendance counsellor (provincial or local) disagree whether or not the child should be excused

§ 24 EA

from attendance, the Provincial School Attendance Counsellor is responsible for directing an inquiry about the validity of the reason or excuse for non-attendance and resolving the dispute.

§ 25 EA

Every school board must appoint one or more attendance counsellors to implement the *Education Act* and jurisdictional bylaws regarding school attendance.° Sometimes, two or more boards may share the same attendance counsellor or counsellors. A school attendance counsellor appointed by a board is responsible for enforcing the compulsory attendance of every child who is required to attend school. When a school attendance counsellor has reasonable and probable grounds for believing that a child is illegally absent from school, the counsellor, at the written request of the parent or guardian or of the principal, take the child to the child's parent or guardian or to the school from which the child is absent. The counsellor may not enter a dwelling place without permission.

The attendance counsellor is responsible to inquire into every case of failure to attend school within his or her knowledge, or when requested to do so by the supervisory officer or the principal, or a ratepayer. The counsellor is required to give written warning of the consequences of the failure to attend school to the parent or guardian, give written notice to the parent or guardian to cause the child to attend school, and advise the parent or guardian in writing of the provisions for legal excuses for non-attendance.

Where a student has not attended school as required, the school principal is to report such student's name, age, and resident to the appropriate school attendance counsellor in writing and provide any other information required for the enforcement of compulsory school attendance. If there is no school attendance counsellor having jurisdiction in respect of a child who has not attended school as required, the appropriate supervisory officer notifies the parent or guardian of the child.

1.1.5 Costs and Fees

§ 32(1) EA

§ 32(1) EA

Every student has the right to attend a school, where they are a qualified resident pupil, without the payment of fees for tuition, transportation, learning materials, supplies, activities, or textbooks.° In addition, students enrolled by a board who are otherwise qualified to attend except as to residence are entitled to attend a regular day school program without payment of fee.° The costs of materials and activities for elementary and secondary education are provided to schools by the Ministry of Education and are incorporated in school board operating budgets. From the perspective of parents and students, the right to attend school and receive instruction appropriate to the student's age and level of educational achievement is at the cost of the school board.

When schools or school boards choose with the support of the school community to offer enhanced or optional programming, parents

A Reasonable Fee?

Under the School Act of Alberta, boards of education are not entitled to charge tuition fees but are allowed to charge parent fees for "instructional supplies and materials." Accordingly, the Peace River School district charged the Whitakers (parents of three children in high school) $492.50 in school fees including student activity fees, course and book rental fees, fees for lost or damaged books and a locker/lock rental fee.

The Whitakers refused to pay the fees and the school board filed a claim to recover the fees. The Provincial Court judge awarded judgment against the Whitakers for $287.47, disallowing the school activity fee and the locker/lock rental fees. The Board saw this judgment as a restriction of their right to recover costs for materials consumed during the year.

The Alberta Court of Queen's Bench ruled in favour of the Board, finding that the charges were a fee and not a tax and therefore properly within the scope of the school district's powers. The court also found that textbooks were included in the phrase "instructional supplies and materials" (From Educational Law Reporter, 13 (10), June 2002).

In Ontario, it is a responsibility of school boards to make sure students are provided with textbooks at the cost of the district school board or schools. Boards, however, are given discretionary powers to collect fees from students associated with the optional programming, trips, events, and student-related activities approved by the school.

Questions to Consider:

- *Are school boards able to charge fees for locker/lock rental?*
- *Are school boards allowed to charge fees for "consumables" such as paper supplies, workbooks, materials used in industrial arts and in home economics?*
- *Should school boards be able to charge fees for activities that are related to the curriculum?"*

may be asked to contribute resources in the way of time, money, or materials to support these programs or activities. In 2011, the Ministry of Education has released Guideline for Fees for Learning Materials and Activities to help parents and school boards follow the rules around fees that are found in the *Education Act*. The fees discussed in this guideline are fees other than tuition fees for visa students, international students, First Nations students attending pursuant to a tuition agreement, adult or continuing education students. Nor do they include fees for early learning programs offered outside the regular school day or other before or after school programs.

In considering fees, school boards need to develop strategies to recognize and reduce barriers to participation and work to effectively include all students in programs and activities. Fees may be charged in cases where school boards or schools choose to offer enhancements or supplementary learning materials beyond the core curriculum. Fee charge is permissible for an activity, material, course or program if it is: not required as part of the regular day school program; voluntary, and alternatives are offered; non-essential or extracurricular in nature and is not required for graduation by an individual student; or a voluntary upgrade or substitute of a more costly material to the material provided for course purposes. Fees should reflect the actual cost of the services or materials being provided to the student.

A transparent accounting of the amounts collected and expenditures allocated must be made available to the school community.

1.1.6 *Non-Residents*

The elementary and secondary qualifications for a resident pupil have been described above. One exception to the secondary geographic qualification of "resident" is in the case of a public and a separate school boards with a coterminous boundary. A student of the faith of the separate school board is a "non-resident" of the public school board. His or her education is the responsibility of the separate school board. The public school board may choose to provide educational services to such a non-resident student, but is not obliged to do so. Also, a parent could be a separate school board supporter, but the child would still qualify as a resident pupil of the coterminous public school board. Similarly, a student not of the faith of the separate school board is considered a "non-resident" of the separate school board. Responsibility for education of that student rests with the public school board, although the separate school board may choose to provide educational services to such a student.

Another exception is when the board may provide for the education of pupils who reside on federal land held by the Crown in right of
§ 187 EA Canada in a school or schools operated by the board.° Also, the board may provide instruction and special services in the schools of the board for First Nations pupils, who are or whose parent or guardian are residents of a First Nations reserve. In that event, the school board may charge any tuition fees agreed to by the board and the First Nations band, council, or educational authority or the Government of
§ 188 EA Canada, or as prescribed by the regulations to the *Education Act*.°

1.1.7 *Tuition Fees*

§ 49(6) EA The *Education Act*° allows for school boards to recover costs of educational services provided to non-resident students and adult students. A board may charge a fee to temporary residents or persons in possession of a study permit within the meaning of the *Immigration*
§ 49(6) EA *and Refugee Protection Act*.° The amount of tuition fees for such students is governed by Ontario Regulation 159/11, Calculation of Fees for Pupils, and is determined in accordance with a fees policy developed by the board that operates the school in which the pupil is enrolled. At the same time, there are exceptions of categories of non-residents or temporary residents to which a board may not charge a
§ 49(7) EA fee for educational services.° In addition to day school program fees, it is also within the powers of school boards of education to offer summer school or continuing education courses and to charge a fee
§ 8(1) Regulation 159/11 to individuals enrolled in any such course.°

In case a pupil chooses to attend a school that is more accessible than any secondary school in the district of which he or she is qualified as a resident, the board that operates the school attended by the pupil will charge the fee to the board of which the person is qualified to be a resident pupil.° A school board may enter into an agreement with another board to provide for a fee accommodation or services for educational, administrative, instructional, and transportation purposes.°

§ 49(1) EA

§ 181(1) EA

1.1.8 Student Records

Ontario Student Record

Each student's educational progress through schools is recorded in the Ontario Student Record (OSR). It is the duty of a principal of a school, in addition to the principal's duties as a teacher, to collect information for inclusion in OSR in respect of each student enrolled in the school and to establish, maintain, retain, transfer, and dispose of the OSR.° As an ongoing record, OSR is transferred if the student transfers to another school in Ontario. The *Ontario Student Record Guideline* (2000)° sets out the policies with regard to the establishment of the OSR; the responsibility for the OSR; the components of the OSR; the access to the OSR; the use and maintenance of the OSR; the transfer of the OSR; the retention, storage, and destruction of information in the OSR; and the correction or removal of information in the OSR.

§§ 265(1)(d) & 266 EA

retrieved May 2013 from http://www.edu.gov.on.ca/eng/document/curricul/osr/osr.pdf

Ontario Student Transcript

A comprehensive record of all course work and diploma requirements achieved by a student is included in the Ontario Student Transcript (OST). An OST must be established for each student enrolled in an Ontario secondary school course, whether or not he or she is taking the course for credit. All information recorded on the transcript must be kept up to date, either in print or electronic form, and must be copied onto an official OST form when a printed copy is required. Upon the student's graduation or retirement, a current and accurate copy of the student's OST must be stored in the OSR folder. The information and guidelines for the establishment, maintenance, issue, and storage of the Ontario Student Transcript is outlined in the *Ontario Student Transcript Manual* (2010).°

retrieved May 2013 from http://www.edu.gov.on.ca/eng/general/elemsec/ost/ost2010.pdf

1.2 OPERATION OF SCHOOLS

This section provides a definition of "school" and outlines the general organization of the school calendar.

1.2.1 Definition of School

The *Education Act* defines "school" as the body of elementary school pupils or secondary school pupils that is organized as a unit for educational purposes under the jurisdiction of the appropriate board, or the body of pupils enrolled in any of the elementary or secondary school courses of study in an educational institution operated by the Government of Ontario. Furthermore, the school includes the pupils who are enrolled in extended day programs in the unit or institution, the teachers, designated early childhood educators and other staff members associated with the unit or institution, and the lands and premises of the unit or institution.

For the vast majority of students this definition of school is a school building with classrooms and all other traditional instructional areas. In recent years the definition of "school" has been expanded to mean other sites and premises including those which are used for outdoor education programs, or those specialized programs, such as work education, held in non-traditional school settings.

1.2.2 The School Year

§§ 1 & 11(7) EA;
§ 2 Regulation 304

The regular school year is the period between September 1 and June 30.° School year consists of school terms, school holidays, instructional days and professional activity days. The school year calendars must be completed in accordance with the *Education Act* and Regulation 304, School Year Calendar, Professional Activity Days. According to the these guidelines, the school board identifies each day of the school year as an instructional day, a professional activity day or a school holiday. School boards are required to prepare, adopt, and submit to the Ministry of Education, on or before May 1st of each year, the school year calendar(s) to be followed in the next school year. A board may designate, and implement with the prior approval of the Minister, a school year, terms, holidays, and instructional days for one or more schools under its jurisdiction that are different from those guidelines. Where a board wishes to adopt a school year calendar that is different from the requirements in section 2 of the regulation, the board shall submit the proposed school year calendar to the Ministry of Education for approval on or before March 1st of the preceding school year.

In practical terms, elementary schools organize themselves in a non-semester fashion. Typically, the school year is divided into three terms in the elementary schools (term 1 ending before Christmas, term 2 ending before March Break, and term 3 ending June 30). Secondary schools are typically semestered with two terms (semester 1 ending January 31st and semester 2 ending June 30th).

1.2.3 School Days

A school day means a day that is within a school year and is not a school holiday. The school year consists of a minimum of 194 school days. While most of school days are instructional days, some school days may be non-instructional days set aside for professional activities. A board may designate half a school day an instructional program and the remainder of the day for professional activities, but such a day constitutes a half-day in determining the number of instructional days in the school year. A board may designate up to 10 instructional days as examination days.

In some boards, there are schools that use a balanced calendar school year, meaning that the start and end dates are different than the norm and the blocks of time for instruction and vacation follow a different schedule. With the exception of province-wide holidays, professional activity days and vacation periods, students attend school from Monday to Friday.

1.2.4 School Hours

Ontario Regulation 298 states that the length of the instructional program of each school day for pupils of compulsory school age should be not less than 5 hours a day.° This excludes recess and scheduled intervals between classes. The program of instruction in Ontario schools is to begin not earlier than 8 a.m. and end not later than 5 p.m. on each school day.° A board may reduce the length of the instructional program on each school day to less than five hours a day for an exceptional pupil in a special education program. Each board may also establish the length of the instructional program on each school day for pupils in junior kindergarten and kindergarten.°

§ 3(1) Regulation 298

§ 3(2) Regulation 298

§ 3(4) Regulation 298

1.2.5 Breaks and Recess

Each pupil and each teacher are entitled to a scheduled interval for a lunch break of not less than forty consecutive minutes. Every school day must include a recess in the morning and in the afternoon, each of which to be not less than ten minutes and not more than fifteen minutes in length, for pupils in the primary and junior divisions In intermediate and senior divisions, with board's approval, principals may provide for recesses or intervals for pupils between periods.°

§ 3(8) Regulation 298

1.2.6 Non-Instructional Days / Professional Activity Days

There are typically a number of non-instructional days or half-days designed for professional activities on a school calendar. Professional activity includes evaluation of the progress of pupils, consultation with parents, the counselling of pupils, curriculum and program evaluation and development, professional development of teachers and attendance at educational conferences, but does not include preparation by teachers for classes or instruction. The provision for professional activity days is made at the school board level and policies vary from jurisdiction to jurisdiction. School boards may designate up to six professional activity days per school year. At least two days in a school year must be devoted to professional development activities related to specific provincial education priorities. Boards may also designate up to four extra days as professional activity days (in doing

§§ 2(3.1)(1) & 2(3.1)(2) Regulation 304

so, boards must ensure that some of the professional activities relate to curriculum development, implementation, and review).°

The Minister of Education has the authority to establish policies and guidelines respecting criteria and topics for the professional activity days and require boards to comply with the policies and guidelines. The required topics for professional activities for the two mandatory professional activity days are grouped according to the following criteria:

Policy/Program Memorandum No. 151, "Professional Activity Days Devoted to Provincial Education Priorities"

a. the professional activities are devoted to the professional learning of teachers with respect to improving student achievement and student success; and
b. the professional activities are devoted to the professional learning of teachers with respect to closing the gaps in student achievement.°

§ 4.1 Regulation 304

Each school board establishes its own professional development programs and scheduled professional activities, assigning dates, times, location, and resources as it sees fit. School boards are required to undertake an annual evaluation of the activities of the professional activity days of the previous year.°

1.2.7 Holidays

§ 2(4) Regulation 304

School holidays include every Saturday and Sundays, statutory holidays (Family Day, Good Friday, Easter Monday, Victoria Day, Canada Day, Labour Day, Thanksgiving Day, Remembrance Day), a day appointed by the Governor General or the Lieutenant Governor as a public holiday, and any civic holidays proclaimed for a municipality in which school is situated. Christmas vacation constitutes fourteen consecutive days starting on the Monday after the Friday preceding December 21 (when December 21 falls on a Thursday or a Friday, a Christmas vacation starts on the following Monday. Mid-Winter Break (called "March Break") constitutes the five consecutive days starting on the Monday after the Friday preceding the March 14. Dates for these holidays may vary in schools that use the balanced calendar school year. Summer vacation constitutes the period after the last day of the previous school year and the first day of the new school year. With prior approval of the Ministry, boards may designate school holidays that are different from those described above.°

1.2.8 Short Term and Emergency Closures

§ 169(1) EA
§ 170(1) EA

School boards are given responsibility for the general control and stewardship over schools and for developing and maintaining policies and organizational structures to deliver effective and appropriate education programs to its pupils.° To do so, boards should keep the schools open during the whole period of the school year.° There are occasions, however, when a board may close or authorise the closing of a school or a class for a temporary period in the interest of student and employee safety. Emergency closures may include inclement weather, fire, flood, failure of transportation arrangements, breakdown of the school heating plant, failure of an essential utility, or other unsafe conditions in the school facility.° Boards may also close schools in case of strike or lockout of members of a teachers' bargaining unit if it believes that in such case the safety of pupils may be endangered, the school building or equipment may not be adequately protected, or the substantial interference will occur with the operation of the school. School boards have developed policies that establish procedures for emergency situations. Procedures may include specific plans to keep students, staff and others safe in the event of a disaster, serious accident, or immediate or threatened emergency situations in, on, or near school property.

§ 19 EA

Ultimately, parents have the daily responsibility of determining whether or not it is safe for their children to go to school, although school divisions might also advise parents that their child's school is closed for a specific time. School board policies include such things as assigning responsibility for making school closure decisions, arrangements for transporting students home, providing billets, communicating with parents, establishing crisis response teams and the like.

1.3 PROVISION OF EDUCATION

This section of the guide covers the general guidelines for provision of education, including goals of education; types of schools; learning programs and curriculum; learning resources; language and culture programs and instruction; particular programs; special education; early childhood education; adult and continuing education; procedures for credit transfer and graduation; and, scholarships and awards.

1.3.1 Goals of Education in Ontario

According to the *Education Act*, the purpose of education is to provide students with the opportunity to realize their potential and develop into highly skilled, knowledgeable, caring citizens who contribute to their society.° The Ministry of Education administers the system of publicly funded elementary and secondary school education in Ontario, in accordance with and under the authority of the *Education Act*. The current goals of education in Ontario were developed in 2003, and include three core priorities:

§ 1(2) EA

- High levels of student achievement;
- Reduced gaps in student achievement;
- Increased public confidence in publicly funded education.

The Minister of Education, through the ministry, issues curricula, sets diploma requirements and sets policy for student assessment.

1.3.2 Types of Schools

Within the *Education Act*, references are made to several distinct types of schools in Ontario: public schools (formerly these were religious majority schools), separate schools (religious minority schools), private schools, and demonstration (or provincial) schools. Other regulations also refer to home schooling.

- A **public school** ("école publique") is a school under the jurisdiction of an English-language or French-language public district school board.
- A **separate school** ("école séparée") is a school under the jurisdiction of a Roman Catholic board or a Protestant separate school board.
- A **private school** ("école privée") is defined as an institution other than a public or separate school at which instruction is provided at any time between the hours of 9 a.m. and 4 p.m. on any school day for five or more pupils who are of or over compulsory school age in any of the subjects of the elementary or secondary school courses of study.
- A **demonstration** (or provincial) school° is operated by the Ministry of Education to serve the needs of students who are deaf, hard of hearing, blind, deaf/blind, low-vision or have severe learning disabilities.

retrieved May 2013 from www.psbnet.ca/eng/index.html

Other Types of Schools in Canada

Other definitions of "school" are similar in meaning to those used in the Act, but are used "outside the provincial education authority," are used in other provinces, or are used in historical contexts. The terms "denominational" or "dissentient" schools, for example, have been used to define separate schools in other provinces and in different historical eras. Other such definitions include:

- A *Charter School* is a publicly funded independent school where the parents whose children attend the school control the administration and operation of the school. Currently, there are no provisions for charter schools in Ontario.
- An *Independent School* is a school that is controlled and administered by a person (or Board) other than a public authority. Independent schools are funded by the parents of children attending the school, and, partly, from government sources.
- A *Sectarian School* is a school that is publicly funded and administered, but with religious instruction as a significant part of the school program.
- An *Associate School* is a school where administration is shared

between public authorities (publicly elected boards) and others, such as parent or church councils. There are a number of Associate schools in Canada where Independent-like schools have made agreements with public or separate boards to form associate relationships. Often associate schools offer specific programs based on language or on a religious or cultural affiliation.

- A *French Immersion School* is a school (usually English public or separate) in which a significant proportion of subjects are taught in the French language. Some schools may offer both a regular English program and a French Immersion program.
- *Community Schools* are characterized by the provision of at least some of the following integrated school-linked services to children and youth and their families: education, health, social service, justice and recreation.
- A *Band School* is a school for Aboriginal students on a First Nations reserve. The school is typically administered by a band council and is funded by the Federal Government.
- *Specialty Schools* emphasize specific subject areas such as the arts or the sciences, and are geared towards students who have strengths in these particular areas. Some specialty schools offer extensive programs in technological studies and aim to prepare students for employment. Some schools are sports-focused, offering programs for developing excellence in one or more sports for all or some of their student body.
- *Alternative Schools* are usually small schools, with a low teacher to student ratio, which have a different approach to curriculum delivery from mainstream schooling. Alternative schools often have high parent involvement. At the secondary level, they tend to focus on independent learning and assist students who have not been successful in regular schools.

Publicly-Funded Schools

Public and separate school boards are funded by the Province. There are four types of publicly-funded schools in Ontario—English public, English Separate (Catholic), French public, and French Separate (Catholic). All of these systems are organized the same way—they are operated by district school boards and share the same standards for teacher and student performance.

Publicly-funded schools in Ontario are divided into four age levels or "divisions":

1. Primary ("cycle primaire")—Junior Kindergarten to Grade 3
2. Junior ("cycle moyen")—Grades 4 to 6
3. Intermediate ("cycle intermédiaire")—Grades 7 to 10
4. Senior ("cycle supérieur")—Grades 11 and 12

Based on these divisions, schools are divided into elementary and secondary. Elementary school ("école élémentaire") provides instruction in some or all of the primary division, junior division and intermediate division but not in the senior division. Also known as grade school or primary school, an elementary school usually offers classes ranging from Junior Kindergarten through to Grade 8. Secondary school ("école secondaire") provides instruction in some or all of the last two years of the intermediate division and the senior division. Also known as high school, a secondary school usually offers classes from Grade 9 to Grade 12.

Considerable variation exists in the way elementary and secondary schools are organized across Ontario. Some elementary schools offer classes only up to Grade 6, whereas students who graduate from these schools often go to Junior High School for grades 7–9, and then high school for grades 10–12. In some instances (often in French language schools), students would go from Grade 6 to a school with grades 7–12. Other than the different grade organization, these schools follow the structures of traditional elementary and secondary schools.

Separate Schools

A separate school is a school that serves the religious minority, either Catholic or Protestant. The *Constitution Act*, 1867, inasmuch as it delegates the responsibility for education to the provinces, also provides the rights for the provinces that had separate (minority) school systems (i.e., Roman Catholic or Protestant) at the time they entered Confederation to keep them and to provide public funding for them. Hence, in Ontario, members of the Roman Catholic and Protestant faiths are entitled to publicly funded, religiously based schools, and do have them. Before that, between 1841 and 1863, a number of acts created the "separate schools" in Canada West and the "dissentient schools" of Canada East, allowing Protestant and Catholic parents to establish their own schools, and, subject to provincial controls over the curriculum and certification of teachers, to receive public funding.° Section 93 of the *Constitution Act*, 1867 entrenched those rights in the Canadian Constitution for Québec and Ontario, and sections 17 of both the *Alberta Act* and *Saskatchewan Act* provide Constitutional protection for such rights in Alberta and Saskatchewan, respectively. If the provincial legislatures do not enact the necessary legislation to ensure that the minority education rights are continued and the schools provided, the Parliament of Canada can enact it for them. Thus, separate schools and school boards in Ontario, Alberta, and Saskatchewan are publicly funded school systems under the jurisdiction of their provincial governments. While subject to the authority of the provincial government, that authority is constrained by the provisions of Section 93 and the many interpretations of the section's intent that have been made by the courts.

Bezeau, LM. (2007). *Educational administration for Canadian teachers* (7th ed.) [Electronic version]. Retrieved August 2009 from http://www.unb.ca/education/bezeau/eact/; Young, J., & Levin, B. (2002). *Understanding Canadian schools: An introduction to educational administration* (3rd ed.). Scarborough, ON: Nelson.

Catholic and Protestant separate schools and school boards exist in a variety of different forms across the country, reflecting in part the existing status of denominational schools in the provinces prior to entry into Confederation, and in part the outcome of legal and political challenges since then. Across Canada, the development of denominationalism has varied. British Columbia and Manitoba have strictly "non-denominational" public school system. Alberta, Saskatchewan, and Ontario have "public and dissentient separate schools" which are protected in law. New Brunswick, Nova Scotia, and Prince Edward Island have "non-denominational with informal concessions" school systems, meaning that denominational schools continue to exist without legal status in these provinces. In Newfoundland, the religiously based school system was secularized a few years ago by constitutional amendment, and Québec has altered its school system so that language, rather than religion is the dominant dividing factor. While in the three territories (Northwest Territories, Yukon, and Nunavut) denominational schooling has statutory status (i.e., permitted administratively), today, constitutionally protected separate schools exist only in Ontario, Alberta, and Saskatchewan.

Specialized and Alternative Schools

School boards may establish schools specializing in areas such as the arts, business studies, the environment, languages, pure and applied sciences, or technological education.° A secondary school may offer programs in subjects in which there is small enrolment—for example, programs in some languages—and these programs may serve several schools. A secondary school should not specialize to the point where it cannot offer the full range of courses that students need in order to obtain a secondary school diploma. School boards may also establish alternative schools to provide an option for some students who have educational needs that cannot be met in their existing schools, and/or to respond to needs expressed in the community.

§ 7.6 Ontario Schools, Kindergarten to Grade 12: Policy and Program Requirements, 2011, *retrieved May 2013 from http://www.edu.gov.on.ca/eng/document/policy/os/ONSchools.pdf*

Private/Independent Schools

Private School is a school funded and operated by a person (or board) other than a public authority. Often called independent schools, these institutions are funded by the parents of children attending the school, and, sometimes partly, from government sources. In Canada at the elementary and secondary levels, about five percent of all students are in private schools. The percentage tends to be higher in provinces that are wealthy, that do not have separate school systems, and that subsidize private schools. Private schools, because they operate in the private sector, have a number of distinguishing characteristics. On the average, private schools are smaller than public schools. They generally charge tuition and can select their students. They do not have a legal obligation to provide education to all resident children as do the public schools.

According to the *Education Act* of Ontario, a private school is deemed as any educational institution that is partially or entirely funded by sources other than the government, and that students of appropriate age attend for instruction between 9:00 to 16:00 on a typical school day. . There are 1000 registered independent (private) schools in Ontario serving about 130,000 students. In Ontario, all private schools that operate in the Province are considered businesses or non-profit organizations. Principals and teachers in private schools are not required to be certified by the Ontario College of Teachers. Further information on private schools in Ontario is provided in Part 12 of the *Guide*.

Overseas Schools

Under agreement with the Ministry of Education, overseas schools are offering credits toward the Ontario Secondary School Diploma. The ministry inspects standard of instruction in each school. If a school receives a satisfactory inspection report, the Principal is authorized to grant credits toward the Ontario Secondary School Diploma. The inspection of the school does not include matters relating to the health, safety or supervision of the pupils. The ministry is not involved in the hiring of teachers for the school. The ministry is not responsible for any claim for injury, loss or other damages to pupils, staff or visitors arising out of the operation of overseas schools.

Provincial and Demonstration Schools

Provincial Schools and Demonstration Schools are under the administration of the Minister of Education. They provide education for students who are deaf, hard of hearing, blind, deaf/blind, low-vision, or who have severe learning disabilities. Prospective students must demonstrate the ability to benefit from the methods and techniques of the school. Admission criteria for students applying for the junior kindergarten program (offered only by Schools for the Deaf) must be 4 years of age by December 31st of the school year for which the application is made. Students applying to the secondary program must be under the age of 21 on the first day of the school year for which the application is made. Admittance to a school for students who are deaf, blind, or deaf/blind is determined by a Provincial Schools Admission Committee in accordance with the requirements set out in Regulation 296. Application for admission to a demonstration school is made on behalf of students by the school board, with parental consent. The Provincial Committee on Learning Disabilities (PCLD) determines whether a student is eligible for admission.

1.3.3 Goals and Requirements for Learning Programs and Curriculum

The Ministry of Education establishes curriculum policy and defines what students are taught in Ontario public schools. The *Education Act*° outlines the minister's responsibility to issue curriculum

§ 8.3(a) EA

guidelines, require that courses of study be developed from them, and establish procedures for the approval of courses of study that are not developed from such curriculum guidelines. The Ministry of Education establishes the requirements that govern the policies and programs of all publicly funded elementary and secondary English-language schools in Ontario.° Numbered policy directives are issued through Policy/Program Memoranda (PPMs) to district school boards and school authorities to outline the Ministry of Education's expectations regarding the implementation of ministry policies and programs. These memoranda are published quite frequently and are official communications from the Minister to Directors of Education. Directors then communicate with Principals who in turn may communicate the contents to teachers as appropriate. They are powerful instruments; they are directives and carry a force close to that of a Regulation. The Policy/Program Memoranda may be active or revoked; therefore, it is necessary to verify their current status before acting upon them.°

Ontario Schools, Kindergarten to Grade 12: Policy and Program Requirements, 2011, *retrieved May 2013 from http://www.edu.gov.on.ca/eng/document/policy/os/ONSchools.pdf*

retrieved May 2013 from http://www.edu.gov.on.ca/extra/eng/ppm/ppm.html

1.3.4 The Full-Day Kindergarten Program

Starting in September, 2010, Ontario has been phasing in the implementation of the full-day kindergarten program for four- and five-year-olds. It was originally intended to be fully implemented in all elementary schools across the province by September 2014. However, the original goal has been revised and the aim is to have it fully implemented by 2015-2016.° This child-centred, developmentally appropriate, integrated, extended-day program of learning aims to establish a strong foundation for learning in the early years, and to do so in a safe and caring play-based environment that promotes the physical, social, emotional, and cognitive development of all children.° The Full-Day Early Learning–Kindergarten program is based on the six over arching principles developed by the Best Start Expert Panel on Early Learning for its report outlining a framework for Ontario early childhood settings entitled *Early Learning for Every Child Today*.° The six principles are as follows:

1. Early child development sets the foundation for lifelong learning, behaviour, and health.
2. Partnerships with families and communities strengthen the ability of early childhood settings to meet the needs of young children.
3. Respect for diversity, equity, and inclusion are prerequisites for honouring children's rights, optimal development, and learning.
4. A planned curriculum supports early learning.
5. Play is a means to early learning that capitalizes on children's natural curiosity and exuberance.
6. Knowledgeable, responsive educators are essential.

Children in the Full-Day Early Learning–Kindergarten program are

Full-Day Early Learning–Kindergarten Program for Four- and Five-Year-Olds: A Reference Guide for Educators, *retrieved May 2013 from http://www.edu.gov.on.ca/eng/curriculum/elementary/kinder2010.pdf*

The Full-Day Early Learning–Kindergarten Program, *retrieved May 2013 from http://www.edu.gov.on.ca/eng/curriculum/elementary/kindergarten_english_june3.pdf*

retrieved May 2013 from http://www.children.gov.on.ca/htdocs/English/topics/earlychildhood/early_learning_for_every_child_today.aspx

expected to demonstrate achievement of the overall expectations for each of the six areas of learning by the end of two years in the Full-Day Early Learning–Kindergarten program.

The full-day learning includes a core day program during regular school hours and, where demand allows, a complementary extended-day program before and after school. The play-based learning core day program provides children with developmental opportunities in six areas of learning – personal and social development, language, mathematics, science and technology, health and physical activity, and the arts.° The extended-day program is offered before and after the core day program. It may be delivered either by the school board directly ("extended-day program") or by a licensed child care provider under an agreement with the school board ("before- and after-school program").°

The Full-Day Early Learning–Kindergarten Program, *retrieved May 2013 from http://www.edu.gov.on.ca/eng/curriculum/elementary/kindergarten_english_june3.pdf*

Full-Day Early Learning–Kindergarten Program: The Extended-Day Program (Draft Version, 2010–11) *retrieved May 2013 from http://www.edu.gov.on.ca/eng/curriculum/elementary/kinderProgram2010.pdf*

1.3.5 *The Ontario Curriculum, Grades 1 to 12*

The Ontario curriculum documents detail the knowledge and skills that teachers are required to teach and students are expected to develop and demonstrate in their class work, on tests, and in various other activities through which achievement is assessed and evaluated in each subject at each grade level. By developing and publishing curriculum documents for use by all Ontario teachers, the Ministry of Education sets standards for the province-wide curriculum. Curriculum documents include policy documents that outline mandatory requirements and standards, and resource documents support implementation of policy and their use is a local decision. Thus, teaching and assessment strategies are left to the professional judgement of teachers, enabling them to address individual student needs and deliver the curriculum in a context that is locally meaningful. Teachers can also access exemplars which were developed to complement the curriculum implementation. They are organized by subject, highlighting key features (with samples of student work) for teachers to look for when designing assessment tasks and when evaluating student learning based on clear criteria.

All elementary curriculum expectations from each relevant curriculum policy document for a grade, and all secondary curriculum expectations for a course, must be accounted for when planning the classroom program (some accommodations, modifications, and alternative expectations for curriculum guidelines may be made for English language learners and students with special education needs).°

Ontario Schools, Kindergarten to Grade 12: Policy and Program Requirements, 2011, *retrieved May 2013 from http://www.edu.gov.on.ca/eng/document/policy/os/ONSchools.pdf*

Program Requirements

The principles underlying the curriculum for each subject are included at the beginning of the curriculum document for that subject.

English-language elementary curriculum documents° span Kindergarten to Grade 8 and require that learning programs include

retrieved May 2013 from http://www.edu.gov.on.ca/eng/curriculum/elementary/subjects.html

the following disciplines: the arts; French as a second language (core French, although boards may offer extended or immersion French); health and physical education; language; mathematics; science and technology; and social studies (in Grades 1 to 6) or history and geography (in Grades 7 and 8). Native languages may also be offered, in accordance with the relevant curriculum policy document. While there is no curriculum mandate to study international languages, parents may request international language courses for their children. Curriculum documents also outline the requirements for the kindergarten program. Schools may also offer such experiential learning programs for students in Grades 7 and 8 as job shadowing and job twinning. In addition, school boards must ensure that all elementary students, including students with special education needs, have a minimum of twenty minutes of sustained moderate to vigorous physical activity each school day during instructional time.

The courses that may be offered in English-language secondary schools are described in curriculum documents° for Grades 9 through 12. They include such subjects as the arts; business studies; Canadian and world studies; classical and international languages; computer studies; English; English as a second language and English literacy development; French as a second language; guidance and career education; health and physical education; interdisciplinary studies; mathematics; Native languages; Native studies; program planning and assessment; science; social sciences and humanities; and technological education. Courses that integrate more than one subject/discipline may also be developed, in accordance with the curriculum policy document for interdisciplinary studies. Schools may also offer, in accordance with the relevant policies of the Ministry of Education, locally developed courses, dual credit courses, and alternative (non-credit) courses, which are not outlined in the curriculum policy documents. All Ontario curriculum courses and locally-developed courses may be offered through the cooperative education mode of delivery. Schools may offer other experiential learning programs and specialized programs. Upon successful completion of courses based on the Ontario curriculum policy documents and other ministry-authorized courses, students receive credits towards the Ontario Secondary School Diploma.

retrieved May 2013 from http://www.edu.gov.on.ca/eng/curriculum/secondary/subjects.html

Curriculum Reviews

Curriculum documents undergo scheduled reviews.° Each year, a number of subject areas enter the review process, to ensure they are kept current, relevant and age-appropriate. The most current review cycle was completed in 2012. Ministry of Education conducts comprehensive reviews by gathering information through studying research in the subject area; comparisons with other jurisdictions; focus groups comprised of educators from all Ontario school boards; technical content analysis conducted by subject experts; and, consultations with education stakeholders (e.g., universities, Faculties of Education, employers, parents, students,

retrieved May 2013 from http://www.edu.gov.on.ca/eng/curriculum/elementary/subjects.html

other ministries and governmental agencies, and NGOs). These sources of information form the basis of recommended revisions to the curriculum. Writing teams drawn from school boards across the province then develop revised English and French documents based on research and consultation, and finalize the curriculum documents. In addition, a group of knowledgeable and committed community leaders were invited to form the Curriculum Council. They provide high level strategic advice to the minister of education on issues related to elementary and secondary school curriculum. In addition, consultations and writing teams, especially at the Intermediate/Senior level, almost always include significant representation from the Ministry-recognized provincial subject councils (e.g., OMLTA [Ontario Modern Language Teachers' Association] or OAEA [Ontario Art Education Association]).

Growing Success: Assessment, Evaluation, and Reporting in Ontario Schools – First Edition Covering Grades 1 to 12, 2010, *retrieved May 2013 from www.edu.gov.on.ca/eng/policyfunding/growSuccess.pdf*

Assessment, Evaluation, and Reporting

From September 2010, assessment, evaluation, and reporting in Ontario schools are based on the guidelines described in *Growing Success: Assessment, Evaluation, and Reporting in Ontario Schools.*° This document outlines the policies and practices for the assessment, evaluation, and reporting of the achievement of curriculum expectations and the development of learning skills and work habits for all students in Grades 1 to 12 in Ontario schools. Aimed at the improvement of student learning, the policy is based on seven fundamental principles designed to ensure that assessment, evaluation, and reporting practices and procedures:

- are fair, transparent, and equitable for all students;
- support all students, including students with special education needs, those who are learning the language of instruction, and those who are First Nation, Métis, or Inuit;
- are carefully planned to relate to the curriculum expectations and learning goals and, as much as possible, to the interests, learning styles and preferences, needs, and experiences of all students;
- are communicated clearly to students and parents at the beginning of the school year or course and at other appropriate points throughout the school year or course;
- are ongoing, varied in nature, and administered over a period of time to provide multiple opportunities for students to demonstrate the full range of their learning;
- provide ongoing descriptive feedback that is clear, specific, meaningful, and timely to support improved learning and achievement;
- develop students' self-assessment skills to enable them to assess their own learning, set specific goals, and plan next steps for their learning.

The document clarifies policy related both to students' demonstration of the learning skills and work habits (responsibility, organization, independent work, collaboration, initiative, self-regulation) and to their achievement of curriculum expectations. It provides a thorough outline of policy related to performance standards, to the role of assessment in the improvement of student learning, to evaluation and reporting procedures, and to considerations pertaining to students with special education needs and students who are learning English. It also includes policies for reporting student achievement demonstrated through e-learning and the credit-recovery process.

The Provincial Report Cards

Student achievement of the curriculum expectations and the learning skills and work habits must be communicated formally to students and parents by means of the Elementary Provincial Report Card, Grades 1–6 and Grades 7 and 8; and the Provincial Report Card, Grades 9–12. The Elementary Progress Report Card, to be used during the fall of the school year in Grades 1–6 and Grades 7 and 8, is designed to show the student's development of the learning skills and work habits and the progress students are making towards achievement of the curriculum expectations. *Growing Success*° policy offers templates and instructions for filling out the elementary and secondary report cards.

retrieved May 2013 from www.edu.gov.on.ca/eng/document/forms/report/card/reportCard.html

1.3.6 Instructional and Learning Resources

Textbooks and Supplementary Resources

A textbook is a comprehensive learning resource, intended for use by an entire class or group of students, in print or electronic form, or any combination of print, electronic, and non-print materials, collectively designed to support a substantial portion (85%) of the Ontario curriculum expectations for a specific grade and subject in elementary school, or for a course in secondary school, or a substantial portion (85%) of the expectations for a learning area in the Kindergarten program. A textbook must be consistent with the philosophy and intent of the curriculum policy for the subject or course and grade.

A supplementary resource is defined as a resource that supports only a limited number of expectations, or the expectations in a single strand, as outlined in the curriculum policy document for a specific subject or course or for a Kindergarten learning area. Such a resource may be intended for use by an entire class or group of students. Examples are readers, novels, spelling programs, dictionaries, atlases, and computer software and instructional guides.

The procedures by which and the conditions under which books and other learning materials are used in Ontario schools are outlined in the *Education Act* and Regulations.°

§§ 8(1), 170(1), 171(1), 264(1), 265(1) EA; § 7 Regulation 298

retrieved May 2013 from http://resources.curriculum.org/occ/trillium/index.shtml

Guidelines for Approval of Textbooks *retrieved May 2013 from http://resources.curriculum.org/occ/trillium/Textbook_Guide_English_2008.pdf*

The textbooks that are approved by the ministry for use in Ontario schools are included in the *Trillium List*.° The Trillium List items are subjected to a rigorous evaluation based on eligibility requirements and content and format criteria to ensure that they conform to ministry standards. School boards may select textbooks from the Trillium List and approve them for use in their schools. However, school boards have the sole responsibility for the selection and evaluation of supplementary resources to support elementary and secondary programs.°

Ontario Public Library System

REGULATION 976

The public library system contributes to education, literacy and life-long learning in Ontario communities. The Ministry of Tourism, Culture, and Sport is responsible for administering the libraries under the *Public Libraries Act* and statutory grants under the Act.° The Public Libraries legislation helps ensure free, equitable access information and establishes free public library services in Ontario through governance and regulations.

The first public facilities to give equitable assess to library services in Ontario were established in Toronto and Guelph in 1883. Ontario residents now have access to basic library services provided through a system of public libraries consisting of autonomous and independent units, under the *Public Libraries Act*, though they are funded by municipal and provincial government sources. Municipal bylaws create Ontario's public libraries and public library boards govern them. Every resident of Ontario who has a valid public library card is entitled to borrow library materials held by any public library in the province (reciprocal borrowing) and make request from home library to borrow items owned by another library (interlibrary loans). Library lending is subject to policies, terms and conditions for borrowing set by the public library board.

1.3.7 Language and Culture Programs and Instruction

Constitutional Rights and Privileges

The official languages of Canada, English and French, are the languages of instruction in English-language and French-language schools in Ontario. French language education is more than just a language immersion program, its goal is also to protect, enhance, and transmit Francophone culture. Linguistic options in education follow overlapping requirements in the *Education Act*, the Canadian *Charter of Rights and Freedoms*, and the *Constitution Act*, 1982.

In fact, the *Education Act* specifically recognizes the rights and privileges inherent in these two documents.

> (4) This Act does not adversely affect any right or privilege guaranteed by section 93 of the *Constitution Act*, 1867 or by

section 23 of the Canadian *Charter of Rights and Freedoms*.

(4.1) Every authority given by this Act, including but not limited to every authority to make a regulation, decision or order and every authority to issue a directive or guideline, shall be exercised in a manner consistent with and respectful of the rights and privileges guaranteed by section 93 of the *Constitution Act*, 1867 and by section 23 of the Canadian *Charter of Rights and Freedoms*.

Additionally, American Sign Language (ASL) and Québec Sign Language (QSL) may be used as languages of instruction.

English-Language Schools

As it is essential for all students in English-language schools to graduate with the ability to use the language of instruction effectively for thinking, learning, and communicating, English is a required subject, and learning opportunities to promote facility in English are integrated into the curriculum in all subject areas. English is taught in each grade in elementary school, and students in secondary schools are required to earn four credits in English (one for each grade) and to meet the provincial secondary school literacy graduation requirement. For English language learners, schools will offer programs and courses to help them develop proficiency in the language of instruction so that they can succeed in all subject areas at school, and later in postsecondary studies, including apprenticeship programs, and/or in the workplace.

French is also taught in the English-language schools of Ontario to provide students with the opportunity to become bilingual in the two official languages of Canada. The study of French as a second language ("français langue seconde") is compulsory in elementary school from Grade 4 to Grade 8, and secondary school students are required to earn at least one credit in French as a second language to graduate. Students may also count two additional French credits as compulsory credits towards their diploma. The mandatory French requirement can be met through core French programs, which involve the study of the French language, or through French immersion and extended French programs, in which French is not only taught as a subject but also serves as the language of instruction in other subjects. Schools must offer at least core French programs from Grade 4 to the end of Grade 12. The delivery of French immersion and extended French programs is optional.

French-Language Schools

In addition to fostering academic achievement and supporting bilingualism in the two official languages of Canada, the education provided in French-language schools is intended to enhance students' bond with the French-language communities of Ontario and to support the development of their sense of cultural identity.°

Aménagement Linguistique: A Policy for Ontario's French-Language Schools and Francophone Community, 2004, *retrieved May 2013 from http://www.edu.gov.on.ca/eng/document/policy/linguistique/policyguide.pdf*

Students study French as a subject from Kindergarten to Grade 12, and they must start the study of English as a subject by Grade 5. The requirements regarding the language of instruction and the other official language of Canada in French-language schools mirror those in English-language schools.

Sign Language

For the instruction of students who are deaf or hard-of hearing, school boards may provide instruction using American Sign Language (ASL) or Quebec Sign Language (QSL). a teacher or temporary teacher may use ASL or QSL as a language of instruction and in communications in regard to discipline and management of the school. °

§ 32 Regulation 298

International Language Programs for Elementary Students

International languages may be offered by boards as subjects to students in Kindergarten to Grade 8 through continuing education.°

§§ 4–10 Regulation 285

These include modern languages other than English or French. A written request to the board from parents, on behalf of twenty-three students or more, for the establishment of a program in an international language, will warrant the board to establish the requested program. Boards may also enter into agreements with other boards to provide the requested program. Boards must deliver the program for the duration of the school year, provided that at least ten students attend the first class and that at least one student continues to attend for the duration of the year. If, at the end of the year, there are fewer than twenty-three students enrolled in the program, the board may discontinue the program.

International language classes may be held during the school day but not within the regular instructional time (for example, over the lunch break) at a school site used by the board, or after school or on weekends at a school or at a location that is not a school site. A student may attend classes in one or more languages. During the school year, a student may attend international language classes for no more than two and one half hours per week. During the summer, a student may attend such classes for a maximum of two and one-half hours per day. School boards establishing international language classes must accept full responsibility for staff, curriculum, and supervision of the classes.

Programs for English Language Learners

One reflection of Ontario's characteristic as the most culturally diverse Canadian province is the demand for classroom support for English Language Learners (ELLs). English language learners are students in provincially funded English language schools, either Canadian born or immigrants from other countries, whose first language is not English, or is a variety of English significantly different from the variety used for instruction in Ontario's schools, and who may require focused educational supports to assist them in attaining proficiency in English. The school system responded by outlining the K-12 language-acquisition policy for providing programs and supports for these students to develop their proficiency in English. Implementation of this policy promotes a consistent approach to the education, capacity building, and academic achievement among English language learners at the level expected of all learners in Ontario. To help school boards implement this policy, the Ministry of Education provides leadership, funding, assessment tools, and other supports intended to be used for the benefit of ELLs.

Boards are to provide reception and orientation for ELLs (and their families), assess their English proficiency, and determine their placements. A student's level of proficiency in English does not influence the choice of grade placement. In elementary schools, English language learners are placed with an age-appropriate group. In secondary schools, placement in a grade or in specific subjects depends upon the student's prior education, background in specific subject areas, and aspirations. English language learners should be placed in a grade-level or subject-specific classroom for at least part of each day. Final decisions regarding placement are made by the principal in consultation with the student, staff, and parents. The principal will communicate the placement decision, and the rationale for the placement, to the student and parents.

According to the policy document, *English Language Learners / ESL and ELD Programs and Services: Policies and Procedures for Ontario Elementary and Secondary Schools, Kindergarten to Grade 12*,[9] boards and schools are required to implement program models that take into consideration the numbers and distribution of English language learners in the board or school. Such program models may include English as a Second Language (ESL) programs; English Literacy Development (ELD) programs; congregated classes for English language instruction; individual assistance on a tutorial/resource basis; core programs; designated sections of secondary courses; participation in international language programs; online support; peer tutoring and/or bilingual tutoring; and others. Furthermore, the implemented programs and services must enable English language learners to continue their education while learning English.

retrieved May 2013 from http://www.edu.gov.on.ca/eng/document/esleldprograms/esleldprograms.pdf

English as a Second Language (ESL) courses are intended to help English language learners develop proficiency in the language of instruction so that they can succeed in all subject areas at school, and later in postsecondary studies, including apprenticeship programs, and/or in the workplace. English Literacy Development (ELD) courses are intended to provide students who had limited access to education prior to admission to an Ontario secondary school with an accelerated literacy program to give them the foundation needed for further study and for employment.

Learning opportunities to enable English language learners to develop

The Ontario Curriculum, Grades 1–8: English as a Second Language and English Literacy Development – A Resource Guide , 2001, *retrieved May 2013 from http://www.edu.gov.on.ca/eng/document/curricul/esl18.pdf*; The Ontario Curriculum, Grades 9–12: English as a Second Language and English Literacy Development, 2007, *retrieved May 2013 from http://www.edu.gov.on.ca/eng/curriculum/secondary/esl912currb.pdf*

proficiency in English are to be integrated into the curriculum in all subject areas.° All teachers share in the responsibility for the English language development of these students. English language learners at different stages of learning English and/or developing literacy in English will need program adaptations in order to be successful. Teachers must adapt the instructional program to address students' different levels of proficiency in English and help these students adjust to a new linguistic, cultural, and educational environment. Appropriate adaptations may include both modifications and accommodations related to instructional and assessment strategies. Modification of some or all of the curriculum expectations may be required, especially for ELLs at the early stages of learning English or those with limited prior access to education. Modifications at the secondary level require the principal to consult with the classroom teacher to determine the integrity of the credit for credit-granting purposes.

Multiculturalism and Citizenship

The 1988 *Multiculturalism Act* of Canada indicates that it is the policy of Government of Canada to facilitate the acquisition, retention, and use of all languages that contribute to the multicultural heritage of Canada. The Federal Minister of Multiculturalism and Citizenship is responsible for the administration of the Canadian *Multiculturalism Act*. This act includes formal policy declarations, requires the Federal Minister to implement those policies and empowers the Federal Minister to enter into agreements with Provinces for the implementation of multiculturalism programs.

Canada's *Immigration Act*

Canada admits about 250,000 new immigrants each year. This process requires significant accommodation on the part of schools and communities. Appropriate care for the educational needs of these people is required. Canada's *Immigration Act* concerns those who enter Canada as a landed immigrant, the selection of immigrants and the levels of immigration, in accordance with established economic, societal and humanitarian principles. The Act specifically provides for the promotion of cooperation between the Federal and "other levels of government" on immigration matters.

1.3.8 Special Education

Special Education Background

The basis of special education law in Ontario is rooted in the Canadian *Charter of Rights and Freedoms* (the "*Charter*") and in the *Education Act*. The *Charter* provides the legal foundation for special education laws in all Canadian jurisdictions. Section 7 and 15 of the *Charter* are particularly relevant. Section 7 deals with legal rights: "Everyone has the right to life, liberty and security of the person and the right not to be deprived thereof except in accordance with the principles of fundamental justice." Some interpretations of the legal decision R *v* Jones° and others suggest a right to an education. Section 15 of the *Charter* describes equality rights as "Every individual is equal before and under the law and has the right to the equal protection and equal benefit of the law without discrimination and, in particular, without discrimination based on race, national or ethnic origin, colour, religion, sex, age or mental or physical disability." Therefore, section 7 may be understood as ensuring the right to an education, and section 15 protects these rights from discrimination.°

R v Jones, [1986] 2 SCR 284

MacKay, AW., Sutherland, L., & Pochini, KD. (2013). *Teachers and the law: Diverse roles and new challenges* [3rd ed.]. Toronto, ON: Emond Montgomery.

The Ontario *Education Act* has been amended to ensure that it complies with the *Charter* to meet the educational needs of exceptional students. Amendments to the *Education Act* (initially through Bill 82 and now Regulation 181) provide the legal structure for these issues in Ontario schools. A variety of policy documents further describe how these laws are enacted in practice in classroom contexts. The purpose of these laws and regulations is to ensure the equity of access to appropriate educational services.

The *Education Amendment Act*, 1980, known as Bill 82, was the first attempt to introduce provisions for special education into the *Education Act*. Although some of the original Bill 82 provisions have been removed or amended to reflect changes in language and program structure based on the evolution of research, practice, and policy, Bill 82 key provisions still remain in place for special education programs in Ontario. These include definitions of special education program and services;° responsibilities of the Minister in regards to provision of special education programs and services;° assigning the responsibility to school boards for provision (or purchasing from another board) of special education programs and special education services for the exceptional pupils;° and the establishment of Ontario Special Education Tribunal.

§ 1(1) EA

§ 8(3) EA

§ 170(1)(7) EA

Students with Special Education Needs

The needs of some students cannot always be met through regular instructional and assessment practices. Therefore, schools offer specific accommodations and modifications to the educational program above or below the age-appropriate grade level expectations for a particular subject or course. The term students with special education needs includes all students receiving special education programs and services, whether or not they have been formally identified as exceptional. Access to special education programs and services need not be limited to students identified through the IPRC process. Boards may provide special education programs and/or services to meet students' educational needs and prepare an IEP even if the student has not been identified as exceptional.

Exceptional Students

§ 1(1) EA

The *Education Act*° defines an exceptional pupil as "a pupil whose behavioural, communicational, intellectual, physical or multiple exceptionalities are such that he or she is considered to need placement in a special education program...." Students are identified according to the following categories and definitions of exceptionalities:

- behaviour:
  - » this refers to a specific behaviour problem of such a degree, nature and duration that it adversely affects academic performance;
- communication:
  - » autism,
  - » deaf and hard-of-hearing,
  - » language impairment,
  - » speech impairment;
- intellectual:
  - » giftedness,
  - » mild intellectual disability,
  - » developmental disability;
- physical:
  - » physical disability,
  - » blind and low vision;
- multiple:
  - » multiple exceptionalities include a combination of learning or other disorders or impairments that will require the provision of appropriate support services.

Special Education Programs and Services

§ 13(1) Regulation 181/98

§ 2 Regulation 464/97

The *Education Act* requires that school boards provide, or purchase from another board, special education programs and services that are appropriate for the needs of their exceptional pupils.° A special education program is defined in the *Education Act* as an educational program that is based on and modified by the results of continuous assessment and evaluation; and includes a plan (currently an Individual Education Plan [IEP]) containing specific objectives and an outline of special education services that meet the needs of the exceptional pupil. Special education services are defined in the *Education Act* as the facilities and resources, including support personnel and equipment, necessary for developing and implementing a special education program. Every school board must also establish a Special Education Advisory Committee (SEAC),° consisting of parents and trustees, whose role is to make recommendations concerning special education services for exceptional students of the board.

According to the most recent statistics from the Ministry of Education, in the 2007/2008 school year, more than 192,000 students in Ontario were identified as exceptional pupils, whereas 96,600 students who were not formally identified were provided with special education programs and services.

Identification of the Exceptional Students' Needs

The identification of exceptional students is conducted by an Identification, Placement, and Review Committee (IPRC). All schools boards are required to set up IPRC consisting of at least three persons, one of whom must be a principal or supervisory officer of the board. Upon receiving a written request from the student's parent(s) or guardian(s), the principal of the school must refer the student to an IPRC who will make a decision about the exceptionality of the student and the type of appropriate educational placement. Alternatively, on written notice to the parent(s)/guardian(s), the student may be referred to an IPRC by the principal. The parent(s) or guardian(s) (as well as students who are sixteen years of age or older), are entitled to be present at and participate in all discussions of the IPRC meetings about the student or about the potential programs that would meet the student's needs. Others (school principal, resource people, representatives, and interpreters) may also attend an IPRC meeting if needed. On the basis of these discussions, the IPRC can recommend the special education programs and/or services that it considers to be appropriate for the student.

Before considering the option of placing a student in a special education class, the committee must first consider whether placement in a regular class, with appropriate special education programs and services, would meet the student's needs and be consistent with the parent's preferences. Where placement in a special education class is deemed most appropriate, the IPRC must provide written reasons for its decision. For exceptional students whose needs cannot be met entirely in the regular classroom, a number of placement options are available:

- A regular class with indirect support where the student is placed in a regular class for the entire day, and the teacher receives specialized consultative services;
- A regular class with resource assistance where the student is placed in a regular class for most or all of the day and receives specialized instruction, individually or in a small group, within the regular classroom from a qualified special education teacher;
- A regular class with withdrawal assistance where the student is placed in a regular class and receives instruction outside the classroom, for less than 50 per cent of the school day, from a qualified special education teacher;

- A special education class with partial integration where the student is placed by the IPRC in a special education class with specific student-teacher ratios depending upon the extent of the exceptionalities of the pupils in the class and the special education services that are available to the teacher,° for at least 50 per cent of the school day, but is integrated with a regular class for at least one instructional period daily.

§ 31 Regulation 298

- A full-time special education class, with specific student-teacher ratios depending upon the extent of the exceptionalities of the pupils in the class and the special education services that are available to the teacher,° for the entire school day.

§ 31 Regulation 298

The IPRC may also consider referring the student to a provincial committee for consideration of eligibility for admission to one of the Provincial Schools for blind, deaf or deaf-blind students, or to one of the Provincial Demonstration Schools for students with severe learning disabilities (discussed above).

If the IPRC has identified the student as an exceptional pupil and the parent agreed with the IPRC identification and placement decision, the board will promptly notify the principal of the school at which the special education program is to be provided of the need to develop an Individual Education Plan (IEP) for the student. Once a child has been placed in a special education program, the parent may request in writing a review IPRC meeting any time after their child has been in a special education program for 3 months. In absence of such request, an annual review IPRC meeting is held within the school year.

Parent(s) or guardian(s) who do not agree with either the identification or placement decision made by the IPRC, may request, within 15 days of receipt of the decision, that the IPRC hold a second meeting to discuss their concerns; or within 30 days of receipt of the decision, file a notice of appeal with the secretary of the board. If the parent does not agree with the decision after the second meeting, he or she may file a notice of appeal within 15 days of receipt of the decision. In case of appeal, the board will establish a special education appeal board consisting of three persons (one of whom is to be selected by the parent) who have no prior knowledge of the matter under appeal. The parent may accept the decision of the school board after the review of appeal, or may appeal to the Ontario Special Education Tribunal.

As an independent adjudicative agency, Ontario Special Education Tribunal, was established to hear appeals from parents regarding the identification and/or the special education placement of exceptional pupils.° OSET renders decisions that are final and binding on the parties (parents and school boards) and are made in the best interest of the pupil. Ontario Special Education (English) Tribunal (OSET) is responsible for appeals from the 60 English Public and Catholic school boards, while Tribunal de l'enfance en difficulté de l'Ontario (français) (TEDO) receives appeals from 12 French Public and

retrieved May 2013 from http://www.oset-tedo.ca/eng/index.html

Catholic school boards.

Individual Education Plan (IEP)

Under Regulation 181/98, "Identification and Placement of Exceptional Pupils," school boards must develop an Individual Education Plan (IEP) for each student who has been identified as exceptional by an Identification, Placement and Review Committee (IPRC), within 30 school days of the student's placement in a special education program. School boards, at their discretion, may also develop an IEP for students who have not been formally identified as exceptional. The IEP must be developed for each exceptional student in consultation with the parent. An IEP must include:

- specific educational expectations;
- an outline of the special education program and services that will be received;

Special Education Placements: Who Decides?

In 1989, a nine-year-old student with cerebral palsy and very limited ability to communicate was identified, in accordance with the *Ontario **Education Act***, as an exceptional student by an Identification, Placement and Review Committee (IPRC). The student, Emily, was placed in a regular classroom on a trial basis, spending two years in Kindergarten and one year in grade one. At that time, her teachers and educational assistants concluded that this placement was not in her best interests, and even might well harm her. As a result, and against her parents' wishes, she was placed in a special education class. As provided by law, her parents appealed the decision to the Special Education Appeal Board, and then the Ontario Special Education Tribunal, both of which upheld Emily's placement in a special education class. Emily's parents then appealed to the court claiming that the Tribunal had made errors in law and that her placement in special education was not in her best interests, considering the *Ontario **Education Act***, the *Canadian **Charter of Rights and Freedoms***, and the *Ontario Human Rights Code*. The Court found no errors in law and upheld the decision of the Tribunal, establishing that Emily's best interests would be served by her placement in a special education class. The court held that the ***Charter*** and the *Human Rights Code* did not presume that one placement or teaching method was superior to another. Equality in the provision of education did not necessarily mean education in the regular class. Emily's parents appealed the Ontario court's decision to the Supreme Court of Canada. In 1997, the Supreme Court approved the placement decision and in so doing provided the standard for determining the appropriateness of exceptional student placements. The Supreme Court determined that children are not disadvantaged by such placement decisions when:

- the best possible placement for the child is considered.
- the child's best interests and special needs are taken into consideration.
- ongoing assessment of the child's best interests and needs may be reflected in the placement.
- the decision is made from a subjective, child-centered perspective, one that tries to make equality meaningful from the child's point-of-view, rather than from that of the adults in the child's life.

EduLaw for Canadian Schools, 6(11), October 1994.

- a statement about the methods by which the student's progress will be reviewed; and
- for students 14 years and older (except those identified as exceptional solely on the basis of giftedness), a plan for transition to appropriate postsecondary school activities, such as work, further education, and community living.

A student's IEP must typically have a direct progress reporting link to the Provincial Report Card.

An IEP is a written plan describing the special education program and/or services required by a particular student, based on a thorough assessment of the student's strengths and needs that affect the student's ability to learn and demonstrate learning. It contains a record of the particular accommodations (not provided to the general student population) needed to help the student achieve his or her learning expectations, given the student's identified learning strengths and needs. As a working document, it identifies learning expectations that are modified from the expectations for the age-appropriate grade level in a particular subject or course, as outlined in the Ministry of Education's curriculum policy documents. In some cases, a student's program will include expectations derived from an alternative program (such as social skills, communication, and behaviour management). Alternative programs are intended to supplement, not replace, the student's access to the provincial curriculum. An IEP contains a record of the specific knowledge and skills to be assessed and evaluated for the purpose of reporting student achievement of modified and/or alternative expectations.

An IEP, thus, is an accountability tool for the student, the student's parents, and everyone who has responsibilities under the plan for helping the student meet the stated goals and learning expectations as the student progresses through the Ontario curriculum. If a parent believes their child will benefit from an IEP and the school board does not agree, the parent has the right to request that an IPRC meet to determine if their child is an exceptional student.

Planning the Entry and Transition to a Postsecondary Setting for Students with Special Education Needs

retrieved May 2013 from http://www.edu.gov.on.ca/eng/general/elemsec/speced/transiti.html

The entry to school for children with special needs is more complex and requires careful planning and coordination.° An entry-to-school plan should provide adequate time for children and parents to learn and practise the skills and routines that will facilitate a smooth move from preschool to school.

Similarly, a plan for the student's transition from secondary school to a postsecondary setting must be developed with input from the student, parent(s)/guardian(s), the principal, school staff, community agencies, and postsecondary institutions. An IEP for a student fourteen years of age or older must include a plan for transition to assist the student in moving from school to work, further education, and/or community living. Students identified as exceptional solely on the basis of giftedness are not required to have a transition plan as part of their IEP; their Individual Pathways Plan should effectively address their education and career planning needs. The principal is responsible for ensuring coordination and development of the transition plan, which could include provisions for helping the student connect with postsecondary educational institutions, community agencies, and/or the workplace, as appropriate.

1.3.9 Particular Programs

Schools in Ontario offer an increasingly wide variety of curricular and co-instructional (co-curricular and extra-curricular) programs. In addition to regular curriculum programs, the *Education Act* and regulations also make specific reference to a number of particular programs.

Religious Instruction

The *Education Act*° allows a student to receive religious instruction as desired by the student's parents or by the student (if the student is an adult). However, no student will be required to read or study in or from any religious book or to join in an exercise of religion if objected to by the parents or student (as an adult).

§ 51(1) EA

Originally, Regulation 262 was concerned with governing religion in schools (Regulation 262 is now Regulation 298). Two major cases affected the current provision of religious education in Ontario public school. Based on the ruling of the Ontario Court of Appeal in 1988 that struck down subsection 28(1) of Regulation 262,° public schools were no longer allowed to open or close the school day with religious exercises that gave primacy to a particular faith. The Ontario Court of Appeal also struck down subsection 28(4) of Regulation 262, which concerned the teaching of religion in the public elementary schools.° In accordance with the court's definition of permissible education about religion, such a program would (a) promote respect for the freedom of conscience and religion guaranteed by the Canadian *Charter of Rights and Freedoms*; and (b) provide for the study of different religions and religious beliefs in Canada and the world, without giving primacy to, and without indoctrination in, any particular religion or religious belief.°

Zylberberg v Sudbury Board of Education (1988), 65 OR (2d) 64.

Canadian Civil Liberties Association v Minister of Education (1990), 71 OR (2d) 341 (CA).

§ 28 Regulation 298

Therefore, Ontario public schools boards may provide programs in education about religion during the regular school day as follows:

1. Boards of education may provide programs in education about religion in Grades 1 to 8 during the school day for up to 60 minutes per week.°

§ 28(3) Regulation 298

2. Boards of education may continue to provide optional credit courses in World Religions in secondary schools, as specified in the curriculum guidelines. The world religion courses introduce

The Ontario Curriculum Grades 11 and 12 Social Sciences and Humanities, 2000, *retrieved May 2013 from http://www.edu.gov.on.ca/eng/curriculum/secondary/sstudies1112curr.pdf*

students to an exploration of religions around the world, and provide them with an awareness of the nature, place, and function of religion in diverse societies. The courses examine the critical issues facing world religions and their followers today.°

3. Schools and programs, including programs in education about religion, under the jurisdiction of boards of education must not be indoctrinational and must not give primacy to any particular religious faith.

4. A board may permit conducting religious exercises or instruction that includes indoctrination in a particular religion or religious belief in a school if the exercises are not conducted or the instruction is not provided by or under the auspices of the board; if they are offered on a school day at a time before or after the school's instructional program, or on a day that is not a school day; if no person is required by the board to attend the exercises or instruction; and if the board provides space for the exercises or instruction on the same basis as it provides space for other community activities.

The above guidelines do not apply to schools under the jurisdiction of separate school boards or to private schools. Roman Catholic school boards are responsible for developing credit courses in religious education. A Roman Catholic board that develops such courses does not have to seek approval for them from the ministry. Students may earn up to 4 credits in religious education. Credit courses may be developed in religious education by inspected private schools, where students may earn up to 4 credits in religious education. These locally developed religious education courses require the approval of the ministry.

Choices into Action: Guidance and Career Education Program Policy for Ontario Elementary and Secondary Schools, 1999, *retrieved May 2013 from http://www.edu.gov.on.ca/eng/document/curricul/secondary/choices/choicee.pdf*

The Guidance and Career Education Program

Choices into Action, a guidance and career education program policy for Ontario elementary and secondary schools,° describes the purpose and importance of Ontario's guidance and career education program, its content, and its unique approach to teaching and learning. It describes the approaches that principals and teachers are expected to take when teaching students how to develop their learning skills, interpersonal skills, and knowledge and skills in the area of career planning. It also outlines program planning strategies, accountability measures, and the roles and responsibilities of all involved—principals, teachers, students, parents, and community partners.

According to this policy, every school is required to develop and implement a guidance and career education program, under the direction of the principal and with the assistance of the school's guidance and career education program advisory team and school staff. The goals of such program are to assist students in understanding the concepts related to lifelong learning, interpersonal relationships

Prayer in Public Schools

In 1993, after attempting for years to change the Saskatoon Public Board of Education's policy on school prayer, a group of nine parents filed a complaint with the Saskatchewan Human Rights Commission alleging that the use of the Lord's Prayer and Bible readings in the public school classrooms violated the Saskatchewan Human Rights Code. After six years of bouncing between the Human Rights Commission and the courts over constitutional, jurisdictional and procedural issues, the complaint was finally heard by Kenneth Halvorson, a one person Board of Inquiry of the Saskatchewan Human Rights Commission.

The Saskatoon Public Board of Education defended its right to allow the Lord's Prayer under section 182 of the ***Education Act*** and under the *Saskatchewan Act,* 1905. Halvorson ruled that, while the Public Board had the constitutional right to "direct" teachers to use prayer in classrooms to start the day, its stated policy of "encouraging" and "supporting" teachers to choose prayer was outdated and discriminatory. He recommended that the board of education develop a multicultural religious proposal that "should not include use of any prayer or readings from any sort of bible" (Saskatchewan Human Rights Board of Inquiry Decision, July 23, 1999, p. 56).

The board of education suspended the use of the Lord's Prayer altogether for the 1999-2000 school year and, amidst considerable debate in the community, searched for other options for school opening exercises. The result was Policy 1030: School Opening Exercises, a policy guided by two fundamental principles:

- No activity will be done for the purposes of indoctrination; and
- The board of education does not mandate compulsory opening exercises with a spiritual dimension.

Instead, where opening exercises were used they were to be restricted to any or all of the following: instruction on the values which have been developed by the Saskatoon Public School Division; opportunities for personal reflection through a moment of silence, writing in a personal journal or sharing a thought for the day; the singing of O Canada (Regulations and Administrative Procedures, Policy 1030, Saskatoon Public Board of Education).

Questions for Discussion:

- How do schools best address the goal of developing moral, ethical and spiritual values?
- How do public schools respect and reflect cultural diversity and traditional religious values and practices?
- How does Halvorson's ruling apply to other school jurisdictions?

(including responsible citizenship), and career planning; developing learning skills, social skills, a sense of social responsibility, and the ability to formulate and pursue educational and career goals; and, applying this learning to their lives and work in the school and the community. The guidance and career education program covers three areas of learning – student development (habits and skills necessary for learning), interpersonal development (knowledge and skills for getting along with others), and career development (knowledge and skills needed to set short-term and long-term goals in planning for the future).

Two of the three areas of learning—student development and interpersonal development—are integrated within the learning skills and work habits described in *Growing Success: Assessment, Evaluation, and Reporting in Ontario Schools – First Edition, Covering Grades 1 to 12*. For each of the learning skills and work habits, the document provides examples of associated behaviours, which are designed to guide teachers in the instruction, assessment, and evaluation of the learning skills and work habits. The third area of learning—career development—helps students reflect critically on their strengths, needs, and interests; set goals; and identify learning opportunities and strategies to achieve their goals. The career development competencies are "knowing self," "exploring opportunities," "making decisions," and "preparing for change and making transitions." The policy outlines these competencies and provides examples of associated behaviours to guide teachers in the integration of these competencies within the delivery of the Ontario curriculum in all disciplines. Schools must offer a range of career exploration activities to support students in the development of these competencies.

To align the guidance and career education program with the Ontario curriculum, teachers in elementary schools need to ensure that classroom learning across all the grades and subjects provides ample opportunity for students to learn how to work independently (including homework completion), to cooperate with others, to resolve conflicts with others, to participate in class, to solve problems, and to set goals to improve their work.

Ontario curriculum policy documents include expectations for secondary school students related to the program goals of guidance and career education. In helping students meet these curriculum expectations, teachers will help them make connections among the knowledge and skills acquired in all disciplines. Students will also learn to make connections between the knowledge and skills they are acquiring at school and the knowledge and skills required by postsecondary educational institutions, apprenticeship programs, and employers.

From Kindergarten to Grade 12, teachers encourage their students to set goals to improve their work and to review the success of their personal efforts and choices. Starting in Grade 7, students also track the growth of their career development competencies and plan for their future in an Individual Pathways Plan (IPP; previously AEP [Annual Education Plan]). Schools are required to put in place a process to support students in Grades 7 through 12 in establishing, reviewing, and revising their IPP at least twice a year. In order to earn an Ontario Secondary School Diploma (OSSD), all students are required to successfully complete the compulsory Career Studies course in Grade 10. Students may also take additional courses from the guidance and career education curriculum policy document, one of which may count as 1 of the 18 compulsory credits (Group 1) within OSSD.

The guidance and career education program policy requires schools to provide orientation and exit programs to help students make smooth transitions. Orientation programs are designed to help students adjust to school at key transition points, such as entry (re-entry) into school and the move from elementary to secondary school. Students who change schools, as well as students enrolled for the first time in schools operated by Ontario school boards, also need such programs.

The goal of an exit program is to help students who leave secondary school on or before graduation to make a successful transition to the next stage of their lives. Exit programs should include a review of the student's Individual Pathways Plan and information to support the student in reaching his or her future goals. Other guidelines require putting in place implementation strategies for transition from Grade 8 to Grade 9 for students who are deemed to be at risk of not graduating.

Co-Instructional Activities

Extracurricular and co-curricular school activities occur on school grounds but are not part of Ontario's curriculum policy documents. In Ontario, extracurricular and co-curricular activities are known as co-instructional activities ("activités complémentaires"). The teacher's participation in co-instructional activities is not required by the province and is regarded as voluntary. However, co-instructional activities are seen as an extremely important part of the educational experience as they support the operation of schools; enrich students' school-related experience within or beyond the instructional program; and, advance students' education and education-related goals. School boards have the authority to incorporate arts, cultural, and athletic activities, youth travel, outdoor education and similar activities into the educational program for schools.

Experiential Learning Programs

Experiential learning programs are designed to provide students with opportunities to apply their classroom learning in a workplace setting and allow them to explore a career of interest as they plan a pathway through secondary school to their postsecondary destination. These programs may include job shadowing and job twinning (starting in Grades 7 and 8), and work experience and cooperative education, which are offered in secondary school.

Cooperative Education

Cooperative education is a program that allows students to earn secondary school credits while completing a work placement in the community.° It allows students to participate in valuable learning experiences that help prepare them for the next stage of their lives, whether in apprenticeship training, college, community living, university, or the workplace. Cooperative education programs must be developed and implemented according to the policy outlined in Cooperative Education and Other Forms of Experiential Learning: Policies and Procedures for Ontario Secondary Schools.°

Cooperative Education Fact Sheet, 2006, *retrieved May 2013 from http://www.edu.gov.on.ca/eng/studentsuccess/pathways/coop/coop_fact_sheet.pdf*

Cooperative Education and Other Forms of Experiential Learning: Policies and Procedures for Ontario Secondary Schools, 2000, *retrieved May 2013 from http://www.edu.gov.on.ca/eng/document/curricul/secondary/coop/cooped.pdf*

A cooperative education program consists, at a minimum, of one cooperative education course, which is monitored by a cooperative education teacher, and the related course, on which the cooperative education course is based. Any course from an Ontario curriculum policy document or any ministry-approved locally developed course may serve as the related course for a cooperative education program.

The cooperative education course consists of a classroom component and a placement component. The classroom component includes 15 to 20 hours of pre-placement instruction, which prepares students for the workplace and includes instruction in areas of key importance such as health and safety, and classroom sessions held at various times during and after the placement, which provide opportunities for students to reflect on and reinforce their learning in the workplace. Placements vary in length, depending on the number of credits students are earning through their co-op program, and may involve work outside the designated hours of the school day, depending on the nature of the program and the placements available in the community.

In their cooperative education program, students may earn up to two cooperative education credits for each related course, whether it is a full- or half-credit course. If the related course is a multiple-credit course, a student may earn a maximum of two co-op credits for each credit earned in the related course

Every student in a cooperative education program must have a Personalized Placement Learning Plan (PPLP). A student's progress in achieving the curriculum expectations and in meeting the requirements identified in the PPLP must be assessed and evaluated by a teacher through regular workplace monitoring meetings with the student and the student's workplace supervisor.

School boards are responsible for providing cooperative education opportunities to all interested students who are considered ready to undertake learning in the workplace, including students with special education needs. Boards should also ensure that the programs are offered through a variety of delivery models such as the regular school program, specialized school and board programs, continuing education day schools, summer and night school programs, or virtual cooperative education ("e-co-op").

Work Experience

Cooperative Education and Other Forms of Experiential Learning: Policies and Procedures for Ontario Secondary Schools, 2000, *retrieved May 2013 from http://www.edu.gov.on.ca/eng/document/curricul/secondary/coop/cooped.pdf*

Work experience is a planned learning opportunity that provides students with a relatively short-term work experience (from one to four weeks). Requirements for work experience programs are similar to cooperative education programs. Work experience placements must comply with the placement assessment criteria.°

Pre-placement preparation must include instruction addressing job-readiness skills, health and safety procedures in the workplace, and school and placement expectations. Based on the curriculum expectations of the unit in which the work experience occurs, a work experience learning plan (WELP) must be developed in collaboration with the participating placement supervisor. Students are required to be monitored at least once at their placement to ensure that their learning is consistent with the WELP. Opportunities must be set in place for students to analyse their work experience and integrate it with their in-school learning.

Job Shadowing and Job Twinning

Students in Grades 7 to 12 can participate in job shadowing and job twinning as part of curriculum delivery or as part of the guidance and career education program. Job shadowing allows a student to spend from ½ to 1 day (in some cases, up to 3 days) on one-on-one observation of a worker at a place of employment. Job twinning provides the opportunity for one-on-one observation of a cooperative education student at his at his or her placement for ½ to 1 day. The preparation of students for job shadowing and job twinning should include review of learning expectations, activity protocols, and workplace health and safety procedures. Students should also be provided with the opportunity to reflect on the experience.

Schools are responsible for ensuring the selection of appropriate placements in safe work environments. Because the emphasis of these placements is on educational experience rather than productivity, students do not normally receive wages (although some students may receive expense allowances or honoraria, these do not necessarily give them employee status).

For students who are fourteen years of age or older and who are participating in experiential learning programs involving more than one day at the workplace, a Work Education Agreement form must be completed to ensure Workplace Safety and Insurance coverage.° If the student is under fourteen years of age or if the experiential learning program activity lasts one day or less, these experiences should be treated as field trips.

Policy/Program Memorandum No. 76a, "Workplace Safety and Insurance Coverage for Students in Work Education Programs"

School-Work Transition Programs

School-work transition programs provide students, who are planning to enter the workforce directly from high school, with workplace experience, to help their transition from school into a particular industry or occupation. These programs offer a progression of experiences from job shadowing through to co-op, giving students the opportunity to complete high school graduation or certificate requirements; develop Essential Skills and work habits outlined in the Ontario Skills Passport (OSP),° as well as industry-specific skills. Employers must be involved in the development and delivery of school-work transition programs. School boards must establish procedures for developing and implementing their school-work transition programs.

retrieved May 2013 from http://skills.edu.gov.on.ca

Specialist High Skills Major (SHSM)

retrieved May 2013 from http://www.edu.gov.on.ca/eng/studentsuccess/pathways/shsm/shsm_fact_sheet.pdf

A Specialist High Skills Major (SHSM) is a ministry-approved specialized program that allows students to focus their learning on a specific economic sector while meeting the requirements to graduate from secondary school.° It also assists in their transition after graduation to apprenticeship training, college, university or the workplace. Boards and schools may offer only the Specialist High Skills Major programs for which they have ministry approval. A school approved to offer an SHSM program must offer the program in all four pathways: apprenticeship training, college, university, and the workplace.

retrieved May 2013 from http://www.edu.gov.on.ca/morestudentsuccess/SHSMBinder.pdf

Each SHSM program must consist of the following five components:°

- a defined bundle of credits consisting of 8 to 10 Grade 11 and Grade 12 credits, including 2 cooperative education credits;
- sector-recognized certifications and training courses and programs;
- experiential learning and career exploration activities appropriate to the sector;
- reach-ahead learning experiences connected with the student's postsecondary plans;
- essential skills and work habits required in the sector and recorded in the Ontario Skills Passport (OSP).

Students must successfully complete all five required components to earn the SHSM designation on their diploma. No substitutions for any of the required components are permitted; however, school boards may add to the SHSM's components to reflect a local emphasis. Students who successfully complete a Specialist High Skills Major (SHSM) program as part of the requirements for their Ontario Secondary School Diploma (OSSD) will receive a diploma with an SHSM red seal. It is interesting to note that the SHSM designation or seal on the OSSD is the only special designation permitted on the OSSD, and it is the first time in the history of Ontario that there has ever been an endorsement or "enhancement" to a diploma.

The Ontario Youth Apprenticeship Program (OYAP)

The Ontario Youth Apprenticeship Program (OYAP) is a specialized program that enables students to meet diploma requirements while participating in a cooperative education program in an apprenticeship occupation. All students participating in an OYAP must be at least sixteen years old, a full-time student, and have accumulated a minimum of 16 credits towards their Ontario Secondary School Diploma (OSSD). An OYAP student earns cooperative education credits for work experience in an apprenticeship occupation. An OYAP student may have the opportunity to become a registered apprentice while attending secondary school. A student may participate in OYAP as part of a Specialist High Skills Major (SHSM) program. The Ontario Youth Apprenticeship Program is guided by policies and procedures in Cooperative Education and Other Forms of Experiential Learning and in the OYAP guidelines established by the Ministry of Training, Colleges and Universities.°

retrieved May 2013 from http://www.tcu.gov.on.ca/eng/eopg/publications/20120411_oyap_2012-12_aa_guidelines.pdf

1.3.10 Graduation Requirements and Procedures

In order to obtain an Ontario Secondary School Diploma (OSSD), a student must earn a minimum of 30 credits (18 compulsory credits and 12 optional credits); meet the provincial secondary school literacy graduation requirement; and complete 40 hours of community involvement activities.

Compulsory Credits

Students must earn the following compulsory credits to obtain the Ontario Secondary School Diploma:°

retrieved May 2013 from http://www.edu.gov.on.ca/extra/eng/ppm/graduate.pdf

- 4 credits in English (1 credit per grade);
  - » The Ontario Secondary School Literacy Course (OSSLC) may be used to meet either the Grade 11 or the Grade 12 English compulsory credit requirement;
  - » The Grade 11 Contemporary Aboriginal Voices course may be used to meet the Grade 11 English compulsory credit requirement;
  - » For English language learners the requirement may be met through earning a maximum of 3 credits in English as a second language (ESL) or English literacy development (ELD); the fourth credit must be a Grade 12 compulsory English course.
- 3 credits in Mathematics (at least 1 credit in Grade 11 or 12);
- 2 credits in Science;
- 1 credit in Canadian History (Grade 10);
- 1 credit in Canadian Geography (Grade 9);
- 1 credit in the Arts;
  - » The Grade 9 Expressing Aboriginal Cultures course may be used to meet the compulsory credit requirement in the arts.
- 1 credit in Health and Physical Education;
- 1 credit in French as a Second Language;
  - » Students who have taken Native languages in place of French as a second language in elementary school may use a Level 1 or 2 Native language course to meet the compulsory credit requirement for French as a second language.
- 0.5 credit in Career Studies;

- 0.5 credit in Civics

Students require 3 additional credits, consisting of 1 credit from each of the following groups:

- Group 1: English (including the Ontario Secondary School Literacy Course), French as a second language, classical languages, international languages, Native languages, Canadian and world studies, Native studies, social sciences and humanities, guidance and career education, cooperative education;
- Group 2: French as a second language, the arts, business studies, health and physical education, cooperative education;
- Group 3: French as a second language, science (Grade 11 or 12), computer studies, technological education, cooperative education.

The following conditions apply to selections from the above three groups:

- A maximum of 2 credits in French as a second language may count as additional compulsory credits, 1 credit from Group 1, and 1 credit from either Group 2 or Group 3;
- A maximum of 2 credits in cooperative education may count as additional compulsory credits, selected from any of Groups 1, 2, or 3.

Students may obtain compulsory credits through the courses locally developed by a board. Seven locally developed compulsory credit courses have been approved by the ministry for use by school boards across the province: Grades 9 and 10 English, Grades 9 and 10 mathematics, Grades 9 and 10 science, and Grade 10 Canadian history.° Locally developed compulsory credit courses may be used only to meet the compulsory credit requirements that they have been designed to meet.

Ontario Schools Kindergarten to Grade 12, 2011, *retrieved May 2013 from http://www.edu.gov.on.ca/eng/document/policy/os/ONSchools.pdf*

§ 3.2 Ontario Secondary Schools, Grades 9 to 12, 1999, *retrieved May 2013 from http://www.edu.gov.on.ca/eng/document/curricul/secondary/oss/oss.pdf*

Subject to certain limitations,° up to three compulsory credits (or the equivalent in half credits) may be substituted with courses from other subject areas specified in the list of compulsory credit requirements (including Groups 1, 2 and 3) above. Such substitutions are made if the principal deems it necessary for promoting and enhancing individual student learning or responding to special needs and interests. The decision to substitute one course for another for a student should be made only if the student's educational interests are best served by such a substitution in consultation with the parent or the adult student and appropriate school staff. Each substitution will be noted on the student's Ontario Student Transcript.

Students may attain compulsory credits by completing music programs outside the school (Option 2 below).

Optional Credits

In addition to the 18 compulsory credits, students must earn 12 optional credits by successfully completing courses that they have selected from the courses listed as available in their school's program and course calendar. The 12 optional credits may include up to 4 credits earned through approved dual credit courses or through a combination of a dual credit program and a program in music taken outside the school (Option 1 below).

Dual credit programs are ministry-approved programs that allow students who are still in secondary school to take college or apprenticeship courses that count towards both an Ontario Secondary School Diploma and a postsecondary certificate, diploma, or degree, or an apprenticeship certification,°

Dual Credit Policy and Implementation, 2010, *retrieved May 2013 from http://cal2.edu.gov.on.ca/november2010/DualCredit_Implement2010.pdf*

A maximum of two credits may be awarded to students taking music programs outside the school through one or both of the following options:

- Option 1: For music programs completed outside the school, the principal of a secondary school may award a maximum of 2 university/college preparation credits (1 Grade 11 credit and 1 Grade 12 credit) towards the Ontario Secondary School Diploma. These credits are optional credits.
- Option 2: Students may be awarded music credits (a maximum of 2 credits, in Grades 10 to 12) through the PLAR process. These credits may be used to meet the compulsory credit requirement in the arts or the additional compulsory credit requirement for Group 2.

Students may obtain optional credits from courses in Grades 9 to 12 in any discipline that are locally developed by a board to accommodate educational and career preparation needs that are not met through courses within the provincial curriculum policy documents.°

Ministry of Education. (2004). *Guide to Locally Developed Courses, Grades 9 to 12, 2004.* Toronto, ON: the Author. *retrieved May 2013 from http://www.edu.gov.on.ca/eng/document/curricul/secondary/localdev/locdeve.pdf*

The Secondary School Literacy Graduation Requirement

All students are required to meet the secondary school literacy graduation requirement in order to earn an Ontario Secondary School Diploma (OSSD). Based on the expectations for reading and writing throughout the Ontario curriculum up to and including Grade 9, the purpose of the secondary school literacy graduation requirement is to determine whether students have the skills in reading and writing that they will need to succeed in school, at work, and in daily life.

The Ontario Secondary School Literacy Test (OSSLT) is administered in Grade 10 to assess the literacy skills of students in Ontario for the purpose of determining whether they meet the provincial secondary school literacy requirement for graduation. The test is scheduled by and administered through the Education Quality and Accountability Office (EQAO) once each year, usually in the spring.

Once students have successfully completed the OSSLT, they may not retake it. Students who do not successfully complete the OSSLT may retake the test in subsequent years or have additional opportunities

The Ontario Curriculum: English – The Ontario Secondary School Literacy Course (OSSLC), Grade 12, 2003, *retrieved May 2013 from http://www.edu.gov.on.ca/eng/curriculum/secondary/english12curr.pdf*

(e.g., remedial assistance, additional credit courses, or the Ontario Secondary School Literacy Course (OSSLC)) to meet the literacy graduation requirement.

If a student has had two opportunities to take the OSSLT and has failed it at least once, the student is eligible to enrol in the OSSLC.° The instructional and assessment core of the course comprises the reading and writing competencies required by the Ontario Secondary School Literacy Test (OSSLT). Students who pass the course are considered to have met the literacy graduation requirement.

• *A mature student is a student who is at least eighteen years of age on or before December 31 of the school year in which he or she registers in an Ontario secondary school program; who was not enrolled as a regular day school student for a period of at least one school year immediately preceding his or her registration in a secondary school program (for mature students, a school year is a period of no less than ten consecutive months immediately preceding the student's return to school); and who is enrolled in a secondary program for the purpose of obtaining an OSSD.*

Mature students have the option to meet the literacy graduation requirement by successfully completing the OSSLT or to enrol directly in the Ontario Secondary School Literacy Course without first attempting the OSSLT.°

The Community Involvement Requirement

Policy/Program Memorandum No. 124a, "Ontario Secondary School Diploma Requirement: Community Involvement Activities in English-Language Schools"

The purpose of the 40-hour community involvement diploma requirement is to encourage students to develop an awareness and understanding of civic responsibility and of the role they can play and the contributions they can make in supporting and strengthening their communities. This diploma requirement applies to students in Grades 9 to 12 (Grade 8 students are allowed to start accumulating the hours for this requirement in the summer before entering Grade 9). Students' community involvement activities are to be planned in consultation with their parents and as part of the Individual Pathways Plan process. °

The Ontario Secondary School Certificate (OSSC)

§ 3.3 Ontario Secondary Schools, Grades 9-12, Program and Diploma Requirements, 1999, *retrieved May 2013 from http://www.edu.gov.on.ca/eng/document/curricul/secondary/oss/oss.pdf*

The Ontario Secondary School Certificate (OSSC) is granted on request to 18-year old students who leave secondary school before earning the Ontario Secondary School Diploma, provided that they have earned a minimum of 14 credits distributed as follows:°

- compulsory credits (total of 7):
  - » 2 credits in English
  - » 1 credit in Canadian geography or Canadian history
  - » 1 credit in mathematics
  - » 1 credit in science
  - » 1 credit in health and physical education
  - » 1 credit in the arts, computer studies, or technological education
- optional credits (total of 7):
  - » 7 credits selected by the student from available courses

The provisions for making substitutions for compulsory credits (above) also apply to the Ontario Secondary School Certificate.

Students who are granted OSSC are not required to complete 40 hours of community involvement or to pass the Ontario Secondary Literacy Test.

The Certificate of Accomplishment

Students who leave secondary school upon reaching the age of eighteen without fulfilling the requirements for the Ontario Secondary School Diploma or the Ontario Secondary School Certificate may be granted a Certificate of Accomplishment.° The Certificate of Accomplishment may be a useful means of recognizing achievement for students who plan to take certain kinds of further training, or who plan to find employment directly after leaving school. The Certificate of Accomplishment is accompanied by the student's Ontario Student Transcript. For students who have an Individual Education Plan (IEP), a copy of the IEP may be included.

§ 3.4 Ontario Secondary Schools, Grades 9-12, Program and Diploma Requirements, 1999, *retrieved May 2013 from http://www.edu.gov.on.ca/eng/document/curricul/secondary/oss/oss.pdf*

1.3.11 Alternative Ways of Completing Courses and Programs

While the majority of secondary school students earn their credits towards the Ontario Secondary School Diploma by enrolling in the courses offered in their secondary school, some may wish to consider alternative ways of earning the required credits. Different options available for such students (as well as adult learners) are discussed below.

E-Learning

E-learning encompasses the use of electronic technologies to support learning and teaching. The Ministry of Education designed the provincial E-learning Ontario Strategy° to assist school boards in providing digital learning opportunities for students. E-Learning Ontario offers access to the wide range of tools and resources at no cost to participating school boards: the digital library (Ontario Educational Resource Bank [OERB]);° the provincial online learning system for blended learning and online courses (Learning Management System [LMS]);° online collaborative and professional development site (E-Community Ontario);° online seat reservation system (SRS);° and online math tutoring (Homework Help).° School boards that participate in the e-Learning Ontario strategy retain full responsibility for the delivery of and access to courses and resources at the local level. Only students who are registered in a provincially funded school are eligible to have access to the e-Learning Ontario resources.

retrieved May 2013 from http://www.edu.gov.on.ca/elearning/strategy.html

retrieved May 2013 from http://www.edu.gov.on.ca/elearning/pdf/5067_OERBhandout_04.pdf

retrieved May 2013 from http://www.edu.gov.on.ca/elearning/courses.html

retrieved May 2013 from http://www.edu.gov.on.ca/elearning/ecomm.html

retrieved May 2013 from http://www.edu.gov.on.ca/elearning/srs.html

retrieved May 2013 from http://www.edu.gov.on.ca/elearning/homework.html

Adult and Continuing Education

Continuing education supports learners of all ages by offering credit and non-credit learning opportunities outside the regular

§ 1 Regulation 285 ► *under the authority of the* Education Act, *1990—not to be confused with* Regulation *285 under the authority of the* Employment Standards Act, *2000*

day school program, and during the summer. Schools boards and various government agencies may provide the following continuing education courses:°

- credit courses for adolescent and adult learners (e.g., English or French as a second language);
- non-credit courses (e.g., driver education or citizenship education);
- international language programs for elementary school students;
- remedial opportunities for students in Grades 7 to 10 to improve their literacy and mathematics skills;
- general-interest community programs and workshops for parents;
- literacy upgrading programs for adults offered by the Ministry of Training, Colleges and Universities;
- English as a second language / French as a second language programs for adults offered by the Ministry of Citizenship and Immigration.

§ 41(6) EA

A person is entitled to enrol in a continuing education course or class that is acceptable for credit towards a secondary school diploma if the principal is satisfied that the person is competent to undertake the work of the course or class.°

A statement of the student's achievement in all credit courses delivered through continuing education will be issued to the student by the principal of the continuing education school. The student's achievement will also be reported to the principal of the school that holds the student's Ontario Student Record for recording on the Ontario Student Transcript.

§ 2(6) Regulation 285 ► *under the authority of the* Education Act, *1990*

§ 10(1) Regulation 285 ► *under the authority of the* Education Act, *1990*

Two or more boards may jointly establish continuing education courses and classes in a school or schools operated by one or more of the school boards where instruction is conducted.° A board may discontinue a program at the end of the school year if the number of qualified persons of the board enrolled in courses or classes provided under the program is fewer than 23 at the conclusion of the school year in which the program is provided.°

Adult Education

School boards may offer classes for adults who return to complete their Ontario Secondary School Diploma (OSSD) requirements and/or to complete specific courses required for entry into postsecondary institutions and apprenticeship programs. Programs may be offered full-time or part-time, during the day or in the evening, allowing adults to learn while fulfilling other obligations that may include working and parenting. Courses may be offered in modules or quadmesters of approximately six to eight weeks and may take place in adult learning centres, centres for continuing education, adult high schools, and secondary schools.

Summer School

School boards may also offer summer school programs° through continuing education, to elementary, secondary, and adult students. The terms of admission to a course offered through summer school will be determined by the board that operates the summer school. A summer school program may not begin until after the last school day in the school year and must end before the first school day of the following school year.

§ 6.8.4.1 Ontario Secondary Schools, Grades 9–12: Program and Diploma Requirements, 1999, *retrieved May 2013 from http://www.edu.gov.on.ca/eng/document/curricul/secondary/oss/oss.pdf*

School boards may offer courses for credit through summer school to enable students to take additional credit courses; allow students to retake or improve achievement in the courses they have not successfully/satisfactorily completed during the school year; allow students to achieve a credit through credit recovery of a course that they have not successfully completed during the school year; or, enable students to complete required components of specialized programs (e.g., Specialist High Skills Major).

Summer school credit courses must fulfil the same credit requirements as courses offered during the regular school year, including the requirement that each one credit course be scheduled for 110 hours. Boards may also offer non-credit summer school courses and programs to address elementary and secondary students' remedial needs and interests.

Night School/Evening Credit Courses

A school board may offer evening credit courses, through continuing education, to regular day school students and to adults who need to complete requirements for the Ontario Secondary School Diploma.

To be considered for admission to a continuing education course offered for credit in the evening, a regular day school student must provide:

- a statement signed by the day school principal about the consultation with the student regarding enrolment in the course and permission to enrol in the course;
- parental approval, if the student is under the age of 18 (unless the student is 16 or 17 years old and has withdrawn from parental control).

The scheduled time in any evening continuing education course taken for credit will not be less than 90 hours. It is the responsibility of the principal of the continuing education program to ensure that each course contains the amount of work that would ordinarily be completed in the time scheduled for the course in a day school program.

The Independent Learning Centre (ILC)

Secondary school credit courses are available through the Independent

retrieved May 2013 from http://www.ilc.org/index-main.php

Learning Centre (ILC).° Courses offered will be courses from the curriculum policy documents and will enable students to fulfil the requirements for an Ontario Secondary School Diploma (OSSD). ILC courses follow a blended learning model, combining print and online components with support from secondary school teachers certified through the Ontario College of Teachers (OCT). When a student has taken a Grade 11 or 12 ILC course, or successfully completed a Grade 9 or 10 ILC course, When a student has successfully completed an ILC course, the principal will record his or her standing on the Ontario Student Transcript (OST).

Independent Study

Independent study is an arrangement by which a student is excused from attending some or all classes in a course in order to study independently but under the supervision of a teacher. Courses delivered through the Independent Learning Centre may form part of independent study. There is no restriction on the number of periods that a teacher may allow for independent study within any given course. The teacher of the course is responsible for assigning components of the course, suggesting available resources, evaluating the achievement of the student, and ensuring that the total work involved is equivalent to that expected in the time scheduled for the course. Students are expected to demonstrate achievement of the overall curriculum expectations of the course. When a student has successfully completed a course through independent study, the principal will make a record on the Ontario Student Transcript.

§ 6.8.2 Ontario Secondary Schools, Grades 9–12: Program and Diploma Requirements, 1999, *retrieved May 2013 from http://www.edu.gov.on.ca/eng/document/curricul/secondary/oss/oss.pdf*

Private Study

§ 6.8.3 Ontario Secondary Schools, Grades 9–12: Program and Diploma Requirements, 1999, *retrieved May 2013 from http://www.edu.gov.on.ca/eng/document/curricul/secondary/oss/oss.pdf*

A student may be permitted to take one or more courses through private study° in one of the following circumstances: (a) the student is deemed to have a valid reason for not attending classes, or (b) the school does not offer the course(s).° The school must be willing to monitor the student's progress and evaluate his or her work. ILC courses may form part of a student's private study program. When a student has taken a course through private study, the principal will record the student's achievement on the Ontario Student Transcript.

1.3.12 Student Transfers

Transfers between Schools within Ontario

Elementary school students who are transferring from one Ontario elementary school to another will be placed in the appropriate grade by the principal, based on the information in the student's Provincial Report Card, Ontario Student Record, and/or other relevant documentation (e.g., Individual Education Plan (IEP), and consultation with parents and the student.

Ontario Student Transcript Manual, 2010, *retrieved May 2013 from http://www.edu.gov.on.ca/eng/general/elemsec/ost/ost2010.pdf*

Secondary school students who are transferring from one Ontario secondary school to another will have their credits recorded on the Ontario Student Transcript° transferred too, along with the information on their progress towards meeting graduation requirements (i.e., whether they have met the literacy graduation requirement; their accumulated community involvement hours). The principal of the receiving school may award credit for work started in the previous school but completed in the receiving school. Where this work cannot be completed in the receiving school, the receiving principal may, after consultation with the principal of the sending school, award a partial credit in recognition of the student's achievement of some of the course expectations.

For students transferring from a French-language to an English-language secondary school, the requirement is to complete at least one compulsory Grade 12 English course in order to meet graduation requirements. For students transferring from an English-language to a French-language secondary school, the requirement is to complete at least one compulsory Grade 12 Français course. A student who transfers before having met the literacy graduation requirement will have to meet the requirement in the language of instruction of the new school.

Transfers from Home Schooling, Non-Inspected Private Schools, or Schools outside Ontario

Elementary school students who are transferring from home schooling, non-inspected private schools, or schools outside Ontario will be placed in an age-appropriate grade by the principal of the receiving school. The placement decision is informed by relevant documentation, such as report cards, various assessment materials, attendance records, and other documentation, as well as consultation with parents/guardians and students.

For secondary students who are transferring from home schooling, non-inspected private schools, or schools outside Ontario, the placement decision by the principal of the receiving school will encompass the total credit equivalency of the student's previous learning and the number of compulsory and optional credits still to be earned. The credit equivalency total and the number of compulsory credits included will be entered on the student's Ontario Student Transcript. Students will have to meet the provincial secondary school literacy requirement. In addition, the principal will determine the number of hours of community involvement activities the student will have to complete. After a consultation with the student, staff, and parents, the final placement decision, and the rationale for the placement, will be communicated to the student and parents. The principal should note the results of his or her assessment and the reasons for the decision in the student's Ontario Student Record.

Both internal (provincial) and external (inter-province) transfers for secondary students may undergo a formal evaluation and accreditation

Policy/Program Memorandum No. 129, "Prior Learning Assessment and Recognition (PLAR): Implementation in Ontario Secondary Schools"

process known as Prior Learning Assessment and Recognition (PLAR),° to evaluate their skills and knowledge against the overall expectations outlined in provincial curriculum policy documents in order to earn credits towards the secondary school diploma. The PLAR process is developed by a school board in compliance with ministry around two components: challenge and equivalency. PLAR procedures are carried out under the direction of the school principal, who grants the credits.

1.3.13 Scholarships and Award Programs

Every year, a number of scholarships and awards are granted to deserving students graduating from Grade 12.

The Ontario Scholar Program

Policy/Program Memorandum No. 53, "Ontario Scholar Program"

The Ontario Scholar Program° recognizes students who have earned an Ontario Secondary School Diploma in either the current school year or the previous school year and who attained an aggregate of at least 480 marks in any combination of ministry-approved courses that provide a total of 6 credits. Upon the recommendation of their principal, these graduating students receive an Ontario Scholar certificate.

Governor General's Medal

The Governor General's Academic Medal was first awarded in 1873 and it continues today as a significant award for academic achievement for secondary, post-secondary and graduate students. In Ontario, a Governor General's Bronze Medal is awarded each year to the student who achieves the highest average upon graduation from his or her high school. It is the responsibility of each high school to determine a clear winner every year based on criteria outlined in the Academic Medal Directives.°

retrieved May 2013 from http://www.gg.ca/honours/awards/acmed/01_e.pdf

Bursaries and Awards

It is the policy of most school boards in Ontario to provide scholarships and other awards to students within their jurisdiction. Other educational institutions and organizations (the universities, colleges, technical institutes, professional organizations, and others) also do the same. As well, numerous fraternal organizations, businesses (both public and private), unions, foundations, individuals, and estates reward excellence and assist students financially in furthering their education.

2.0 PARENTS AND SCHOOL COMMUNITIES IN ONTARIO

Part 2.0 provides an overview of the rights and obligations of parents, and the opportunities for community involvement in the educational affairs of individual schools and of school districts.

2.1 WHO IS A "PARENT"?

The Ontario *Education Act* does not define who a "parent' is, but for the purpose of the Act, a parent is a person, either a natural parent or a guardian, who is responsible for the care of a child. The Act typically references "parent or guardian" as a person legally appointed and recognized as guardian, or a person who has the child in his or her home or care or custody. For example, Section 277.15 indicates that "a parent includes a person who has lawful custody of a child."

2.2 RIGHT TO INFORMATION

A student's records are privileged and only available to designated educational personnel and parents. These records may only be provided to others with written permission from a parent, with a few extraordinary exceptions (for example, as stipulated in the *Personal Health Information Protection Act*, the *Child and Family Services Act* and the *Occupational Health and Safety Act*). Parents may have access to a child's personal information under both the *Municipal Freedom of Information and Protection of Privacy Act* and section 266(3) of the *Education Act*. The *Education Act* provides for the right of access to a student's Ontario Student Record (or OSR) by a parent or guardian if the child is under the age of 18.° According to Section 54(c) of the *Municipal Freedom of Information and Protection of Privacy Act*, the rights and powers of a child may be exercised by any person having lawful custody of the child so that a parent with lawful custody of a child may consent to disclosure of a child's personal information or make a request for access to the personal information. Separated or divorced parents of a child have a right to access the child's school records regardless of who has custody of the child. In

Cavoukian, A. (2011). *A Guide to Ontario Legislation Covering the Release of Students' Personal Information*. Toronto, ON: Information and Privacy Commissioner. *retrieved May 2013 from http://www.ipc.on.ca/images/Resources/educate-e.pdf*

§ 266(3) EA

§ 20(5) Children's Law Reform Act
§ 16(5) Divorce Act (Canada)

the *Education Act*,° the parent or guardian of a child under the age of 18 is entitled to examine the OSR, and this section allows access for both custodial parents and non-custodial parents. This provision is further reinforced by the provincial *Children's Law Reform Act*° and the federal *Divorce Act*.°

2.2.1 Correction of Information

§ 266(4)(a) EA

§ 54 Municipal Freedom of Information and Protection of Privacy Act

The *Education Act* .°and in the *Municipal Freedom of Information and Protection of Privacy Act*,° provide for the corrections of fact (inaccuracies) on individual student's personal information held school records. In the case of adult students, this request may be made by the student themselves.

> The process for correction is provided in the OSR *Guideline*, which states that a parent (or an adult student) must submit a written request to the school principal. Only matters of fact, not opinion, may be corrected. If the principal refuses to correct the alleged inaccuracy, the matter may be referred to a supervisory officer of the school board and ultimately, the parent may request a hearing from the Ministry of Education. (p. 11 °)

(Cavoukian, 2011)

§ 36(2) Municipal Freedom of Information and Protection of Privacy Act

The *Municipal Freedom of Information and Protection of Privacy Act* gives a child (or any person) the right to request the correction of their personal information that is in the custody of an institution such as a school.°

2.3 DUE PROCESS

§ 300 EA

§§ 306, 310 EA

When an employee of the School Board becomes aware that a student may have engaged in a prohibited activity or an activity that might impact on the school climate they are to report this to the school principal.° Prohibited activities include: uttering a threat to inflict serious bodily harm on another person; possessing alcohol or illegal drugs; being under the influence of alcohol; swearing at a teacher or at another person in a position of authority; committing an act of vandalism that causes extensive damage to school property at the pupil's school or to property located on the premises of the pupil's school; bullying; possessing a weapon, including possessing a firearm; using a weapon to cause or to threaten bodily harm to another person; committing physical assault on another person that causes bodily harm requiring treatment by a medical practitioner; committing sexual assault; trafficking in weapons or in illegal drugs; committing robbery; giving alcohol to a minor or any activity "motivated by bias, prejudice or hate based on race, national or ethnic origin, language, colour, religion, sex, age, mental or physical disability, sexual orientation, gender identity, gender expression, or any other similar factor."° It is then the principal's duty to investigate and report his or her findings. If a student is believed to have been harmed then the principal must notify the parent or guardian as soon as possible. The same is true in terms of notification of parent or guardian of a student who is believed to have engaged in any of the above activities. If the student is 18 years of age or older or has withdrawn from parental control then the student must give consent to principal before notification. The principal will not notify parents if this notification is not in the student's best interests. The principal will disclose nature of activity (resulting in harm), the effect or harm suffered, together with the protection, discipline measures, and support provided in response to situation. The principal may not identify the student who has allegedly caused the harm. The principal will invite a discussion with parents about supports for the child.

In terms of due process involving parents in cases of student suspension or an expulsion, the *Education Act*° stipulates that each board will have polices and guidelines governing appeals of a decision to suspend a student. Unless the student is at least 18 years old, or is 16 or 17 years old and has withdrawn from parental control, parents may appeal, a principal's decision to suspend a child to the Board. In the case of an expulsion,

§ 302(6) EA

> If a principal recommends to the Board that a pupil be expelled, the board shall hold an expulsion hearing and, for that purpose, the Board has powers and duties as specified by board policy. The Board may authorize a committee of at least three members of the board to exercise and perform powers and duties on behalf of the board and may impose conditions and restrictions on the committee. (p. 57 °)

Ontario Educational Services Corporation. (2012). *Good governance: A guide for trustees, school boards, directors of education and communities*. Toronto, ON: the Author. *retrieved May 2013 from http://www.opsba.org/files/GoodGovernance.pdf*

Where a child is under 18, their parents or guardians have the right to participate in the hearing. To reinforce the above, the *Keeping Our Kids Safe at School Act* (effective February 1, 2010) requires all Board employees to report serious student incidents that must be considered for suspension or expulsion to the principal. This Act requires school staff who work directly with students to respond to inappropriate and disrespectful student behaviour.

2.4 INSTRUCTIONAL PROGRAM CONCERNS

Ultimately, the courts have upheld the rights of school officials to make the final decisions in matters of instruction programs for students. However, there are many formal.° and informal means for parents to interact with the school regarding program concerns. Most boards of education have policy statements that suggest that the consideration of controversial issues may have a legitimate place in the instructional program of the schools when properly handled. Typically, these policies stipulate that students are not required to participate in activities that are contrary to the religious convictions of the student or his/her parents or guardians. Schools will typically honour a written request from a parent or guardian for his/her child to be excused from a particular class for specified reasons.

see 2.5, below

2.5 PARENT INVOLVEMENT COMMITTEE

Ontario Educational Services Corporation. (2012). *Good governance: A guide for trustees, school boards, directors of education and communities*. Toronto, ON: the Author. *retrieved May 2013 from http://www.opsba.org/files/GoodGovernance.pdf*

Ministry of Education. (2010). *Ontario's new Parent Engagement Policy and Regulation 330/10: School Councils and Parent Involvement Committees*. Toronto, ON: the Author. *retrieved May 2013 from http://www.edu.gov.on.ca/eng/policyfunding/memos/september2010/2010ParentEngagement.pdf*

In 2009, the *Student Achievement and School Board Governance Act* provided for Parent Involvement Committees (PIC). In 2010, after the amending of Regulation 612/00 (and 330/10) each school board was required to have such a committee. The purpose of the PIC is to encourage and enhance parent involvement at the board level to support student achievement and well-being. The PIC is a parent-led committee that is an important advisory body to the board.° The Ontario Parent Engagement Policy

> recognizes, encourages and supports many forms of parent engagement, recognizes and supports the important role parents have contributing to their children's learning at home and at school, identifies strategies to remove barriers to parent involvement (e.g., communications and language), supports parents in acquiring the skills and knowledge they need to be engaged and involved in their child's learning, and provides a parent voice at the local level. (p. 2 °)

2.6 SCHOOL COUNCILS

In January 1995, the For the Love of Learning, the Royal Commission

Attendance, Religion and Parental Rights

DK and her second husband, AK, enrolled her son, J, in the Christian Centre Academy in Saskatoon, against the wishes of his natural father, HM. At the time, the curriculum at the Academy was known as Accelerated Christian Education (ACE), a program not approved by the Minister of Education. As J had not been given an exemption to attendance by either the Saskatoon Public Schools Division, or the Saskatoon Separate School Division, the DK and AK were charged under the compulsory attendance requirements of the *Education Act*. They were found guilty and appealed their conviction.

In his decision on the matter, Mr. Justice Hrabinsky noted the case of R. vs. Jones. Jones, a fundamentalist pastor, in Alberta, established an "academy" in the basement of his church to educate his own and 20 other children. He refused to apply for approval of his academy as a private or independent school and refused to ask for an exemption for his children from attendance at a public school, as provided under the ***Education Act*** of Alberta. Jones contended that it would be sinful to ask the government for permission to do God's will. Ultimately, the Supreme Court of Canada ruled against Jones, stating that the state had the authority to pass laws requiring compulsory education. The court also found that the ***Education Act*** did not violate the pastor's freedom of conscience, or right to liberty.

Applying these findings to the DK and AK case, Justice Hrabinsky dismissed their appeal. He found that the DK and AK were not deprived of their rights under the ***Charter***, and that the actions of the educational authorities were not unfair or arbitrary when they refused to exempt J from attendance

Saskatchewan Report, 76, pp. 116-130, 1990.

Note that enabling legislation was passed in the early 1990s to "legitimize" education outside the public and separate systems.

on Learning recommended that because of the importance of parental involvement in Ontario schools that school community councils be established. In April 1995, the Ministry of Education and Training issued Policy/Program Memorandum (PPM) No. 122: School Board Policies on School Councils, which required boards to develop policies that would establish school councils in the schools operated by them by June 1996. This memorandum outlined the requirements for the composition and functioning of school councils.° The *Education Act* requires each school board to establish a school council for each school under their jurisdiction.° School councils serve as advisory bodies to improve student achievement and enhance the accountability of the education system to parents.° To help school councils with their work of influencing decisions that affect students' education and the effective operation of schools, Ontario Regulation 612/00 and Regulation 298 address three key areas: the purpose of school councils, operational matters, and the obligation of boards and principals to consult with school councils. Regulation 612/00 confirms that school councils are advisory bodies and clearly states that they may make recommendations to their principals or school boards on any matter. The regulations require boards and principals to report back on how the recommendations have been taken into account.°

Ministry of Education. (2002). *School Councils: A Guide for Members*. Toronto, ON: the Author. *retrieved May 2013 from http://www.edu.gov.on.ca/eng/general/elemsec/council/council02.pdf*

§ 170 EA

Regulation 610/00; Ontario Educational Services Corporation. (2012). *Good governance: A guide for trustees, school boards, directors of education and communities*. Toronto, ON: the Author. *retrieved May 2013 from http://www.opsba.org/files/GoodGovernance.pdf*

Ministry of Education. (2002). *School Councils: A Guide for Members*. Toronto, ON: the Author. *retrieved May 2013 from http://www.edu.gov.on.ca/eng/general/elemsec/council/council02.pdf*

Each year, potential new council members are recruited for election and the newly elected members will be oriented to their tasks. Ontario Regulation 612/00 established that a school council will consist of the following members:

- a majority of parents, as specified in a bylaw of the school council or by the board if such a bylaw does not exist;
- the principal or vice-principal of the school (the principal may delegate membership responsibility to the vice-principal);
- one teacher employed in the school, other than the principal or vice-principal;
- one non-teaching employee of the school;
- one student, in the case of secondary schools (optional for elementary schools);
- one or more community representatives appointed by the elected council; and
- one person appointed by an association that is a member of the Ontario Federation of Home and School Associations, the Ontario Association of Parents in Catholic Education, or Parents Partenaires en Éducation, if the association is represented at the school.

School councils are to focus their work on student learning and the best interests of all students; setting school priorities for improving student achievement; promoting meaningful parental and community involvement and seeking the perspectives of their school communities; keeping well informed about school and board policies and procedures; communicating with their communities; and maintaining high ethical standards.°

see 12.0, below

2.7 MINORITY LANGUAGE

In keeping with Section 23 of the *Canadian Charter of Rights and Freedoms*, which indicates that Canadian citizens belonging to the English- or French-language minority in a province or territory have a right to have their children educated in that language, at the elementary and secondary levels, where numbers of students warrant, the *Education Act*°gives residence minority parents the right to send their children to Francophone schools.°

§ 294 EA

Canada–Ontario Agreement on Minority Language Education and Second Official Language Instruction 2009–10 to 2012–13 *retrieved May 2013 from http://www.pch.gc.ca/pgm/lo-ol/entente-agreement/education/ont/2009-2013/09-13EntenteEducationON-eng.pdf*

2.8 RELIGION AND PARENTAL RIGHTS

The *Education Act*° indicates that pupils should be allowed to receive religious instruction according to their parent or guardian. Ontario school districts have guidelines that outline religious accommodations available to students and staff. The guidelines were developed in partnership with multiple faith communities and with individuals who do not belong to a religion or practice any specific faith. The provisions of the guideline are actively communicated to students, teachers, parents, school staff, school councils, and volunteers.° However, students in public schools can not be "required to read or study in or from a religious book, or to join in an exercise of devotion or religion, objected to by the pupil's parent or guardian, or by the pupil, where the pupil is an adult".° The *Education Act* a Roman Catholic board (minority religion) is allowed to establish and maintain programs and courses of study in religious education for students in all its schools.° As will be indicated later in this guidebook, members of minority religion can provide faith-based private schools for their children.°

§ 51 EA

Ministry of Education. (2009). Equity and Inclusive education in Ontario: Guidelines for Policy Development and Implementation. Toronto, ON: the Author. retrieved May 2013 from http://www.edu.gov.on.ca/eng/policyfunding/inclusiveguide.pdf

§ 51 EA

§ 52 EA

retrieved May 2013 from http://www.ourkids.net/ontario-private-schools.php

2.9 OBLIGATIONS OF PARENTS

Along with parent rights come obligations. Under the *Education Act*,°parents (or guardians) of a person who is required to attend school (in other words a child who has attained the age of six years on or before the first school day in September)° must not neglect or refuse to ensure that their youngster attend school, unless the person is 16 years old or older.

§ 30 EA

§ 21 EA

2.10 PARENTS AND THE ONTARIO CODE OF CONDUCT

In the *Ontario Code of Conduct*,° parents are recognized for the important role they play in their child's education and for the support they can provide to school personnel in maintaining a safe and respectful learning environment for all students. The *Code* specifically indicates that

> parents fulfill this responsibility when they: show an active interest in their child's school work and progress; communicate regularly with the school; make sure their child is neat, properly dressed and prepared for school; ensure that their child attends school regularly and on time; inform the school promptly about their child's absence or late arrival; become familiar with the provincial code of conduct, the board's code of conduct and school rules; encourage and help their child follow the rules of behaviour and help school staff deal with disciplinary issues involving their child. (p. 4)

retrieved May 2013 from http://www.edu.gov.on.ca/eng/safeschools/code.pdf
► POLICY/PROGRAM MEMORANDUM NO. 128, "THE PROVINCIAL CODE OF CONDUCT AND SCHOOL BOARD CODES OF CONDUCT"

2.11 COMMUNITY USE OF SCHOOL FACILITIES

School buildings and facilities serve a significant role in the life of many communities. Schools provide locations for a wide variety of community activities including meetings, social functions, recreational and cultural activities.

Although schools are "public" buildings, the community does not have automatic access to school facilities. Boards of education are responsible for providing and maintaining school buildings and facilities as well as regulating their use during school and out-of-school hours.

Community groups who wish to use school facilities must obtain a permit to access the school district facilities. Each school district has their own policies and procedures for community use of its facilities. In partnership with the Ministry of Education and Ministry of Tourism and Recreation, the school boards in Ontario often make school space more affordable and accessible to communities.

3.0 THE SCHOOL TEACHER

In Part 3.0 of the Guide, topics such as teacher qualification and certification, professional status of teachers, teacher hiring, contracts, and conditions of employment will be briefly described. The guide also outlines the duties and responsibilities of teachers, professional and ethical codes of conduct, professional misconduct, and disciplinary actions against teachers. The section concludes with the discussion of a teacher's role in copyright protection and use of technology in classrooms. Attention is also given to the role and duties of teachers' assistants.

3.1 TEACHER QUALIFICATION AND CERTIFICATION

In order to be employed as a teacher in Ontario, an individual must meet certain requirements as specified in the *Education Act*, the *Ontario College of Teachers Act*, the *Teaching Profession Act*, and the regulations thereunder. Applicants for teaching positions in public schools must be certified to teach within the province by the Ontario College of Teachers (the College). Some private schools in the province may have the same requirement.

3.1.1 *Ontario College of Teachers*

Ontario's Royal Commission on Learning in its 1994 report For the Love of Learning stated that "the teaching profession in Ontario must now be considered equal to other established professions" and recommended establishing the Ontario College of Teachers. The government of Ontario passed the *Ontario College of Teachers Act*, 1996 to allow the teaching profession to regulate itself. Under this Act, that took effect in 1998, the College is authorized to licence, govern, and regulate the teaching profession in the public interest.° In doing so it sets the requirements for entering teaching; issues, suspends, or revokes teaching certificates; accredits teacher education programs and courses; sets ethical standards; and, investigates and hears complaints against its members. It is governed by a 37-member Council: 23 are College members and 14 are government appointees. The Registrar, the chief executive officer of the college, is directly

§ 3 Ontario College of Teachers Act

§§ 3, 18 Ontario College of Teachers Act

accountable to the council.

3.1.2 Who is a Teacher?

§ 1(1) EA

§ 1(h) Teaching Profession Act

The *Education Act* defines a "teacher" ("enseignant") as a member of the Ontario College of Teachers (OCT).° *The Teaching Profession Act*° also clarifies that a teacher means a person certified by OCT and is employed by a board as a teacher but does not include a supervisory officer, a principal, a vice-principal or an instructor in a teacher training institution. No person can be employed in an elementary or secondary school to teach or to perform any duty for which membership in OCT is required unless the person is a member of the Ontario College of Teachers.°

§ 262 EA

There are many types of teaching positions besides those of classroom teacher. Non-classroom teachers include those designated as teacher-librarian, guidance counselors, consultants, special assignment teachers and the like. All must hold valid teaching certificates.

Private schools do not have to conform to the requirements of the *Education Act* to employ only the certified teachers; however, more and more private schools prefer their teachers to be certified with the College.

3.1.3 Ontario Certified Teacher (OCT) Designation

In September of 2008, the Council of the Ontario College of Teachers has approved the use of a professional designation. Ontario Certified Teacher—or OCT—is the designation in English, and Enseignante agréée de l'Ontario, enseignant agréé de l'Ontario—or EAO—is the equivalent French terminology for use by French-language College members. Only qualified teaching professionals who have been certified by and remain in good standing with the Ontario College of Teachers can use the abbreviation OCT beside their name.°

Ontario College of Teachers. (n.d.). Ontario Certified Teacher OCT: Your Professional Designation. Toronto, ON: the Author. *retrieved May 2013 from http://www.oct.ca/~/media/PDF/Professional%20Designation%20Brochures/OCT_member_guide_e.ashx*

3.1.4 Teacher Certification

An Ontario teaching certificate is a licence to teach in Ontario. It is the teacher's responsibility to ascertain eligibility for a teaching certificate before beginning to teach in the province. Certified teachers as members of the OCT pay an annual membership fee to maintain their membership and certification.

retrieved May 2013 from http://www.oct.ca/becoming-a-teacher/applying/application-guide

For certification teachers must:°

- have completed a minimum three-year postsecondary degree from an acceptable postsecondary institution
- have successfully completed a one-year acceptable teacher education program
- apply to the College for certification and pay the annual membership and registration fees. Application process includes

providing proof of identity and a Canadian Criminal Record Check Report.

Teachers of Technological Studies do not require a postsecondary degree for certification. They must, however, provide the following in addition to the rest of the items listed above:

- a secondary school diploma;
- evidence of five years of wage-earning experience;
- proof of competence in their field of specialization (for example, a trade certificate).

Teachers who completed their teacher education outside of Ontario in a language other than English or French or who are not Canadian citizens must also provide:

- proof of proficiency in either English or French;
- Canadian employment authorization;
- proof of certification/authorization to teach in a jurisdiction outside of Ontario even if they have never taught there;
- a Statement of Professional Standing, which is a letter from a licensing institution such as an education ministry, that says the teacher's right to teach has never been suspended, revoked, or cancelled.

While a valid teaching certificate is a requirement for teaching, obtaining a certificate is not analogous to employment as a teacher; an individual may hold a valid certificate without teaching under contract. Nor does certification confer membership in the Ontario Teachers' Federation; membership in the Federation is a condition of employment under the *Teaching Profession Act*.°

§ 1(h) Teaching Profession Act

Any member of the public may confirm if a teacher does, in fact, hold a valid teaching certificate by referring to the public registry where the College publicly lists the name of every public school teacher, along with her or his credentials and current status.°

retrieved May 2013 from http://www.oct.ca/findateacher

3.1.5 Teaching Qualifications

There are four divisions in Ontario education: Primary (kindergarten to Grade 3), Junior (Grade 4 to Grade 6), Intermediate (Grade 7 to Grade 10), and Senior (Grade 11 to Grade 12). The Ontario College of Teachers requires that a teacher is certified in two consecutive divisions prior to certification. Normally, teachers who complete their teacher education program in Ontario have the required areas of study, commonly known as Basic Qualifications (BQ), in either Primary-Junior or Intermediate-Senior divisions. Furthermore, through additional study a teacher may become certified in more than two divisions (e.g., through Additional Qualifications (AQ) courses in education methodology completed after pre-service training).

The Basic Qualification determines if a member is qualified as a general education or a technological education teacher, and in what language, grades and subjects one may teach. In order to become a general studies teacher, a candidate needs an acceptable postsecondary degree, which is at least three years of full-time study, and one year of full-time study (or equivalent) in an acceptable teacher education program, which includes at least 30 credits, in total, in practice teaching and in courses on foundations and teaching methods related to two consecutive divisions: Primary/Junior (Kindergarten to Grade 6); Junior/Intermediate (Grades 4 to 10); Intermediate/Senior (Grades 7 to 12).

In order to become a teacher of technological education, a candidate needs an Ontario Secondary School Diploma or equivalent, a completed degree from an acceptable teacher education program, a proof of competence and five years of work experience in the area of technological studies corresponding to the teacher education program completed, or a combination of work experience and postsecondary education. Any combination must include at least two years of work experience with continuous employment of no less than 16 months.

Primary-Junior teachers are qualified to teach all subjects in Ontario's elementary schools. Junior -Intermediate teachers are qualified to teach all subjects at the Junior level and have a single subject speciality for Grades 7 to 10. Intermediate and Senior teachers have two subject specialities that cover Grades 7 to 10 and 11 and 12. Basic qualifications in Technological Education cover Grades 9-10 and Grades 11-12.

3.1.6 *Types of Teaching Certificates*

§ 2 Regulation 176/10

According to Regulation 176/10,° under the *Ontario College of Teachers Act*, the College provides: certificate of qualification and registration, and transitional certificate of qualification and registration.

The Certificate of Qualification and Registration provides proof of registration with the College and is an annual licence to teach in Ontario. Each year, after the membership fee is paid, the College updates and mails it to members. This certificate outlines teaching qualifications, is separated into four sections:

- Degree(s);
- Program of Teacher Education;
- Basic Qualifications; and,
- Additional Qualifications.

Under certain circumstances, the Registrar may grant a general certificate of qualification and registration to an applicant who has not completed the requirements or to an applicant with qualifications outside of Ontario but within Canada.

A Transitional Certificate of Qualification and Registration is for College members who are still completing their professional education as part of the College-accredited, multi-session program or an equivalent in another Canadian province or territory. The transitional certificate is provided to:

- people of First Nations, Métis or Inuit ancestry preparing to teach in the Primary and Junior divisions
- teacher candidates preparing to teach technological education, a Native language or in a the French-language school system
- teacher candidates who are enrolled in a multi-session program that will prepare them to teach students who are Deaf or Hard of Hearing.

This certificate is valid for six years, with the option of one-year extension if professional education program is not completed within six years. Transitional certificate is either converted to a Certificate of Qualification and Registration upon the successful completion of the program of professional education or expires if the program is not completed within the specified timeframe. Those with expired certificates must complete their teacher education program before reapplying to the College.

3.1.7 Additional Qualifications

§ 3(10) ONTARIO COLLEGE OF TEACHERS ACT

In the *Ontario College of Teachers Act*,° one of the College's objectives is to develop, provide and accredit educational programs leading to certificates of qualification additional to the certificate required for membership. This system of regulated Additional Qualifications (AQs) allows educators to expand their knowledge and skills within the divisions and/or subjects in which they are already qualified or to acquire knowledge in new areas.°

retrieved May 2013 from http://www.oct.ca/members/additional-qualifications/prerequisites

Teachers may add a division or subject area to what they are already qualified to teach by taking Additional Basic Qualification (ABQ) courses that prepare teachers to teach at the Primary, Junior, Intermediate or Senior level or in Technological Education. They also offer an opportunity for English or French-speaking teachers to develop the skills to work in the other language.

Teacher may expand their knowledge and skills within the divisions and subjects in which they are already qualified or acquire knowledge in new subject areas by taking Additional Qualification (AQs) courses. Specialist and honour specialist courses allow teachers to focus on curriculum development and leadership. In order to qualify for admission to AQ courses or programs, teachers must hold a General Certificate of Qualification and Registration. Transitional certificate holders are not eligible to enrol in College-accredited AQ programs including ABQs.

Additional Basic Qualifications (ABQs) and Additional Qualifications

§ 2 Regulation 176/10

(AQs) that teacher can earn by successfully completing courses and programs are outlined in the Regulation 176/10.° Other provisions in the regulation include AQ programs for principals, supervisory officers and for teachers of students who are deaf and hard of hearing. The College develops schedules and guidelines for courses,° approves the providers,° accredits the courses, and records a successfully completed qualification on a teaching certificate. The College itself does not offer AQ courses or programs.

retrieved May 2013 from http://www.oct.ca/members/additional-qualifications/schedules-and-guidelines

retrieved May 2013 from http://www.oct.ca/members/additional-qualifications/course-providers

When a member of the College completes an Additional Qualification course, the faculty of education or other provider confirms successful completion of the course to the College. All Additional Qualifications appear on the members' registry and on the teaching certificate.

3.1.8 Registration Appeals Committee

In case when application for certification has been denied or when certain terms, conditions or limitations have been imposed on the certificate, educators may appeal the decision to the Registration Appeals Committee. The goal of this Committee is to ensure impartial and objective licensing process. It is made up of five members of Council, three teachers elected by the profession and two members of the public appointed by the provincial Cabinet. Registration appeal process usually includes an appeal request, committee review, an oral presentation, and in exceptional cases, a hearing for the appeal.°

retrieved May 2013 from http://www.oct.ca/becoming-a-teacher/applying/appealing-registration-decisions

3.2 TEACHER AS PROFESSIONAL

3.2.1 Ontario Teachers' Federation

According to the *Teaching Profession Act*, 1944, a teacher is considered a professional. This *Act* established the Ontario Teachers' Federation (OTF) in English, or Fédération des enseignantes et enseignants de l'Ontario (FEO) in French, an umbrella organization for various affiliates member organizations representing teachers in Ontario.° Any licensed teacher working for a publicly funded school board is a member of the Ontario Teachers' Federation. In addition, every teacher is a member of one of the Ontario Teachers' Federation's affiliates.

§ 4(1) Teaching Profession Act

A teacher candidate in an accredited teacher education program in Ontario by law is an associate member of the Ontario Teachers' Federation° and is bound by the behaviour code of the Federation. Upon graduation and employment as a teacher in Ontario, he or she will no longer be an associate member, but a member of the Ontario Teachers' Federation and an affiliate.

§ 4(2) Teaching Profession Act

The objectives of the Ontario Teachers' Federation are:°

§ 4(3) Teaching Profession Act

- to promote and advance the cause of education;
- to raise the status of the teaching profession;
- to promote and advance the interests of teachers and to secure conditions that will make possible the best professional service;
- to arouse and increase public interest in educational affairs;
- to co-operate with other teachers' organizations throughout the world having the same or like objects; and
- to represent all members of the pension plan established under the *Teachers' Pension Act* in the administration of the plan and the management of the pension fund.

3.2.2 Ontario Teachers' Federation's Affiliates

A licenced teacher in Ontario is a member of one of the four Ontario Teachers' Federation affiliates, depending on the type of school and the kind of board where he or she is employed. Elementary school teachers for public school boards are members of the Elementary Teachers Federation of Ontario / Fédération des enseignantes et des enseignants de l'élémentaire de l'Ontario (ETFO/FEEO).° Secondary school teachers for public school boards are members of the Ontario Secondary School Teachers Federation/Federation des enseignantes-enseignants des ecoles secondaires de l'Ontario (OSSTF/FEESO).° All teachers for Catholic separate boards are members of the Ontario English Catholic Teachers Association (OECTA).° All teachers for francophone boards are members of Association des enseignantes et des enseignants franco-ontariens (AEFO).° Included in the membership in the affiliate member organizations are also teacher librarians, guidance teachers, consultants, and teachers on special assignment (excluded are principals, vice-principals, supervisory offices, and instructors in the teacher training institutions).°

retrieved May 2013 from http://www.etfo.ca

retrieved May 2013 from http://www.osstf.on.ca

retrieved May 2013 from http://www.oecta.on.ca

retrieved May 2013 from http://www.aefo.on.ca

§ 1 Teaching Profession Act

3.2.3 Canadian Teachers' Federation

Founded in 1920, the Canadian Teachers' Federation (CTF) / Fédération canadienne des enseignantes et des enseignant (FCE) is a national alliance of provincial and territorial teacher organizations that represent nearly 200,000 elementary and secondary school teachers across Canada.° Its functions include lobbying of the federal government on school-related matters; liaising with federal departments and organizations whose work affects education, children and youth; supporting teachers in the collective bargaining process; advancing teacher interests by holding seminars and conferences on educational issues; offering teacher opportunities or international exchange and volunteer service to colleagues from other countries; among other activities.

retrieved May 2013 from http://www.ctf-fce.ca

3.2.4 Education International

retrieved May 2013 from http://www.ei-ie.org

The Canadian Teacher's Federation is a member of Education International (EI),° an international organization representing organisations of teachers and other education employees across the globe. Its headquarters are in Brussels. Education International promotes and represents the interests of teachers and other education employees on the international level.

3.3 CLASSIFICATION OF TEACHERS

Once a teacher is certified and has signed a contract with a school board, that teacher is classified for salary purposes.

3.3.1 Classification Authority

In Ontario, evaluation of teacher qualifications for salary purposes is administered by Qualifications Evaluation Council of Ontario (QECO) for teachers at elementary, Catholic and French schools and by Ontario Secondary School Teachers' Federation (OSSTF) for teachers in public secondary schools. The terminology for the process varies depending on the administering authority, therefore terms "evaluation" and "certification" are used in the following sections to denote "classification."

3.3.2 Salary Categories

QECO Evaluation

retrieved May 2013 from http://www.qeco.on.ca/qeco/download/program5.pdf

Membership in a participating Ontario Teachers' Federation Affiliate (ETFO, OECTA, and AEFO) is a requirement for evaluation by QECO. QECO evaluates teacher qualifications based on the documentation supplied by the teacher. QECO teacher evaluations operate following a consistent set of policies found in Program 5.° Two charts are used for QECO evaluation purposes.

The General Studies Chart consists of 5 categories (A, A1, A2, A3, and A4), all of which require a valid certification from the Ontario College of Teachers and other conditions (e.g., undergraduate university degree, additional qualification courses, other diplomas, etc.).

The Technological Studies Chart consists of 4 categories (A1, A2, A3, and A4), which all require a valid certification from the Ontario College of Teachers with basic qualifications in Technological Studies and other conditions (e.g., diploma from an accredited Institute of Technology or College of Applied Arts and Technology (CAAT), Art or Music Diploma, courses, certificates, etc.).

OSSTF Evaluation

OSSTF/FEESO provides Certification Rating Statements to its teacher members which are then used to determine the pay rate according to four possible groups.° Teacher ratings are based on their academic backgrounds and trade records according to the constitution and bylaws and policies and procedures° governing the OSSTF/FEESO Certification Plan.°

retrieved May 2013 from http://www.osstf.on.ca/Default.aspx?DN=fe32e83b-feeb-4956-88e5-ae349b167c70

retrieved May 2013 from http://www.osstf.on.ca/2012-2013-policies-and-procedures.pdf

retrieved May 2013 from http://www.osstf.on.ca/2012-2013-constitution-and-bylaws.pdf

The OSSTF Certification charts are significantly different from the QECO charts. OSSTF regulations outline three Programs or Charts which reflect the various areas and levels of specialization in teacher qualifications.° These charts are:

retrieved May 2013 from http://www.osstf.on.ca/2012-2013-policies-and-procedures.pdf

- Honour Specialist Program (Chart 1 Regulations, Specified Subject Area)
- Three Session Specialist Program (Chart 2 Regulations, In the Discipline)
- Honour Technological Studies Specialist Program (Chart 3 Regulations)

The Certification Regulations are the sole criteria used in the evaluation of Members' qualifications.

Each Program or Chart is divided into four groups (Groups 1, 2, 3, 4) based on various levels of specialization and teacher training from the basic, Group 1, through to the most advanced, Group 4. For placement in Group 1, a member must be a qualified secondary school teacher holding a valid Certificate of Qualification. Placement in subsequent groups requires meeting the requirements listed under each chart, such as additional qualifications and training.

3.3.3 Change of Classification

Teachers who improve their qualifications are eligible for reclassification. Both QECO and OSSTF emphasize that teachers need to apply regularly for upgrading of their certification for salary purposes. According to QECO, it is the responsibility of the individual teacher to apply in writing for an evaluation or for any change in evaluation after additional qualifications have been achieved. OSSTF notes that changes to guidelines governing the placement of teachers in groups occur on a regular basis; therefore, members are responsible for reviewing the changes to determine if a re-evaluation for a new Certification Rating Statement should be requested.

3.3.4 Teacher Classification Councils

The QECO Evaluation Council members are practicing teachers appointed by the three Affiliates at a ratio of one Certification Council member per each 10,000 teacher members or major fraction

retrieved May 2013 from http://www.qeco.on.ca/qeco/download/program5.pdf

thereof, in the respective Affiliates, with no Affiliate having fewer than two members. The Evaluation Council recommends policies and procedures governing the evaluation of qualifications.°

Procedure 8 OSSTF POLICY AND PROCEDURES

The OSSTF Certification Council is composed of six Members from across Ontario who are practicing teacher members of OSSTF. Council formulates and interprets the OSSTF Certification Regulations and is responsible for recommending any changes to the Regulations to the Annual Meeting of the Provincial Assembly.°

3.3.5 *Appeal of Classification*

retrieved May 2013 from http://www.qeco.on.ca/qeco/index.cfm?do=c.appeals

When a teacher is not satisfied with the evaluation or certification for salary purposes, the teacher may appeal the decision.

QECO Appeal Protocol is a two-step process.° Step 1 comprises a review of an evaluation based on teacher's written request within 60 days of the teacher's category placement. It is conducted by the Executive Director who makes a decision upon the completion of the review. If a teacher is not satisfied with this decision, he or she may proceed to Step 2, an appeal of the Executive Director's decision to the Affiliates Committee.

Procedure 8 OSSTF POLICY AND PROCEDURES

An OSSTF member who is not satisfied with Certification Rating Statement may appeal to the Certification Appeal Board. It is composed of three teacher members who are appointed by the Provincial Executive. The Certification Appeal Board provides federation members with a route for appealing decisions of the Certification Department. The role of the Certification Division (Department) is two-fold: to evaluate qualifications of individual Members in accordance with the Certification Plan, and; to assist individual Members in improving their qualifications.°

3.4 HIRING OF TEACHERS

In Ontario, all hiring is the responsibility of publicly funded school boards, the provincial school authority, demonstration schools or private schools. School boards as employers assign and appoint the College members to teaching and administrative roles according to their qualifications.

3.4.1 *Teacher Assignments*

§ 262 EA

According to the *Education Act*, "no person shall be employed in an elementary or secondary school to teach or to perform any duty for which membership in the College is required under this Act unless the person is a member of the Ontario College of Teachers."° Section 19 of Regulation 298 provides guidelines for the assignment and appointment of teachers. Each board is responsible for appointing a principal and an adequate number of teachers for each school of the board.° § 170(1.12) EA

It is the principal of the school who is ultimately responsible for teacher assignments. Specifically, teaching assignments must be made:

- with due regard for the provision of the best possible program and the safety and well-being of the pupils.° § 19(1) Regulation 298
- in accordance with the qualifications recorded on the teacher's certificate of qualification and registration.° § 19(2) Regulation 298

In some instances, school boards are unable to find professionals with the qualifications they need to fill certain subject areas or teaching needs. In this case, principals may assign a teacher who does not have the required qualifications but who is nevertheless considered competent to teach a particular subject, teach in a division, or hold a certain position. Regulation 298 allows for the following assignments to be made by mutual agreement between the school's principal and the teacher and with the approval of the appropriate supervisory officer.° § 19(3) Regulation 298

1. A teacher who has a qualification and certification to teach in the primary division, the junior division, the intermediate division in a general education subject or the senior division in a general education subject may be assigned to teach in any division and in most general education subjects.
2. A teacher who has a qualification and certification to teach in a technological education subject in Grades 9 and 10 or Grades 11 and 12 may be assigned to teach any other technological education subject in Grades 9 to 12.

Principals' decisions must ensure the safety and well-being of students and align with any existing assignment decisions made by the school board staffing committee and any relevant provisions regarding teacher assignment in collective agreements.

In specified circumstances, teaching assignments may be made outside of a teacher's specific qualifications with the granting of a Temporary Letter of Approval (TLA) by the ministry of education.° § 19.2 Regulation 298 TLA authorizes a school board to assign a teacher to teach a subject, teach in a division, or hold a position for a period of up to one year where the teacher does not have the required qualifications.° § 8(11) EA School boards apply for a TLA when they cannot find teaching professionals with the qualifications they need to fill certain subject areas or teaching needs. A TLA does not provide permanent approval for a board to assign a teacher to a subject or position for which they are not fully qualified. The board must ensure that a teacher in respect of whom the application is made holds a certificate of qualification and registration, is considered competent to teach the subject, teach in the division or hold the position, and has agreed to the assignment or appointment.° § 19.2(b) Regulation 298

Policy/Program Memorandum No. 153, "Applications for Temporary Letters of Approval"

PPM No. 153° details board requirements for submitting an application for a Temporary Letter of Approval, a description of the application process, and the application form. According to PPM 153, a TLA is commonly required to:

- allow a teacher who does not have a qualification in any division to be assigned to teach in the primary or junior division or to teach a general education subject in the intermediate or senior division;
- allow a teacher who does not have a qualification in any technological education subject to be assigned to teach a technological education subject;
- allow a teacher who does not have a qualification in French as a second language (FSL) to be assigned to teach FSL;
- allow a teacher who does not have French-language qualifications in a division to be assigned to teach in the primary or the junior division where French is the language of instruction;
- allow a teacher who does not have English-language qualifications in a division to be assigned to teach in the primary or the junior division where English is the language of instruction;
- allow a teacher who does not have a qualification in special education to be assigned to teach or be placed in charge of a special education program or class;
- allow a teacher who does not have a qualification in teaching students who are deaf or hard of hearing or students who are blind or who have limited vision to be assigned to teach these students;
- allow a teacher who does not have principal's qualifications to be assigned to hold a position as a principal or vice-principal.

Ministry of Education. (2010). *Teacher Assignment in Ontario Schools: A resource guide*. Toronto, ON: the Author. *retrieved May 2013 from http://www.edu.gov.on.ca/eng/teacher/pdfs/assignment.pdf*

TLA is also required when the board wishes to appoint a teacher who does not have the required specialist qualifications or honour specialist qualifications to supervise or coordinate subjects or programs or to act as a consultant for teachers in the subjects or programs. The specialist or honour specialist qualifications must be in one or more of the subjects or programs in question.°

Without a TLA, a teacher who holds a Transitional Certificate of Qualification and Registration may only be assigned to teach a subject indicated on his or her transitional certificate. Similarly, without a TLA a teacher trained in a single additional qualification subject may only be assigned to teach that subject.

3.4.2 Hiring Non-Members of the Ontario College of Teachers

Two provisions in the regulations under the *Education Act* allow a school board, under special circumstances, to hire a non-member of the College to teach in one of the schools.

Upon school board's request, the Minister of Education may grant a Letter of Permission authorizing the school board to employ a person who is not a member of the College to teach in an elementary or a secondary school if the Minister is satisfied that no teacher is available. According to Regulation 142/08 under the *Education Act*, a Letter of Permission is issued only after a school board has pursued all recruitment requirements as laid out in regulation and found that no member of the College is available to fill the position. A Letter of Permission is effective only for a specified time and a specified position and may not exceed one year. PPM No. 147° outlines requirements for submitting an application for a Letter of Permission, a description of the application process, and the application form.

POLICY/PROGRAM MEMORANDUM NO. 147, "APPLICATIONS FOR LETTERS OF PERMISSION"

According to the *Education Act*, in the case of emergency, a school board may appoint a person who is not a teacher or a temporary teacher to teach in school in the event that no member of the College is available.° In the emergency circumstances, a board may employ a person for up to 10 school days who is 18 years or older and who holds an Ontario Secondary School Diploma, a secondary school graduation diploma or a secondary school honour graduation diploma, or an equivalent to any of them.

§ 21 EA

3.4.3 Teaching Contracts and Tenure

The *Education Act* provides for two types of contractual arrangements: a teacher contract and an occasional teacher contract. However, the Policies of the Ontario Teachers' Federation° state that a teacher should sign a form of contract of employment as soon as possible after the appointment of the member to a teaching position and before commencement of duties. The policies further differentiate between the permanent, probationary, long-term occasional, and continuing education contracts. Although not further defined in the policies, permanent contract means contractual agreement with the teacher that has successfully completed the probationary requirements. Probationary contract means contractual agreement with a teacher who has not actively completed a continuous period of successful teaching as determined by the board. Long-term occasional contract is a contractual agreement with a teacher for a determined period of time (12 or more school days in the same assignment) within the school year replacing a specific teacher and assuming his or her duties. Continuing education contract means contractual agreement with a teacher employed for the instruction of continuing education courses.

Part IV A # 1 POLICIES OF THE ONTARIO TEACHERS' FEDERATION

A school board makes an offer of employment to a teacher which if accepted requires that the teacher is on probation during which time she or he is assessed and during which time the teacher will complete Ontario's New Teacher Induction Program. The probationary period for teachers when they first become employed by a board must not exceed two years.° For teachers with three or more years of experience probationary period cannot exceed one year.° Following

§ 261 EA

Part IV A # 4 POLICIES OF THE ONTARIO TEACHERS' FEDERATION

A Question of Faith: Employment in Denominational Schools

The teaching contract of Margaret Caldwell, a Roman Catholic teacher in a Roman Catholic school in British Columbia, was not renewed after she married a divorced man in a civil ceremony. In doing so, she broke two Church rules: marrying a divorced person and marrying outside the Church.

Caldwell lodged a complaint, under the *British Columbia Human Rights Code*, alleging her dismissal was on unreasonable grounds and was discrimination on a religious basis. A Board of inquiry ruled that, under the circumstances, marital status and religion were both *bona fide* occupational qualifications. It also held that, while the *Human Rights Code* was valid provincial legislation, section 93(1) of the ***Constitution Act*** (1867) protected denominational rights of Catholic schools. Consequently, the Board dismissed her complaint.

Caldwell appealed the ruling thereby initiating a series of appeals culminating in a Supreme Court decision in 1985 that ruled against her. Writing for the Court, Justice McIntyre noted that while religion and marital status normally cannot constitute reasonable grounds for dismissal, where employment includes religious conformance as a bona fide occupational requirement, an employer has the right to insist on that conformance. If an employer no longer meets those requirements, he or she may be dismissed. In the Court's view, when Caldwell contravened the Church's requirements, she deprived herself of a bona fide qualification for employment.

As Justice McIntyre stated, denominational schools are special cases in which "observance of standards forms a part of the contract of employment of teachers." They are required to exhibit the "highest model of Christian behaviour." Citing an earlier case, he also noted that "a Catholic teacher must exhibit to the students an example that is consistent with what is being taught. For a Catholic teacher to be credible, he must proclaim the Catholic philosophy by his actions, both within the school and outside it"

(Case taken from: *Western Weekly Reports*, Vol 1, January 5, 1985).

a successful probationary period the teacher's employment with the school board crystallizes into a "permanent" contractual arrangement the terms and conditions of which are governed by the local collective agreement, school board policy and the *Labour Relations Act*, 1995. This ongoing or continuing contact of employment is what is often referred to as tenure, for example in the Policies of the Ontario Teachers' Federation.

Besides an ongoing contract of employment the *Education Act* provides for a second category of agreement, the Occasional Teacher category (i.e., daily casual and long term occasional teacher contracts), the terms and conditions of which are determined by the collective agreements negotiated with school boards by the bargaining unit representing occasional teachers. The *Education Act* defines occasional teacher as the person employed by a board to teach as a substitute for a teacher or temporary teacher who is or was employed by the board in a position that is part of its regular teaching staff including continuing education teachers but,

a. if the teacher substitutes for a teacher who has died during a school year, the teacher's employment as the substitute for him or her shall not extend past the end of the school year in which the death occurred; and

b. if the teacher substitutes for a teacher who is absent from his or her duties for a temporary period, the teacher's employment as the substitute for him or her shall not extend past the end of the second school year after his or her absence begins.° § 1.1 EA

Occasional teachers fall into two categories, casual and long-term. Casual occasional teachers are hired on a day-by-day basis and are paid a daily rate, while long-term occasional teachers are occasional teachers on long-term or extended teaching assignments.

3.4.4 Hiring Practices

Regulation 274/12 "Hiring Practices" provides steps that all publicly funded school boards must follow when hiring for long term occasional positions (LTO) and new permanent teacher positions.

For hiring, every occasional teacher (OT) of a board must be ranked in accordance with teacher's seniority and placed on the occasional teacher roster.° Furthermore, every board must establish and maintain a long-term occasional teachers (LTO) list.° Those who have been placed upon the Occasional Teachers Roster for a minimum 10 months and have taught as an occasional teacher in one or more schools of the board are qualified to apply to be on the LTO list. Boards may interview occasional teachers who qualify to determine whether an individual will be added to the LTO List. For appointments to long-term assignments, the board will interview the five (or fewer, if five are not available) qualified, highest-ranked teachers from the long-term occasional teachers list. When permanent contract positions come available as per collective agreement provisions, the board will interview the five (or fewer, if five are not available) qualified, highest-ranked teachers who have completed a long-term assignment in a school of the board that was at least four months long and in respect of which the teacher has not received an unsatisfactory evaluation.

§§ 2, 3 Regulation 274/12
§ 4 Regulation 274/12

3.4.5 New Teacher Induction Program

Sections 268 to 276.2 of the *Education Act* describe the new teacher induction process for teachers who are employed by the board and whose "new teaching period" has not elapsed (e.g., the 24-month period that follows the day on which the teacher (other than as an occasional teacher) first begins to teach for a board).° All new teachers (including teachers trained out-of-province) certified by the College who have been hired into permanent positions (full-time or part-time) in publicly funded schools must complete the New Teacher Induction Program (NTIP). Regulation 266/06 stipulates that every new teacher who has never previously taught in any jurisdiction or has only taught as an occasional teacher must participate in the elements

§ 267(2) EA

§§ 1(2), 1(3) Regulation 266/06

§ 268(2) EA

§ 18(1.1) Ontario College of Teachers Act

retrieved May 2013 from http://www.edu.gov.on.ca/eng/teacher/induction.html

of this program.° Every board must establish an NTIP consisting of an orientation for new teachers; mentoring for new teachers; professional development and training appropriate for new teachers; and other elements prescribed by the board.° Teachers have up to two years to complete the program, and a notation thereupon is added to their teaching certificate.° A new teacher successfully completes the program when he or she receives two satisfactory ratings in performance appraisals before the end of his or her new teaching period. Beginning long-term occasional teachers (i.e., certified occasional teachers who are in their first long-term assignment, of 97 or more consecutive school days as a substitute for the same teacher) are included in the induction elements of the NTIP.°

3.4.6 Teacher Redundancy

retrieved May 2013 from http://www.otffeo.on.ca/english/docs/WTT_TPA_policiesbylawsetc.pdf

• *The purpose of the* School Boards and Teachers Collective Negotiations Act, 1990 *is "the furthering of harmonious relations between boards and teachers by providing for the making and renewing of agreements and by providing for the relations between boards and teachers in respect of agreements"* (§ 2)

Under the *Teaching Profession Act,* the Ontario Teachers' Federation deals with redundancy in Policies° Part VI (Contract and Tenure), section F. It is the Policy of the Ontario Teachers' Federation that the minimum number of teachers to be employed by a Board be negotiated under the *School Boards and Teachers Collective Negotiation Act.*° Where staff reductions are required, redundancy should be determined solely on the basis of seniority. Every collective agreement should provide for the process of identification, declaration and recall of redundant teachers, and severance allowances, retraining and re-qualification programs.

These points are significant as they implicitly declare that the student teacher ratio in the classrooms of Ontario are of great importance to the Federation, as well as seniority, and means of ameliorating the effect of layoffs on members due to redundancy. Where permanent teacher contracts have been terminated because they are surplus to the board and who have not refused position with the board, they are eligible for severance pay (subject to collective bargaining unit terms).

3.4.7 Contract Termination

When the board or teachers wish to terminate the contract, the written notice is required. A teacher may terminate his contract at the end of June. A teacher may resign the membership in the College by completing the notice of resignation. Upon such resignation, the person will no longer be a member of the College and will not be able to teach in publicly funded schools in Ontario until the member has applied for reinstatement and paid the applicable fee. Many teachers maintain continuous membership in the College regardless of whether they are teaching or not, as it is easier to apply for positions if one is already a member of the OCT. In those cases they pay their membership themselves in the spring of each year. When employed, the dues are collected automatically by the school board.

If a board wishes to terminate a contract of a teacher, policies of the Ontario Teachers' Federation provide that a termination of the contract "shall be in accordance with the terms of the contract or for just and sufficient cause"° and be accompanied with written reasons. This Part of the policies also excludes marital status as a ground for termination as well as other matters.

Part IV A # 5 Policies of the Ontario Teachers' Federation

Part IV A # 6 Policies of the Ontario Teachers' Federation

A principal may terminate the employment of an occasional teacher on a long-term contract with five teaching days notice or five days pay in lieu of notice (or according to the collective agreement).°

retrieved May 2013 from http://www.etfo.ca/Resources/ForTeachers/Documents/Governance.pdf

The *Education Act* provides guidelines for termination of contract where the welfare of a school is involved.° If teacher employment is deemed to adversely affect the welfare of the school in which the teacher is employed, the teacher's employment can be terminated with the thirty-day written notice of termination or with the written notice of immediate termination. In the latter case, the termination is accompanied with one-tenth of the teacher's yearly salary in addition to the amount to which the teacher would otherwise be entitled.

§ 263(1) EA

3.5 CONDITIONS OF EMPLOYMENT FOR TEACHERS

While the *Education Act* and regulations afford all teachers throughout the province the same general conditions of employment, the same rights and benefits, certain conditions vary based on the type of publicly funded school board that employs teachers.

3.5.1 Denominational Rights and Employment

Constitutional protection for separate schools in Canada is set out in Section 93(1) of the *Constitution Act*, 1867. Separate school boards establish and maintain programs and courses of study in religious education for pupils in all schools under its jurisdiction, and therefore may hire and dismiss teachers, impose duties and obligations upon teachers, and ensure that their schools are operated according to the provisions of the relevant legislation. This may include, among other things, preferential employment, or the preference to hire Catholic teachers over others and the preference to require all teachers within the school system to live as examples of the Catholic faith. Since in a practical sense, all teachers in a separate school are required to integrate religious instruction into all programs, courts have held that all teachers (and other employees) in a separate school board must adhere to qualifications set by their school boards.

Preferential employment may be deemed as discrimination on the basis of religion under section 5 of the Ontario *Human Rights Code*, which states that "every person has a right to equal treatment with respect to employment without discrimination because of race, ancestry, place of origin, colour, ethnic origin, citizenship, creed, sex, sexual orientation, gender identity, gender expression, age, record of offences, marital status, family status or disability."

However, special employment provisions are provided in section 24 of the *Code*, specifying that the right under section 5 to equal treatment with respect to employment is not infringed where,

> (1)(a) a religious, philanthropic, educational, fraternal or social institution or organization that is primarily engaged in serving the interests of persons identified by their race, ancestry, place of origin, colour, ethnic origin, creed, sex, age, marital status or disability employs only, or gives preference in employment to, persons similarly identified if the qualification is a reasonable and bona fide qualification because of the nature of the employment.

3.5.2 Teacher Performance Appraisal

§§ 3(e), 3(g), 3(h), 3(i) REGULATION 298

§ 277.14 EA

retrieved May 2013 from http://www.edu.gov.on.ca/eng/teacher/appraise.html

Ministry of Education. (2010). *Teacher Performance Appraisal: Technical Requirements Manual.* Toronto, ON: the Author. *retrieved May 2013 from http://www.edu.gov.on.ca/eng/teacher/pdfs/TPA_Manual_English_september2010l.pdf*

The principal is responsible for the general supervision of and the conducting of any school activity authorized by the board, and specifically, for conducting performance appraisals of members of the teaching staff and reporting to the board or supervisory officer (including the written report on the effectiveness of members of the teaching staff for whom performance appraisal is not required).° The purpose of teacher performance appraisal is to ensure that pupils receive the benefit of an education system staffed by teachers who are performing their duties satisfactorily; to provide for fair, effective and consistent teacher evaluation in every school; and to promote professional growth.°

Teacher performance appraisal (TPA) is conducted under a province-wide system outlined by the Ontario Ministry of Education.° This system looks at a teacher's ability to use his or her skills effectively in the classroom. TPA requirements are set out in Part X.2 of the *Education Act*, Regulation 98/02 – Teacher Learning Plans, and Regulation 99/02 – Teacher Performance Appraisal. Ontario's TPA system consists of two parts: for "new teachers" and for "experienced" teachers. Depending on whether the teacher is "new" or "experienced," the application of appraisal components and the frequency of appraisal differs. The common components to the appraisal of both new and experienced teachers are competency statements, classroom observation, appraisal meetings, summative report, rating, and process for providing additional support.°

Teachers are considered "new" until they successfully complete the NTIP or until 24 months have elapsed since the date on which they first began to teach for a board. The performance appraisal process for new teachers includes two evaluations within a 12 month period of being hired into a permanent position. New teachers are evaluated according to eight areas of competency and receive an overall rating of "satisfactory" or "development needed." Additional evaluations are required if an appraisal in the first year results in a performance rating of "development needed." The overall rating options in the subsequent appraisals are "satisfactory" or "unsatisfactory."

All teachers who have completed the NTIP, or who held permanent positions in Ontario's publicly funded schools prior to the NTIP's implementation in September 2006, as well as temporary teachers (those teaching on a Letter of Permission), are appraised as "experienced" teachers. Experienced teachers are evaluated once every five years according to 16 areas of competency and receive an overall rating of "satisfactory" or "unsatisfactory."

3.6 TEACHERS' DUTIES AND RESPONSIBILITIES

Teachers working in government funded public and separate school systems assume statutory and regulatory duties described in section 264 of the *Education Act* and in section 20 of Regulation 298. In addition, duties outlined in the regulations under the *Teaching Profession Act* and in the *Ontario College of Teachers Act* apply to teachers through their membership in the Ontario Teacher's Federation (OTF) and the Ontario College of Teachers (OCT). Furthermore, the policies of the OTF outline responsibilities of teachers.

3.6.1 *General Duties*

Section 264(1) of the *Education Act* lists duties of a teacher and a temporary teacher:

(a) to teach diligently and faithfully the classes or subjects assigned to the teacher by the principal;

(b) to encourage the pupils in the pursuit of learning;

(c) to inculcate by precept and example respect for religion and the principles of Judaeo-Christian morality and the highest regard for truth, justice, loyalty, love of country, humanity, benevolence, sobriety, industry, frugality, purity, temperance and all other virtues;

(d) to assist in developing co-operation and co-ordination of effort among the members of the staff of the school;

(e) to maintain, under the direction of the principal, proper order and discipline in the teacher's classroom and while on duty in the school and on the school ground;

(f) in instruction and in all communications with the pupils in regard to discipline and the management of the school,

(i) to use the English language, except where it is impractical to do so by reason of the pupil not understanding English, and except in respect of instruction in a language other than English when such other language is being taught as one of the subjects in the course of study, or

(ii) to use the French language in schools or classes in which French is the language of instruction except where it is impractical to do so by reason of the pupil not understanding French, and except in respect of instruction in a language other than French when such other language is being taught as one of the subjects in the course of study;

(g) to conduct the teacher's class in accordance with a timetable which shall be accessible to pupils and to the principal and supervisory officers;

(h) to participate in professional activity days as designated by the board under the regulations;

(i) to notify such person as is designated by the board if the teacher is to be absent from school and the reason therefor;

(j) to deliver the register, the school key and other school property in the teacher's possession to the board on demand, or when the teacher's agreement with the board has expired, or when for any reason the teacher's employment has ceased; and

(k) to use and permit to be used as a textbook in a class that he or she teaches in an elementary or a secondary school,

(i) in a subject area for which textbooks are approved by the Minister, only textbooks that are approved by the Minister, and

(ii) in all subject areas, only textbooks that are approved by the board;

(l) to perform all duties assigned in accordance with this Act and the regulations.

§§ 264.1(3), 264.1(4) EA

Furthermore, the *Education Act* stipulates that it is the duty of teachers and temporary teachers maintain a healthy physical, emotional and social learning environment and to communicate with families.°

§ 20 Regulation 298

Regulation 298° further clarifies the duties assigned to the teacher under the *Education Act* and by the board. According to this regulation, a teacher has the following duties:

(a) be responsible for effective instruction, training and evaluation of the progress of pupils in the subjects assigned to the teacher and for the management of the class or classes, and report to the principal on the progress of pupils on request;

(b) carry out the supervisory duties and instructional program assigned to the teacher by the principal and supply such information related thereto as the principal may require;

(c) where the board has appointed teachers under section 14 or 17, co-operate fully with such teachers and with the principal in all matters related to the instruction of pupils;

(d) unless otherwise assigned by the principal, be present in the classroom or teaching area and ensure that the classroom or teaching area is ready for the reception of pupils at least fifteen

A Case of Too Much "Whooptsie"?

Two teachers employed by the Calgary Board of Education claimed sick leave for 11 days during which time they performed in a children's television production, "The Whoopties." Even though both teachers were highly qualified and talented, the board of education terminated their contracts. The teachers appealed the terminations to a Board of Reference.

Representing the board of education, the Superintendent of Personnel claimed that the teachers' contracts were terminated as a result of dishonesty, misrepresentation, lack of candor, and absence of contrition. The teachers acknowledged that if they were well enough to participate in the television production, they were well enough to teach, but they characterized their conduct as "indiscretion" and a "mistake."

The Board of Reference set aside the termination and substituted six month suspensions without pay. The reasons for its decision were both procedural and substantive. In the first instance, the procedure used to terminate the contracts were not officially board policy and thus could not apply. Secondly, the Board of Reference ruled that the conduct of the teachers was very foolish and dishonest, and their claims of sickness represented a gross misunderstanding of proper adherence to sick leave policies and to their ethical and professional responsibilities. Nevertheless, these teachers were gifted, related well to students and had been a help and "inspiration" to many students. Taking these mitigating factors into consideration, the Board of Reference felt that the terminations were not reasonable and appropriate and that, in this case, dishonest conduct did not constitute just cause for dismissal.

(From *EduLaw, 2*(5), January 1991)

minutes before the commencement of classes in the school in the morning and, where applicable, five minutes before the commencement of classes in the school in the afternoon;

(e) assist the principal in maintaining close co-operation with the community;

(f) prepare for use in the teacher's class or classes such teaching plans and outlines as are required by the principal and the appropriate supervisory officer and submit the plans and outlines to the principal or the appropriate supervisory officer, as the case may be, on request;

(g) ensure that all reasonable safety procedures are carried out in courses and activities for which the teacher is responsible;

(h) co-operate with the principal and other teachers to establish and maintain consistent disciplinary practices in the school;

(i) ensure that report cards are fully and properly completed and processed in accordance with the English and French guides;

(j) co operate and assist in the administration of tests under the Education Quality and Accountability Office Act, 1996;

(k) participate in regular meetings with pupils' parents or guardians;

(l) perform duties as assigned by the principal in relation to co-operative placements of pupils; and

(m) perform duties normally associated with the graduation of pupils.

§ 300.1 EA

Teachers may sometimes assume powers, duties, and functions of the principal, delegated to them in writing, in the event when both principal and vice-principal are absent from the school.° Teachers are generally asked if they are willing to accept the role of acting principal. Many collective agreements stipulate that teachers who have Principals' Qualifications are to be asked first. Furthermore, teachers may be required to assume the role of acting principal in cases of emergency or necessity.

3.6.2 Teachers' Responsibilities

As outlined in the policies of the OTF, the role of the teacher includes the following responsibilities.

1. diagnosis of the needs of students;
2. awareness of the resources available to meet pupils needs;
3. establishment of performance goals related to both the learning and development of each student;
4. grouping of students where appropriate to meet these needs and goals;
5. use of the best pedagogical techniques and materials available;
6. ongoing evaluation of goals, programs and techniques in the context of progress achieved;
7. ongoing appraisal of the progress of each student.

3.6.3 Duty to Protect Student Records

According to section 266 of the *Education Act*, student records are privileged information, and teachers (among others) are required to keep them confidential. The information may be divulged only in certain circumstances. For example, the medical officer of health must be given certain, very limited information upon request to the principal. This information includes the student's name, address, phone number, birthdate; and name, address and phone number of the student's parent or guardian. Also, a student, or his or her parent or guardian if the student is a minor, is entitled to examine the record of the student. In the latter case, if the student (if an adult) or the parent or guardian (if the student is a minor) feel that information contained in the file is inaccurate, or not conducive to the improvement of instruction of the student, such student, parent or guardian may request in writing to the principal that the alleged inaccuracy be corrected, or the impugned information be removed from the record. For complete details, please read. The privacy of student records is also protected through the *Municipal Freedom of Information and Personal Privacy Act* (MFIPPA). Ontario College of Teachers emphasizes the importance of teachers to safeguard student information.°

Scott, G. (2008, March). Student Privacy and You. *Professionally Speaking: Magazine of the Ontario College of Teachers.* *retrieved May 2013 from http://professionallyspeaking.oct.ca/march_2008/privacy.asp*

3.6.4 Common Law Responsibilities

This Guide is limited in what it can describe and even more limited in what it might prescribe with respect to legal obligations. Common law does provide some extremely helpful understandings that point to ways of behaving and the way the justice system typically responds to difficult legal situations. For example, we know from common law that a person may be successfully sued for negligence only if all four factors can be shown to have been involved:

- the person had a legal duty of care toward the one who is suing them;
- the person has failed to fulfill this duty of care;
- the person suing was injured, in whole or in part, as a result of this failure;
- the person suffered some actual loss or damage.

Obviously, educators should be certain that activities involving students (such as field trips, evening activities etc.) have been approved by the school board and are, therefore, covered by the school board's insurance. Also, educators who transport students in their own vehicles should have adequate liability coverage.°

see 14.10 and 14.11, below

3.6.5 Academic Research in Schools

Many teachers are now attending classes at post-secondary institutions in order to achieve a Masters' Degree or other designation as part of the requirement for advancement into educational administration and other roles. That phenomenon has resulted in many such adult students seeking to do academic research in schools either for a particular course or for a thesis/project. Such activities are laudable but fraught with ethical issues given the fiduciary relationship between students and teachers. This is particularly the case when teachers seek to use their own classroom students as participants in research. To ensure that the sensitive nature of the student teacher relationship is protected, school boards require that all research in schools is vetted by a school board's ethics committee or, in the absence of such, by at least the supervisory officer of the school board. Each school board has its own process, procedures, and policy for such vetting and teachers are advised to seek advice before making their application for ethics clearance from their school board. Moreover, post-secondary academic institutions are committed to follow the ethical procedure outlined in the 2010 Tri-Council Policy Statement: *Ethical Conduct for Research Involving Humans* (TCPS),° in order to receive prior approval from the relevant academic institution to commence academic research that involves humans. All research in

retrieved May 2013 from http://www.ethics.gc.ca/pdf/eng/tcps2/TCPS_2_FINAL_Web.pdf

schools must adhere to this policy that stipulates that consent for participation should be voluntary, informed, and an ongoing process (e.g. participants may choose to withdraw from the study). Post-secondary institutions will have a general (and sometimes, unit-specific) Research Ethics Board (REB).

3.7 PROFESSIONAL CONDUCT

The teaching profession, like all other professions, has standards of professional conduct and practice to which all members of the profession are expected to conform. These standards are codified in provincial statutes and regulations, as well as other documents. Failure to abide by these norms may lead to serious disciplinary action against the offending teacher. Professional conduct of teachers

Termination for Cause

On May 1987, the board of education of Eston-Elrose School Division gave notice of termination of contract to RS, a teacher with 16 years of experience. Reasons for the termination (in accordance with Sec 214(1) of the ***Education Act***) included incompetence and failure to demonstrate certain qualities and characteristics expected of teachers. RS appealed the termination to a Board of Reference as was her right under section 216(1) of the ***Education Act***. The Board of Reference concluded that the board of education had acted in bad faith when it did not follow its usual procedures, when it had tried to coerce her into resigning, and when it failed to consider her full record of employment. In August 1987 the Board of Reference ordered that her contract be continued.

The board of education appealed to the Court of Queen's Bench to overturn that decision and in January 1988, Justice Macleod heard the appeal. He held that the board of education did not act in bad faith and thus set aside the order from the Board of Reference. The matter was referred back to the Board of Reference to determine if the reasons for dismissal were sufficient and whether the decision was reasonable considering all circumstances.

In November 1988, the Board of Reference reconsidered the matter and affirmed its original decision. It ordered the teacher's reinstatement, but the board of education appealed once again to the Court of Queen's Bench alleging that the Board of Reference had erred in law. Justice Lawton heard that appeal in March 1989. He held that the board of education did not act in bad faith, but that it did not follow its own policy of evaluation to establish a good cause for termination. Most importantly, he found that the Board of Reference did not make an error of law. The result was that RS won her case.

This case serves as an illustration of the procedures used in the termination of a teacher's contract and the appeals available under the Act. It also raises the question of what could or should the parties involved have done differently to resolve the situation and points out the following:

- Cases of termination of teachers' contracts can be lengthy and sometimes tortuous affairs.
- Judges have traditionally been reluctant to interfere in the decision of professional educators. They will rule on matters of law rather than on purely educational issues.
- The ***Education Act*** provides a statutory appeal process, but principles of administrative law and common law also apply.
- When a board of education establishes policies of supervision and evaluation, they must be followed conscientiously

(From *EduLaw, 1*(2), October 1989).

in Ontario is guided by regulations issued by Ontario College of Teachers (OCT) and Ontario Teachers' Federation (OTF).

3.7.1 Standards of Professional Conduct and Practice

As a self-regulating body that governs the teaching profession in Ontario, and Ontario College of Teachers (OCT) is responsible for establishing and enforcing standards of professional conduct and practice. The standards describe the principles of ethical behaviour, professional practice, and ongoing learning for the teaching profession in Ontario. They are organized under the notion of Foundations of Professional Practice,° and include Ethical Standards for the Teaching Profession, Standards of Practice for the Teaching Profession, and The Professional Learning Framework for the Teaching Profession.

retrieved May 2013 from http://www.oct.ca/~/media/PDF/Foundations%20of%20Professional%20Practice/Foundation_e.ashx

The Ethical Standards for the Teaching Profession describe the professional beliefs and values that guide the decision-making and professional actions of teachers in their professional roles and relationships. The ethical standards include four key statements concerning Care, Respect, Trust and Integrity that are central to the ethics of the teaching profession in Ontario.

The Standards of Practice for the Teaching Profession include five interdependent domains: commitment to students and learning, professional knowledge, teaching practice, leadership and community, and ongoing professional learning. Under each of the five statements there are several "key elements" that expand upon the standards of practice statements.

The Professional Learning Framework for the Teaching Profession outlines the responsibility and the opportunities for continuing professional growth for teachers in Ontario. This framework identifies accredited pre-service and in-service programs of professional teacher education designed to reflect the ethical standards and standards of practice as well as a wide range of other opportunities for professional growth and development.

The above standards are not intended to be the criteria for the ongoing performance appraisal of individual members. However, these standards are used as the criteria for professional misconduct investigations by the College.

3.7.2 Code of Professional Ethics and Conduct

The Federation and its affiliates also have a code of professional ethics and conduct that all members are expected to abide by. This code of professional ethics and conduct is found in the *Regulation Made Under the Teaching Profession Act*, sections 13 through 18.° It contains provisions with respect to the general duties of members and duties of members to the public, educational authorities, an affiliate within OTF, and fellow members:

retrieved May 2013 from http://www.otffeo.on.ca/english/docs/WTT_TPA_policiesbylawsetc.pdf

General Duties of Members

13. A member shall strive at all times to achieve and maintain the highest degree of professional competence and to uphold the honour, dignity, and ethical standards of the teaching profession.

Duties of a Member to His or Her Pupils

14. A member shall,

(a) regard as his first duty the effective education of his pupils and the maintenance of a high degree of professional competence in his teaching;

(b) endeavour to develop in his pupils an appreciation of standards of excellence;

(c) endeavour to inculcate in his pupils an appreciation of the principles of democracy;

(d) show consistent justice and consideration in all his relations with pupils;

(e) refuse to divulge beyond his proper duty confidential information about a pupil; and

(f) concern himself with the welfare of his pupils while they are under his care.

Duties of a Member to Educational Authorities

15. (1) A member shall, (a) comply with the Acts and regulations administered by the Minister;

(a) co-operate with his educational authorities to improve public education;

(b) respect the legal authority of the board of trustees in the management of the school and in the employment of teachers;

(c) make in the proper manner such reports concerning teachers under his authority as may be required by the board of trustees; and

(d) present in the proper manner to the proper authorities the consequences to be expected from policies or practices which in his professional opinion are seriously detrimental to the interests of pupils.

(2) A member shall not,

(a) break a contract of employment with a board of trustees;

(b) violate a written or oral agreement to enter into a contract of employment with a board of trustees; or

(c) while holding a contract of employment with a board of trustees, make application for another position the acceptance of which would necessitate his seeking the termination of his contract by mutual consent of the teacher and the board of trustees, unless and until he has arranged with his board of trustees for such termination of contract if he obtains the other position.

Duties of a Member to the Public

16. A member shall,

(a) endeavour at all times to extend the public knowledge of his profession and discourage untrue, unfair or exaggerated statements with respect to teaching; and

(b) recognize a responsibility to promote respect for human rights.

Duties of a Member to the Federation

17. A member shall co-operate with the Federation to promote the welfare of the profession.

Duties of a Member to Fellow Members

18. (1) A member shall,

(a) avoid interfering in an unwarranted manner between other teachers and pupils;

(b) on making an adverse report on another member, furnish him with a written statement of the report at the earliest possible time and not later than three days after making the report;

(c) notwithstanding section 18 (1) (b), a member who makes an adverse report about another member respecting suspected sexual abuse of a student by that other member need not provide him or her with a copy of the report or with any information about the report.°

Note: Sexual abuse is a criminal matter. This is to ensure that the rights of the potential victims and the accused persons are pretected and to prevent possible destruction of the evidence.

(d) refuse to accept employment with a board of trustees whose relations with the Federation are unsatisfactory; and regulation made under the teaching profession act

(e) where he is in an administrative or supervisory position, make an honest and determined effort to help and counsel a teacher before subscribing to the dismissal of that teacher.

(2) Under clause (c) of subsection (1), the onus shall be on the member to ascertain personally from the Federation whether an unsatisfactory relationship exists.

(3) A member shall not attempt to gain an advantage over other members by knowingly underbidding another member, or knowingly applying for a position not properly declared vacant, or by negotiating for salary independently of his local group of fellow-members.

Under Ontario law, any student who is registered in a pre-service teacher education program in a Faculty of Education in Ontario is automatically an associate member of the Ontario Teachers Federation (but not of any of the affiliate organizations). Therefore, section 18(1) of the above Regulation is applicable for teacher candidates when they are at the practicum placements and when they start looking for a teaching position.

§ 18(1)(b) REGULATION MADE UNDER THE TEACHING PROFESSION ACT

According to section 18(1)(b),° teacher candidates must not deliver negative reports or make negative statements about their associate teachers or other teachers to anyone unless they are willing to tell them in writing what they have said or are going to say about them. (The only reasonable exception would be a situation in which they disclose a significant difficulty to a university faculty member in the context of a university student having a private, and therefore, confidential conversation with their instructor or if they need to make a complaint consistent with the guidelines set up by the Practicum Office).

In the profession itself, the issue of negative reports is a significant challenge. In addition, the requirement to furnish a written report to the target of a negative report outlining any negative statements that were made within three days is deceptively simple in way it is worded in 18(1)(b). Such a letter is fraught with pitfalls and a member should seek advice from their affiliate in cases such as this. Members must be discouraged from writing letters that outright admit to having slandered or libeled another member. At minimum, such letters should carry the disclaimer "Without Prejudice."

According to Section 18(1)(d), teacher candidates must not accept a teaching position with a school board with whom the Federation judges its relations to be unsatisfactory. This section of the regulation relates to the issues that may arise between the federation and board are a result of negotiations of new or renewals of collective agreements, which may result in the application of sanctions on the part of federation (or its affiliates). The application of sanctions during the bargaining process is regulated by Ontario *Labour Relations Act*. The federation (by its affiliates) will issue, during the course of negotiations for a new or renewal collective agreement, an Information Bulletin advising current or prospective members of difficulties arising in the bargaining process. This information bulletin is issued on pink paper—and is called "Pink Slip" or "Pink Letter"—and details sanctions which could include changes to the terms of agreements and conditions of employment, partial withdrawal of services or full withdrawals of services by the members, or lockouts. The "pink slips" advise members (and associate members) against applying for or accepting employment with the board identified in the bulletin. Failure to abide by this directive is a violation of Section 18 (1) (d). The restriction against seeking or taking employment with a particular board identified in a "Pink Letter" only ends with the issuance of an Information Bulletin on green paper—a "Green Letter." It is the individual member's responsibility to check the Green/Pink Letters prior to applying for or accepting employment with any school board to ensure that there are advisories are being applied by the federation. Usually, the list of "pink lettered" board will appear on the federation affiliate's website (e.g., OSSTF Green/ Pink Letters list).°

retrieved May 2013 from http://wwwa.osstf.on.ca/Default.aspx?DN=d37ec6ec-b6a1-4556-8ea9-e82860ee1c8f

3.8 COMPLAINTS AND DISCIPLINE

Under authority of the *Ontario College of Teachers Act* and Regulations under that Act, the College investigates and resolves complaints and conducts hearings regarding professional misconduct, incompetence or incapacity of teachers employed in the publicly funded system, including principals, vice-principals and academic supervisory officers. The College handles expressions of concern received from the public, members of the College, the Minister of Education, and the College Registrar acting on behalf of the public interest. Complaints regarding the conduct or actions of a member of the College are considered and investigated by the Investigation Committee.° Upon investigation, the committee may decide to dismiss the complaint; resolve the issue by a voluntary and mutually-consented Complaint Resolution program; caution or admonish the member; or, provide advice. Alternatively, the Investigation may refer the matter in whole or in part to a Discipline Committee° or a Fitness to Practice Committee.° The Discipline Committee deals with teachers who are alleged to have been incompetent or have committed professional misconduct. The Fitness to Practice Committee deals with allegations of incapacity (i.e., health-related physical or mental issues affecting the member's ability to teach).

§ 26 Ontario College of Teachers Act

§ 30(1) Ontario College of Teachers Act

§ 31(1) Ontario College of Teachers Act

3.8.1 Professional Misconduct

Failure to adhere to the professional and ethical standards of conduct and practice is considered professional misconduct. Regulation 437/97 "Professional Misconduct under the *Ontario College of Teachers Act*" lists acts (behaviours) that are defined as professional misconduct for the purpose of subsection 30(2) of the *Act* and for which teachers are subject to disciplinary action by the Discipline Committee of the Ontario College of Teachers.

The following acts are defined as professional misconduct:

1. Providing false information or documents to the College or any other person with respect to the member's professional qualifications.

2. Inappropriately using a term, title or designation indicating a specialization in the profession which is not specified on the member's Certificate of Qualification and Registration.

3. Permitting, counselling or assisting any person who is not a member to represent himself or herself as a member of the College.

4. Using a name other than the member's name, as set out in the register, in the course of his or her professional duties.

5. Failing to maintain the standards of the profession.

6. Releasing or disclosing information about a student to a person other than the student or, if the student is a minor, the student's parent or guardian. The release or disclosure of information is not an act of professional misconduct if,

   a. the student (or if the student is a minor, the student's parent or guardian) consents to the release or disclosure, or

   b. if the release or disclosure is required or allowed by law.

7. Abusing a student verbally.

8. Abusing a student physically.

9. Abusing a student psychologically or emotionally.

10. Abusing a student sexually.

11. Practising or purporting to practise the profession while under the influence of any substance or while adversely affected by any dysfunction,

    a. which the member knows or ought to know impairs the member's ability to practise, and

    b. in respect of which treatment has previously been recommended, ordered or prescribed but the member has failed to follow the treatment.

12. Contravening a term, condition or limitation imposed on the member's Certificate of Qualification and Registration.

13. Failing to keep records as required by his or her professional duties.

14. Failing to supervise adequately a person who is under the professional supervision of the member.

15. Signing or issuing, in the member's professional capacity, a document that the member knows or ought to know contains a false, improper or misleading statement.

16. Falsifying a record relating to the member's professional responsibilities.

17. Failing to comply with the Act, the regulations or the bylaws.

18. Failing to comply with the *Education Act* or the regulations made under that Act, if the member is subject to that Act.

19. Contravening a law if the contravention is relevant to the member's suitability to hold a Certificate of Qualification and Registration.

20. Contravening a law if the contravention has caused or may cause a student who is under the member's professional supervision to be put at or to remain at risk.

21. An act or omission that, having regard to all the circumstances, would reasonably be regarded by members as disgraceful, dishonourable or unprofessional.

22. Conduct unbecoming a member.

23. Failing to appear before a panel of the Investigation Committee to be cautioned or admonished, if the Investigation Committee has required the member to appear under clause 26(5)(c) of the Act.

24. Failing to comply with an order of a panel of the Discipline Committee or an order of a panel of the Fitness to Practise Committee.

25. Failing to co-operate in a College investigation.

26. Failing to take reasonable steps to ensure that requested information is provided in a complete and accurate manner if the member is required to provide information to the College under the Act and the regulations.

27. Failing to abide by a written undertaking given by the member to the College or an agreement entered into by the member with the College.

28. Failing to respond adequately or within a reasonable time to a written inquiry from the College.

29. Practising the profession while the member is in a conflict of interest.

30. Failing to comply with the member's duty under the Child and Family Services Act.

Furthermore, the regulation stipulates that

> a finding of incompetence, professional misconduct or a similar finding against a member by a governing authority of the teaching profession in a jurisdiction other than Ontario that is based on facts that would, in the opinion of the Discipline Committee, constitute professional misconduct as defined in section 1, is defined as professional misconduct for the purposes of subsection 30 (2) of the Act.°

§ 2 Regulation 437/97

3.8.2 *Disciplinary Hearings Process*

Under the rules set by *Statutory Powers Procedures Act* and the *Ontario College of Teachers Act*, the College operates a quasi-judicial hearing process.° Members accused of professional misconduct have a right to procedural fairness, including the right to answer and defend, to be presumed innocent until proven otherwise, to have

Ontario College of Teachers. (2011) *Rules of Procedure*. Toronto, ON: the Author. *retrieved May 2013 from http://www.oct.ca/public/complaints-and-discipline/fitness-to-practise-committee/rules-of-procedure*

matters dealt with in a timely manner, and to appeal the committees' decisions.

When a complaint is fully investigated and referred by the Investigation Committee to a disciplinary hearing, a notice of hearing containing charges of incompetence or professional misconduct against the member is prepared and served on the member. This notice of hearing is intended to advise the member and members of the public that the allegations as described in the notice will be considered by a panel to determine if the allegations are founded or not. Discipline Committee hearings involving allegations of incompetence or professional misconduct are usually held in public; however, the committee may direct that the public be excluded from a hearing under certain circumstances.

§ 30(2) ONTARIO COLLEGE OF TEACHERS ACT

After a hearing, the Discipline Committee may find a member guilty of professional misconduct as defined in the Regulation 437/97.° The Discipline Committee may, after a hearing, find a member to be incompetent if he or she displayed a lack of knowledge, skill, or judgment or disregard for the welfare of a student of a nature or extent that demonstrates that the member is unfit to continue to carry out his or her professional responsibilities or that a certificate held by the member should be made subject to terms, conditions or limitations.°

§ 30(3) ONTARIO COLLEGE OF TEACHERS ACT

3.8.3 *Fitness to Practise Hearing*

The Fitness to Practise Committee conducts hearings in matters related to the alleged incapacity of members. The hearings are generally closed to the public, unless a member makes a written request in for a public hearing. The purpose of these hearings is to determine whether a member is physically or mentally unfit to carry out his or her professional responsibilities and, if so, to specify any appropriate terms, limitations, change of certificate status, or conditions. The penalties are similar to the ones imposed by the Disciplinary Committee and may involve the following:

- revoking a member's certificate;
- suspending a certificate for up to 24 months;
- requiring the member to provide evidence that any physical or mental condition or disorder has been resolved before removing any terms, limitations, or conditions imposed;
- fixing a period during which the teacher is ineligible for reinstatement or variation of the committee's order.

3.8.4 *Ontario Teachers' Federation's Complaints Review and Disciplinary Action*

According to the *Regulations Made under the Teaching Profession Act*,° Relations and Discipline Committee of the Ontario Teachers'

§§ 19 through 28 REGULATIONS MADE UNDER THE TEACHING PROFESSION ACT

Federation also consider complaints regarding professional misconduct or unethical conduct of a member. It also considers applications for reinstatement of the teaching certificate of a former member or the lifting of an imposed suspension. A member may be found guilty by the Committee of a professional misconduct or unethical conduct if in the opinion of the Committee the teacher has contravened any of the provisions of code of professional ethics and conduct in the *Regulation Made Under the Teaching Profession Act*, sections 13 through 18.° If a member is found guilty, the committee may recommend one of the following options: cancelling a teaching certificate of the member; suspending the member's certificate for a stated fixed period; reprimanding a member; or, any combination of the foregoing.

Ontario Teachers' Federation. (2012). *We the Teachers of Ontario*. Toronto, ON: the Author. *retrieved May 2013 from http://www.otffeo.on.ca/english/docs/WTT_TPA_policiesbylawsetc.pdf*

3.9 TEACHERS AND TECHNOLOGY IN THE CLASSROOM

3.9.1 *Teachers and Copyright*

One of the most prevalent questions asked by teachers is "What is copyright and what does or should the law mean to me as a teacher?" Essentially, copyright refers the right to copy or proper use of intellectual property. According to Section 3(1) of the *Copyright Act*, copyright in relation to a work, means:

> the sole right to produce or reproduce the work or any substantial part thereof in any material form whatever, to perform the work or any substantial part thereof in public or, if the work is unpublished, to publish the work or any substantial part thereof.

Copyright implies the legal protection of literary, dramatic, artistic, cinematographic, and musical works, sound recordings, performances, computer program, etc. The intent of copyright is the legal protection given to a person or a legal entity, who is the creator of an original piece of work. Only the owner of copyright, usually the creator of the work, is allowed to produce or reproduce the work in question or to permit anyone else to do so. Copyright law rewards and protects a person's creative endeavour by giving them the sole right to publish or use their work in any number of ways. Copyright is authorized by the *Copyright Act*, a piece of federal legislation applicable to all provinces and territories.

Protection under copyright laws is automatic in Canada: as soon as an original work has been written down, recorded, or entered as a computer file, it is immediately copyright-protected even if the author does not choose to register the work for added protection. Copyright infringement occurs in cases when someone reproduces a copyrighted work (in any of the forms discussed in Section 3(1) of the *Copyright Act*) without the permission of the owner of the copyright.

Canadian Copyright Licensing Agency. (2010). *Ensuring Quality Content for Educators and Students*. Toronto, ON: the Author. *retrieved May 2013 from http://www.accesscopyright.ca/educators/*

In schools, copyright is often associated with photocopying practices, and all publicly funded (non-profit) schools across Canada are covered by Access Copyright licence with the Canadian Copyright Licensing Agency (CANCOPY).° This licence provides permission to educational institutions to make reprographic copies, the most common form of which are photocopies. In our digital and electronic classrooms, the implications of copyright legislation extend beyond the Xerox machine, as copyright protects the rights of those who created text, audio, and media works.

Copyright law has become more challenging in recent years with the advent of the Internet. One of the major problems with respect to copyright protection is that legislators have been unable to keep up with technological advances. After many years of deliberation, *Copyright Modernization Act*, Bill C-11, had received royal assent on June 29, 2012. This new copyright law clarified Canada's approach to copyright, striking a balance between the needs of creators and users and establishing a clearer legal framework for the digital age and its ever-changing technologies.

By adding "education" as an allowable purpose within the copyright "fair dealing" provision in the *Copyright Act*, this recent development in copyright law permits educational institutions to act "in fair dealing" with copyrighted materials. Copyright-protected materials can be used for educational purposes, provided the dealing is "fair." This measure of fair dealing is meant to promote "balanced copyright," that is, fairness is interpreted in terms of protecting the interests of copyright holders while at the same time actions on behalf of using copyrighted materials in educational institutions must be set on reducing administrative and financial costs for users of copyrighted materials that enrich the educational environment.

The *Copyright Act* provides that it is not an infringement of copyright to deal with (or make use of) a work for the purposes of research, private study, criticism, review, news reporting, education, satire, and parody, providing that the dealing is "fair." Since teachers use copyrighted materials in their work as well as to educate their students about issues of (or related to) copyright, they have a unique responsibility to demonstrate how to use copyrighted materials "fairly." Teachers and students are now permitted to access and use publicly available Internet materials in the process of teaching and learning, while respecting the rights of those creators and other copyright holders who post materials on-line for commercial purposes. The use of materials in the classroom must be consistent with provisions of usage of copyrighted materials as set out in the *Copyright Act* or any of its regulations.

Noel, W. & Snel, J. (2012). *Copyright Matters: Some Key Questions and Answers for Teachers*. Toronto, ON: Council of Ministers of Education. *retrieved May 2013 from http://cmec.ca/Publications/Lists/Publications/Attachments/291/Copyright_Matters.pdf*

Three organizations (the Council of Ministers of Education, Canada, the Canadian School Boards' Association, and the Canadian Teachers' Federation) have cooperated to produce a booklet titled "Copyright Matters: Some Key Questions and Answers for Teachers."° It answers the everyday questions which teachers have with regard to Canadian copyright and its application in school.

3.9.2 *Intellectual Property and Teachers*

A related area of law deals with ownership of materials developed by teachers. Intellectual property is a term which is used to describe the law relating to copyright, patents, designs, trademarks and other related areas. One of the objects of intellectual property law is to protect the output of human intellectual endeavour in a similar way as the law protects, say, ownership of goods or land. It has been long assumed by teachers that they own the lesson plans that they have created. With the increase of teachers' involvement in curriculum development, the issue arises whether individual teachers own the materials that they have created or whether the school boards as their employers own the materials created in the course of employment. The issue arises because of the Section 13 of the *Copyright Act* that states:

> 13. (1) Subject to this Act, the author of a work shall be the first owner of the copyright therein ...
>
> (3) Where the author of a work was in the employment of some other person under a contract of service or apprenticeship and the work was made in the course of his employment by that person, the person by whom the author was employed shall, in the absence of any agreement to the contrary, be the first owner of the copyright, but where the work is an article or other contribution to a newspaper, magazine or similar periodical, there shall, in the absence of any agreement to the contrary, be deemed to be reserved to the author a right to restrain the publication of the work, otherwise than as part of a newspaper, magazine or similar periodical.

The issue has been debated for some time, as proponents argue that teaching materials or handouts can attract copyright protection even if the materials are a compilation of existing matter, as the literary element lies in the selection, ordering and arrangement of the compiled matter. Relying on a well-established practice that copyright in a lecture delivered by an employee who is employed to lecture lies with that employee, teachers have generally been presumed to own the copyright in the materials that they have created. Opponents argue that teachers are professionals working under contracts of service with the employing school boards, and therefore materials created by a teacher that clearly relate to the teacher's position with the board are owned by the board. The issue is far from being resolved because of the lack of case law and the ongoing disagreements among legal analysts and will depend on further developments in copyright legislation in Canada.

Overall, educators have a responsibility to respect the value of intellectual property in their classrooms. As students, we were taught the value of original thinking and the importance of not plagiarizing the work of others. Since teachers use copyright materials as well as educate the copyright owners and users of tomorrow, they have a unique responsibility to set the right example.

3.9.3 Technology in the Classroom

ICT provides exciting new opportunities to use in the classroom. Social networking has redefined the way that students communicate with one another. However, technology also provides some new "grey areas" that teachers should be aware of. Some school boards have specific policies regarding the use of technology in classroom to protect student and teachers (and the boards themselves). Often this involves blocking (or prohibiting) the use of such devices in schools. Some of the potential uses of technology in classroom are detailed below.

Teacher websites (either using a school template or your own) may provide an excellent resource to post homework information, course syllabi, planning information, as well as teacher contact information.

Email can provide an excellent opportunity to communicate with both students and their parents. However, emails may also be misinterpreted, taken out of context, or edited to portray a different meaning than intended.

The advent of social media provides a technological way to meet friends, share photos and communicate to large groups of people. Caution is advised on publicly sharing information that may affect the role of a teacher as a professional. Teachers need to consider the importance of keeping your professional and personal life separate.

The popularity of cellphones, smart phones, iPods, digital cameras, have resulted in a very "plugged-in" student population. Many schools and school boards have policies in place that limit/prohibit/control the presence of these devices in classrooms. The use of communication technologies in classrooms (including cell phones, text messaging, internet, etc.) often has negative consequences (e.g., distraction, bullying or harassment).

Finally, technology gives the illusion of anonymity. Often this facilitates serious antisocial behaviour, in the form of cyber bullying through texting, email, among others. Teachers need to be aware of changes in a student's behaviour that might be the result of cyber-bullying.

3.9.4 Teachers and Social Media

Social media has become a ubiquitous part of modern culture for adults and for students. Social media generally refers to a class of web sites that allow users to publish user-generated content to a network of designated peers. The ability to share text, photos, videos, and other digital resources make for an engaging experience for adults and young people alike. For these reasons, web sites like Facebook, Twitter, LinkedIn, Pinterest, Tumblr/Wordpress/Blogger, Wiki, and YouTube have a pervasive presence in society. It is important for teachers to be aware not only of potential benefits, but also potential pitfalls of professional uses of social media.

Social media is often used for professional development and pedagogical approaches that makes use of technology. Professional bodies are increasingly using social media channels to communicate to their members. For instance, OSSTF maintains both a Facebook° and a YouTube° page. Social media can also become a source of professional learning for educators when used strategically. For instance, teachers and educators regularly meet online to participate in a topical discussion. These communities can be found on Twitter, among others. Many organizations are turning to Twitter to push out news items. By "following" and subscribing to the accounts of various organizations, one can assemble own newsfeed.

retrieved May 2013 from https://www.facebook.com/osstfnews

retrieved May 2013 from http://www.youtube.com/user/OSSTF

For members of the teaching profession it is important to remember that their conduct, both professional and personal, matters beyond the walls of a school. Unlike some professions that enjoy greater anonymity, the teaching profession is held to a greater standard of care because of the nature of their work and the role in teaching children and other vulnerable persons. What is often considered to be a post of a personal nature may not always be so, whereas a private photo could become "leaked" and made public when a screen shot is made of it. Once something is online, it is difficult to fully destroy its existence; a file may not be retrievable by public means, but may still be archived. Teachers need to consider their digital footprint, or the traces of information found online representing their behaviors, actions, and digital content that may lead to their identity. In some cases, it may be a post left on a public forum, or a review left on an online retailer's site. In other cases, it may be a photo on a social networking site, or something as innocuous as "liking" a photo on another individuals' profile page.

A number of professional teacher organizations have offered advice to its members in relation to the use of social media. For example, the Ontario College of Teachers' has a Professional Advisory on the Use of Electronic Communication and Social Media° and Elementary Teachers' Federation of Ontario issued Electronic Communication and Social Media—Advice to Members.°

retrieved May 2013 from http://www.oct.ca/resources/advisories/use-of-electronic-communication-and-social-media

retrieved May 2013 from http://www.etfo.ca/AdviceForMembers/PRSMattersBulletins/PDF%20Versions/Electronic%20Communication%20and%20Social%20Media.pdf

3.10 NON-TEACHING STAFF

In recent years, the number of non-teaching employees in Ontario schools has increased substantially. In practice, and dependent on school size and other factors, a school board may employ a variety of non-teaching personnel: building maintenance staff and custodians, clerical employees, education or teacher assistants, bus drivers, social workers, and other "support staff." Many individual boards of education have collective agreements with their non-teaching staffs, who are often represented by locals of trade unions such as CUPE. Conditions of employment for non-teaching staff are included in such local agreements and in board policy. Other statutes of a more general application are relevant to the hiring and employment of these employees, particularly the *Employment Standards Act*, 2000 and its regulations, which set out the minimum standards that employers and employees must follow.

3.10.1 Educational Assistants

An increasingly vital role in today's classroom is played by educational assistants who work alongside and under the guidance of teachers to support their working with individual, or groups of, students. The development of the educational assistant role can be traced back to the introduction of Bill 82 in 1980, under which all school boards in Ontario became obliged to serve all children including those with exceptional needs. Various titles are used for persons performing this role: Educational Resources Assistant; Lunch Room Supervisor; Teacher's Aide; Teacher's Assistant; Educational Assistant; Special Education Assistant; Staff Assistant Education; or Program Assistant Education.

§ 170.3 EA

Employment Ontario. (2009). *Elementary and Secondary School Teacher Assistants*. Toronto, ON: the Author. *retrieved May 2013 from http://www.tcu.gov.on.ca/eng/labourmarket/ojf/pdf/6472_e.pdf*

The *Education Act* makes special reference° to the role of schools boards to determine the duties and minimum qualifications of teachers' assistants, who are assigned to assist teachers or to complement instruction by teachers in elementary or secondary schools. Elementary and secondary school teacher assistants perform some or all of the following duties:°

- Assist students with lessons under direct supervision of classroom teacher;
- Monitor and report to classroom teacher on student progress;
- Accompany and supervise students during activities in school gymnasiums, laboratories, libraries, resource centres, and on field trips;
- Assist special needs students, such as those with mental or physical disabilities, with mobility, communication, and personal hygiene;
- Prepare classroom displays and bulletins;
- Operate or assist teacher in the operation of projectors, tape recorders, and other audio-visual or electronic equipment;
- Carry out behaviour modification, personal development and other therapeutic programs under supervision of professionals such as special education instructors, psychologists or speech/ language pathologists;

- Work with special needs students using techniques such as sign language, Bliss symbols, or Braille;
- Monitor students during recess or noon hour;
- Assist with marking of tests and worksheets;
- Assist with classroom inventory;
- Assist in school library or office and perform other duties assigned by a school principal.

Educational assistant positions are considered to be non-teaching, complementary, or paraprofessional. They may be full-time or part-time contract positions (usually 10-month contract agreement renewed at an annual basis). Teacher assistants do not require certification from the Ontario College of Teachers, but boards may require a combination of education, experience or other attributes. Boards' minimum qualification requirements usually include completion of secondary school and proficiency in English or French. Most boards will prefer experience and/or training in working with young people and college diplomas in the human services field (e.g., Early Childhood Education (ECE), Youth Care Worker (YCW), Nursing or Nursing Assistant (NA), Educational Assistant (EA), etc.). Teacher assistants who aid students with special needs may require specialized training and experience.

4.0 THE SCHOOL PRINCIPAL

Part 4.0 of the Guide deals with in-school administration: the principal and vice-principal.

4.1 QUALIFICATIONS AND APPOINTMENTS

The staff of each school consists of a principal and any number of teachers, designated early childhood educators and other staff members considered necessary for the operation of the school.° § 1 EA
A principal is appointed by the board of education to that specific position, usually upon the recommendation of the Director of Education or another supervisory officer of a board.° All principals § 9 Regulation 298
of schools with more than 125 students must be qualified teachers; each must have a school principal's qualification or certificate.° § 9(1) Regulation 298

Members of the Ontario College of Teachers who

1. have an Ontario Certificate of Qualification or Interim Certificate of Qualification (Temporary Letter of Standing),

2. have taught for a minimum of five years in an elementary or secondary school,

3. hold qualifications in teaching methodology studies (as shown on their Certificate of Qualification) for three of the four provincial divisions—i.e., primary (kindergarten to grade 3), junior (grades 4 to 6), intermediate (grades 7 to 10), and senior (grades 11 to OAC)—inclusive of the intermediate division, and

4. hold one of the following three credentials

   (a) a Specialist or Honour Specialist qualification and

   (i) have successfully completed at least half of the credit units required for the granting of a Master's degree from a recognized university program, or

   (ii) have a second Specialist or Honour Specialist qualification;

   (b) a Master's degree from a recognized university program; or

(c) sufficient credit units at a graduate level that would be equivalent to the number required for the granting of a Master's degree from a recognized university program

may earn qualifications for the position of school principal by engaging in the Principals' Qualification Program (PQP), established by the Ontario College of Teachers for that purpose. Completion of the PQP is prerequisite of employment as a school principal or vice-principal in Ontario.°

§ 9 Regulation 298

The PQP is operationally divided into two parts, each of which offers modules focused on specific learning objectives defined by the College of Teachers. Universities and professional associations throughout Ontario offer both parts of the PQP. Part one is focused on the study of leadership, and is a prerequisite for completion of part two, which is focused on the study of change.

4.2 PROFESSIONAL STATUS

§§ 1, 3(3) Provincial Schools Negotiation Act, 1990; § 9 Regulation 298

§ 1 Provincial Schools Negotiation Act, 1990

§§ 1, 4(1) Teaching Profession Act, 1990; § 1 Provincial schools Negotiation Act, 1990; § 277.1 EA

§ X(A), Policy of the Ontario Teachers' Federation, 2012

Principals are teachers under contract to carry out administrative duties and must hold valid certificates of qualification (OCQ) to teach in Ontario° or be otherwise approved by the Minister of Education and Training to fulfill such purposes.° When employed by publicly funded boards, they are members of the Ontario College of Teachers but are not considered teachers for basic salary and classification purposes. They are not members of the Ontario Teachers' Federation° although it remains a policy statement of the OTF that principals and vice-principals ought to be members.° Care should be taken in the interpretation of policy and statutes given the legal status of this distinction.

Membership in provincial or national professional associations or societies for the promotion of the collective interests of principals is voluntary in Ontario. The Ontario Principals' Council (OPC) claims 5000 members and offers access to legal council, long-term disability insurance coverage, professional development, and peer support and advice. Membership is contingent on payment of annual fees. The OPC operates within the Ontario College of Teachers guidelines for ethical conduct.° The Catholic Principals' Council of Ontario (CPCO) offers similar services for principals and vice-principals in Catholic school divisions, and l'Association des directions et directions adjointes des écoles franco-ontariennes (ADFO) is the francophone analogue.

retrieved May 2013 from http://www.principals.ca

The Canadian Association of Principals (CAP) is a national professional advocacy organization that offers membership to principals and vice-principals automatically through provincial professional associations. Ontario principals and vice-principals who are not members of provincial bodies may independently become members of the CAP.°

retrieved May 2013 from www.cndprincipals.org

4.3 DUTIES AND RESPONSIBILITIES OF THE PRINCIPAL

4.3.1 Duties

The *Education Act* spells out the duties and responsibilities of principals in both general and specific terms. Subject to the *Education Act*, the regulations made under the authority of the *Education Act*, and the policies of a board of education, the principal is responsible for the general organization, administration, and supervision of the school, its programs and professional staff.

The specific duties of the principal° include all of those duties of a teacher, as well as the duty to § 265 EA

- maintain proper order and discipline in the school;
- develop co-operation and co-ordination of effort among the members of the staff of the school;
- register the pupils and to ensure that the attendance of pupils for every school day is recorded either in the register supplied by the Minister in accordance with the instructions contained therein or in such other manner as is approved by the Minister;
- collect information for inclusion in a record in respect of each pupil enrolled in the school and to establish, maintain, retain, transfer and dispose of the record, in accordance with the *Education Act* and the regulations and the guidelines issued by the Minister;
- prepare a timetable, to conduct the school according to such timetable and the school year calendar or calendars applicable thereto, to make the calendar or calendars and the timetable accessible to the pupils, teachers and supervisory officers and to assign classes and subjects to the teachers;
- hold, subject to the approval of the appropriate supervisory officer, such examinations as the principal considers necessary for the promotion of pupils or for any other purpose and report as required by the board the progress of the pupil to his or her parent or guardian where the pupil is a minor, and otherwise to the pupil;
- promote such pupils as the principal considers proper and to issue to each such pupil a statement thereof, subject to revision by the appropriate supervisory officer
- ensure that all textbooks used by pupils are those approved by the board and, in the case of subject areas for which the Minister approves textbooks, those approved by the Minister;
- furnish to the Ministry and to the appropriate supervisory officer any information that it may be in the principal's power to give respecting the condition of the school premises, the discipline of the school, the progress of the pupils and any other matter

affecting the interests of the school, and to prepare such reports for the board as are required by the board;

- give assiduous attention to the health and comfort of the pupils, to the cleanliness, temperature and ventilation of the school, to the care of all teaching materials and other school property, and to the condition and appearance of the school buildings and grounds;
- report promptly to the board and to the medical officer of health when the principal has reason to suspect the existence of any communicable disease in the school, and of the unsanitary condition of any part of the school building or the school grounds;
- refuse admission to the school of any person who the principal believes is infected with or exposed to communicable diseases requiring an order under section 22 of the *Health Protection and Promotion Act* until furnished with a certificate of a medical officer of health or of a legally qualified medical practitioner approved by the medical officer of health that all danger from exposure to contact with such person has passed;
- subject to an appeal to the board, to refuse to admit to the school or classroom a person whose presence in the school or classroom would in the principal's judgment be detrimental to the physical or mental well-being of the pupils; and
- maintain a visitor's book in the school when so determined by the board.

§ 11 Regulation 298

Additionally, the regulations° indicate a collection of specific duties that stand independent of those found in the Act, or through their reinforcement, underline their statutory importance:

- The principal of a school, subject to the authority of the appropriate supervisory officer, is in charge of, the instruction and the discipline of pupils in the school; and the organization and management of the school.°

§ 11(1) Regulation 298

Furthermore, the principal's duties and responsibilities focus upon safety, good order, and the progression of students toward the goals of the education program. To this end, he or she shall:°

§§ 11(3), 11(4) Regulation 298

- supervise the instruction in the school and advise and assist any teacher in co-operation with the teacher in charge of an organizational unit or program;
- assign duties to vice-principals and to teachers in charge of organizational units or programs;
- retain on file up-to-date copies of outlines of all courses of study that are taught in the school;
- upon request, make outlines of courses of study available for examination to a resident pupil of the board and to the parent of the pupil, where the pupil is a minor;

- provide for the supervision of pupils during the period of time during each school day when the school buildings and playgrounds are open to pupils;
- provide for the supervision of and the conducting of any school activity authorized by the board;
- where performance appraisals of members of the teaching staff are required under a collective agreement or a policy of the board, despite anything to the contrary in such collective agreement or board policy, conduct performance appraisals of members of the teaching staff;
- subject to the provisions of the policy of the board or the provisions of a collective agreement, as the case may be, in respect of reporting requirements for performance appraisals, report thereon in writing to the board or to the supervisory officer on request and give to each teacher so appraised a copy of the performance appraisal of the teacher;
- where the performance appraisals of members of the teaching staff are not required by board policy or under a collective agreement, report to the board or to the supervisory officer in writing on request on the effectiveness of members of the teaching staff and give to a teacher referred to in any such report a copy of the portion of the report that refers to the teacher;
- make recommendations to the board with respect to the appointment and promotion of teachers, and the demotion or dismissal of teachers—whose work or attitude is unsatisfactory—after warning the teacher in writing, giving the teacher assistance and allowing the teacher a reasonable time to improve;
- provide for instruction of pupils in the care of the school premises;
- inspect the school premises at least weekly and report forthwith to the board,
- any repairs to the school that are required, in the opinion of the principal, any lack of attention on the part of the building maintenance staff of the school, and where a parent of a pupil has been requested to compensate the board for damage to or destruction, loss or misappropriation of school property by the pupil and the parent has not done so, that the parent of the pupil has not compensated the board;
- where it is proposed to administer a test of intelligence or personality to a pupil, inform the pupil and the parent of the pupil of the test and obtain the prior written permission for the test from the pupil or from the parent of the pupil, where the pupil is a minor;
- report promptly any neglect of duty or infraction of the school rules by a pupil to the parent or guardian of the pupil;

- promote and maintain close co-operation with residents, industry, business, and other groups and agencies of the community;
- provide to the Minister or to a person designated by the Minister any information that may be required concerning the instructional program, operation, or administration of the school and inform the appropriate supervisory officer of the request;
- assign suitable quarters for pupils to eat lunch.

4.3.2 *Additional Responsibilities*

Elsewhere in the Act and the regulations, specific provisions are made for the powers and responsibilities of the principal in the day-to-day operation and administration of the school. In some cases, these apply exclusively to principals in schools catering to elementary, intermediate, or secondary division students.

General Operation of the School

The role of the principal in the general operation of the school is paramount. Within the regulations, the Ministry offers several clarifications of specific management expectations for principals.

§ 3(6) Regulation 298

- Principals of the intermediate or senior divisions may, subject to the approval of the board, provide for recesses or intervals for pupils between periods.°

§ 4(4) Regulation 298

- If parents of pupils under the age of 18, or pupils 18 years of age and older, apply to the principal for an exemption from participation in opening and closing exercises in a school, a pupil will not be required to participate.°

§ 6(2) Regulation 298

- Every principal, including the principal of an evening class or classes or of a class or classes conducted outside the school year, shall hold at least one emergency drill in the period during which the instruction is given.°

§§ 7(1), 7(2) Regulation 298

- The principal of a school, in consultation with the teachers concerned, shall select from the list of the textbooks approved by the Minister the textbooks for the use of pupils of the school, and the selection shall be subject to the approval of the board and, where no textbook for a course of study is included in the list of the textbooks approved by the Minister, the principal of a school, in consultation with the teachers concerned, shall, where they consider a textbook to be required, select a suitable textbook and, subject to the approval of the board, such textbook may be introduced for use in the school.°
- A principal shall notify the appropriate supervisory officer in writing if his or her fluency in English or French would result in the impracticability of the duty, having regard to the qualifications of the principal, to supervise the instruction, to conduct performance

appraisals, and to assist and advise the teachers referred to in his or her assigned school.° § 11(5) Regulation 298

- Where, after reasonable notice by the principal, a pupil who is an adult, or the parent of a pupil who is a minor, fails to provide the supplies required by the pupil for a course of study, the principal shall promptly notify the board.
- A principal shall transmit reports and recommendations to the board through the appropriate supervisory officer.
- A principal, subject to the approval of the appropriate supervisory officer, may arrange for home instruction to be provided for a pupil, where medical evidence that the pupil cannot attend school is provided to the principal, and the principal is satisfied that home instruction is required.
- The principal of a school shall provide for the prompt distribution to each member of the school council of any materials received by the principal from the Ministry that are identified by the Ministry as being for distribution to the members of school councils. Further, the principal shall post any materials distributed to members of the school council in the school in a location that is accessible to parents.
- In each school year, the principal of a school shall make the names of the members of the school council known to the parents of the pupils enrolled in the school, by publishing those names in a school newsletter or by such other means as is likely to bring the names to the attention of the parents not later than 30 days following the election of parent members of the school council.
- The principal of a school shall promptly provide the names of the members of the school council to a supporter of the board that governs the school or to a parent of a pupil enrolled in the school, on the request of the supporter or the parent.
- The principal of a school shall attend every meeting of the school council, unless he or she is unable to do so by reason of illness or other cause beyond his or her control.
- The principal of a school shall act as a resource person to the school council and shall assist the council in obtaining information relevant to the functions of the council, including information relating to relevant legislation, regulations and policies.
- The principal of a school shall consider each recommendation made to the principal by the school council and shall advise the council of the action taken in response to the recommendation.
- In addition to his or her other obligations to solicit the views of the school council under the Act and the regulations, the principal of a school shall solicit the views of the school council with respect to at least° the following matters: § 11(20) Regulation 298

- » The establishment or amendment of school policies and guidelines that relate to pupil achievement or to the accountability of the education system to parents, including,
  - » a local code of conduct established under sections of the Act° governing the behaviour of all persons in the school, and

§§ 303(1), 303(1) EA

  - » school policies or guidelines related to policies and guidelines established by the board under the section of the Act° respecting appropriate dress for pupils in schools within the board's jurisdiction.

§ 303(5) EA

- » The development of implementation plans for new education initiatives that relate to pupil achievement or to the accountability of the education system to parents, including,
  - » implementation plans for a local code of conduct established under sections of the Act° governing the behaviour of all persons in the school, and

§§ 303(1), 303(1) EA

  - » implementation plans for school policies or guidelines related to policies and guidelines established by the board under the section of the Act° respecting appropriate dress for pupils in schools within the board's jurisdiction.

§ 302(5) EA

- » School action plans for improvement, based on the Education Quality and Accountability Office's reports on the results of tests of pupils, and the communication of those plans to the public.°

§§ 11(9) through 11(19) Regulation 298

- A vice-principal shall perform such duties as are assigned to the vice-principal by the principal.
- In each non French-language school, of sufficient size, offering French-language classes, the board shall appoint one of the teachers of such classes or a teacher who holds the qualifications required to teach such classes to be responsible to the principal for the program of education in such classes.°

§ 13 Regulation 298; §§ 290, 291 EA

- A board may appoint for each organizational unit (department) of an elementary or secondary school a teacher to direct and supervise, subject to the authority of the principal of the school, such organizational unit.°

§ 14 Regulation 298

- In assigning or appointing a teacher to teach in a division or to teach a subject in a school, the principal of the school shall have due regard for the provision of the best possible program and the safety and well-being of the pupils.°

§ 19 Regulation 298

- No principal, vice-principal, or teacher, without the prior approval of the board that operates the school at which they are employed, shall authorize any canvassing or fund-raising activity that involves the participation of one or more pupils attending the school.°

§ 25 Regulation 298

- The appropriate supervisory officer, in addition to the duties under the Act, may, during a visit to a school, assume any of the authority and responsibility of the principal of the school.° § 26 Regulation 298
- Psychiatrists, psychologists, social workers, and other professional support staff employed by a board shall perform, under the administrative supervision of the appropriate supervisory officer, such duties as are determined by the board and, where such persons are performing their duties in a school, they shall be subject to the administrative authority of the principal of that school.° § 26 Regulation 298

4.3.3 *Student Discipline*

In February, 2008, changes in the *Education Act* related to safe schools and student discipline came into force. The purpose of these changes was to more closely align disciplinary measures taken by school board officials (including principals and vice-principals) with opportunities for students to maintain connections to educational programing.° Additional information detailing progressive discipline programming is provided in Chapter 14, but within this framework the principal holds particular responsibilities outlined below.

Policy/Program Memorandum No. 145, "Progressive Discipline and Promoting Positive Student Behaviour"

- In addition to his or her other obligations to solicit the views of the school council under the Act and the regulations, the principal of a school shall solicit the views of the school council with respect to at least° the following matters: § 11(20) Regulation 298
  - » The establishment or amendment of school policies and guidelines that relate to pupil achievement or to the accountability of the education system to parents, including,
    - » a local code of conduct established under sections of the Act° governing the behaviour of all persons in the school, and §§ 303(1) or 303(2) EA
    - » school policies or guidelines related to policies and guidelines established by the board under the section of the Act° respecting appropriate dress for pupils in schools within the board's jurisdiction. § 302(5) EA
  - » The development of implementation plans for new education initiatives that relate to pupil achievement or to the accountability of the education system to parents, including,
    - » implementation plans for a local code of conduct established under sections of the Act° governing the behaviour of all persons in the school, and §§ 303(1) or 303(2) EA
    - » implementation plans for school policies or guidelines related to policies and guidelines established by the board under the section of the Act° respecting appropriate dress for pupils in schools within the board's jurisdiction.° § 302(5) EA § 11(19) Regulation 298

4.3.4 *Teacher Evaluation*

Regulations dictate a specific process for the evaluation of teachers under the authority of a principal. Operationally, regulations provide different evaluation processes for teachers classified as "new teachers" and "teachers other than new teachers." For teachers other than new teachers, the evaluation cycle is five years and the first year in which a teacher is employed by a board will be an evaluation year. Within the first 20 school days of an evaluation year, the principal will ensure that the teacher is notified that he or she will be evaluated in that year; in each evaluation year the teacher must be evaluated at least once, but the principal may decide to evaluate the teacher as frequently as he or she feels appropriate. Additionally, the teacher may request a performance appraisal in a year other than an evaluation year, and the principal may choose to accommodate this request.°

§§ 2 through 6 Regulation 99/02

The evaluation of teachers other than new teachers involves a competency-based performance appraisal (competencies are provided in Schedule 1 of Regulation 99/02, and are discussed elsewhere in Chapter 3 of this text) where (a) the principal meets with the teacher in advance of a classroom observation in order to review the teacher's current learning plan; (b) the principal observes classroom instruction of the teacher to evaluate the teacher's knowledge and use of practices offered in guidelines issued by the Minister; (c) the principal and teacher meet to discuss the results of the observation and to finalize the teacher's learning plan for that year; (d) the principal prepares a formal written summative report of the evaluation of the teacher including an overall performance rating (of either "satisfactory" or "unsatisfactory") and explanation for the rating; (e) the principal and teacher sign the summative report and both the report and the teacher's learning plan are forwarded to the board, who must keep these documents on file for at least six years; and (f) at the request of either the teacher or the principal, the two may meet to discuss the evaluation process.°

§§ 7 through 9 Regulation 99/02

The evaluation of new teachers is more complex than, but similar to, the process outlined above. As with teachers other than new teachers, the evaluation of new teachers involves a competency-based performance appraisal but one that does not include categories focused on "leadership and community" and "ongoing professional learning" (competencies are provided in Schedule 2 of Regulation 99/02, and are discussed elsewhere in Chapter 3 of this text).

Performance Appraisals of Teachers

§ 277.29(3) EA

§ 269 EA

A principal is responsible for the appraisal of the performance of teachers under his or her supervision.° This involves the determination of the degree to which any new teacher in his or her school will participate in the new teacher induction program offered by the Board of Education,° the ongoing appraisal of new teachers' performance and reconsideration of the degree to which any new teacher in his or her school will participate in the new teacher induction program, as well as the scheduling° and written notice of rating of performance appraisals of each member of the school teaching staff.° § 277.29(4) EA § 277.29(5) EA

4.4 PERFORMANCE OF THE PRINCIPAL

The process defined for the appraisal of the performance of Ontario principals and vice-principals is identical in all ways, except in terms of the individuals to whom the principal or vice-principal is responsible. Generally speaking, a principal is responsible to a supervisory officer or director of education, and a vice-principal is responsible to his or her principal, a supervisory officer, or the director of education.

The principal is responsible to a supervisory officer of the board for his or her performance° on a five-year cycle.° Performance appraisals must not be conducted in the first year in which a principal is employed as a principal, but may otherwise be conducted at times in addition to the five-year cycle when deemed appropriate to do so by the supervisory officer. Principals may request that a performance appraisal be conducted at a time in addition to the five-year cycle; supervisory officers will oblige unless they reasonably believe that conducing an appraisal will not result in an improvement.°

§ 278.4 EA; § 4 Regulation 234/10

§ 3 Regulation 234/10

§ 5 Regulation 234/10

4.4.1 *The Review Process*

The board is responsible for ensuring that every principal it employs develops (a) a performance plan in each year in which the principal is appraised, and (b) an annual growth plan every year in which the principal is employed by the board. The performance plan includes each of the following items:

- one or more goals focused on improving student achievement and well-being, which takes into account,
  - the school improvement plan,
  - the board improvement plan, and
  - provincial educational priorities;
- the actions that a principal will take during the evaluation year to attain the goals;
- the leadership competencies and practices that will assist the principal to attain the goals; and
- the methods by which a principal's success in attaining the goals are to be measured.°

§ 6 Regulation 234/10

The annual growth plan includes each of the following:

- the leadership competencies and practices that will be the focus of the principal's professional growth for that year;

- the professional growth activities that the principal will undertake to assist him or her to develop the leadership competencies and practices identified under the previous bulleted item; and
- if the principal has developed a performance plan, the professional growth activities that will assist him or her to attain the goals identified in the performance plan.°

§ 7 Regulation 234/10

§ 8 Regulation 234/10

The process prescribed for the appraisal of principals is outlined in regulations.° Three meetings are scheduled between a principal and the supervisory officer. At the first meeting, the principal's performance plan is developed and, if necessary, the annual growth plan for the year is reviewed and updated. At the second meeting, the progress of the principal toward achieving the goals contained in his or her performance plan is reviewed, and other information relevant to the performance plan is discussed. At the third meeting, the results of the actions taken by the principal to achieve the goals contained in his or her performance plan are reviewed, other information relevant to the performance plan is again discussed, and the principal's annual growth plan for the year is reviewed and updated if necessary.

§ 9(1) Regulation 234/10

Principals in Ontario receive either a satisfactory or unsatisfactory rating.° The rating is determined through a consideration of several factors related to the diligence, consistency, perseverance, and collegiality of his or her work toward the successful completion of goals identified in the performance plan. Furthermore, within the assessment the supervisory officer also considers the principal's explanation and willingness to persevere if the goals were not successfully achieved within the appraisal timeframe.°

§ 9(2) Regulation 234/10

Following the three meetings between principal and supervisory officer, a summative report on the performance appraisal is prepared by the supervisory officer that includes the evaluation of the principal, the performance rating of the principal, and the supervisory officers explanations. Within 10 days of receipt of the summative report, the principal may request a meeting with the supervisory officer. Following this 10 day window, a copy of the summative report signed by both the supervisory officer and the principal, a copy of the principal's performance and growth plans for that year, and all other documents relied upon for the appraisal must be submitted to the board.°

§ 8 Regulation 234/10

4.4.2 *Unsatisfactory Ratings*

The consequence of an unsatisfactory rating in a principal's performance appraisal is not imminently dire, although it would be cause for concern. Following receipt of the supervisory officer's summative report, the principal who has received an unsatisfactory rating must be apprised of the reasons undergirding this conclusion. Furthermore, the supervisory officer will explain the areas in which the principal's performance is lacking and the expectations for performance. The supervisory officer will seek input from the principal on the manner in which the performance expectations might be achieved and will develop a written improvement plan for the principal. Improvement plans signed by both the supervisory officer and the principal are included in the summative report that is submitted to the director of education.

A second performance appraisal is conducted by the supervisory officer at a time believed by the supervisory officer to be appropriately balanced when consideration is made of both (a) a reasonable time for the principal to improve his or her performance, and (b) the best interests of the school.° The process related to the creation of a summative report found in section 4.4.1 above is repeated, but this time the rating is withheld for 40 to 80 days, unless otherwise decided by mutual agreement of the supervising officer and the principal.°

§ 10(7) Regulation 234/10

§§ 10(5), 10(6) Regulation 234/10

Should the principal receive a second consecutive unsatisfactory performance rating, the principal will be placed under review status° and the director will be informed in writing of that fact. The second summative report will include the reasons for which an unsatisfactory rating was made, the areas in which the performance remains lacking, the expectations for performance, and the manner in which the principal's performance has changed since the first review. Again, the supervisory officer will seek input from the principal on the manner in which the performance expectations might be achieved and will develop a written improvement plan, in consultation with the director of education, for the principal. Second improvement plans signed by both the supervisory officer and the principal are included in the summative report that is submitted to the director of education.°

see 4.4.3, below

§ 11 Regulation 234/10

4.4.3 Review Status

The supervisory officer, who regularly consults with the director of education and offers feedback and recommendations to the principal for the purpose of improving the principal's performance, monitors principals placed under review. A third performance appraisal is conducted by the supervisory officer at a time believed by the supervisory officer to be appropriately balanced when consideration is made of both (a) a reasonable time for the principal to improve his or her performance, and (b) the best interests of the school.° The process related to the creation of a summative report found in section 4.4.1 above is repeated, but this time the rating is provided 20 to 60 days following the date on which the principal is informed of his or her review status, unless otherwise decided by mutual agreement of the supervising officer and the principal.°

§ 12(6) Regulation 234/10

§§ 12(4), 12(5) Regulation 234/10

Should the supervisory officer find the performance of the principal under review to be satisfactory, the review status of the principal will be removed and both the principal and the director will receive a written statement to this effect.° The principal will remain in his or her position, unless mutual agreement between the principal and the board is otherwise found.°

§ 13(1) Regulation 234/10

§§ 12(12), 13(7) Regulation 234/10

4.4.4 Disciplinary Actions

The regulations stipulate that at any time up until 60 days following the date on which the principal is informed of his or her review status, the supervisory officer may elect to suspend any action on a third performance appraisal and recommend in writing to the board that the principal under review be reassigned, demoted to vice-principal, have his or her employment terminated, or take other appropriate actions.° Similar action may be taken following the completion of a third appraisal.° Any decision on action taken by the board—which may include a finding contrary to the conclusion drawn by the supervisory officer with respect to satisfactory performance°—must be made within 60 days of the supervisory officer's recommendation to the board.°

§§ 12(7), 12(8) Regulation 234/10

§§ 13(2), 13(3) Regulation 234/10

§§ 12(10)(a), 12(12), 13(5)(a), 13(7) Regulation 234/10

§§ 12(11), 13(6) Regulation 234/10

While a process for the disciplining of principals based upon performance appraisal is outlined above, this does not exclude a board from the reassignment of duties, suspension, or termination of employment of a principal in the absence of a performance appraisal,° so long as provisions for cause and natural justice are made.

§ 287.7 EA

4.5 VICE-PRINCIPALS

Each school board in Ontario may appoint one or more individuals to the position of vice-principal in each school. A vice-principal is defined as a teacher appointed to take charge of a school in the absence of the school's principal.° As a teacher, the vice-principal may be called upon to perform any duties of a teacher, no matter the wording of any provision in a collective agreement.° The qualifications for a vice-principal are the same as those of a principal,° but the duties of a vice-principal are not specifically identified in law. The vice-principal of a school performs duties assigned by the principal° and is responsible to the principal for his or her performance.°

§ 12(3) Regulation 298; § 1 Provincial Schools Negotiation Act, 1990

§ 278.1 EA

§ 9 Regulation 298

§ 12(2) Regulation 298

§ 278.4 EA; § 28 Regulation 234/10

4.6 PERFORMANCE OF THE VICE-PRINCIPAL

The process defined for the appraisal of the performance of Ontario principals and vice-principals is identical in all ways, except in terms of the individuals to whom the principal or vice-principal is responsible.

The vice-principal is responsible to the principal for his or her performance° on a five-year cycle. Performance appraisals must not be conducted in the first year in which a vice-principal is employed as a vice-principal,° but may otherwise be conducted at times in addition to the five-year cycle when deemed appropriate to do so by the principal. Vice-principals may request that a performance appraisal be conducted at a time in addition to the five-year cycle; principals will oblige unless they reasonably believe that conducting

§ 278.4 EA; § 28 Regulation 234/10

§§ 27 Regulation 234/10

an appraisal will not result in an improvement.° § 29 Regulation 234/10

4.6.1 The Review Process

The board is responsible for ensuring that every vice-principal it employs develops (a) a performance plan in each year in which the vice-principal is appraised, and (b) an annual growth plan every year in which the vice-principal is employed by the board. The performance plan includes each of the following items:

- one or more goals focused on improving student achievement and well-being, which takes into account,
  - » the school improvement plan,
  - » the board improvement plan, and
  - » provincial educational priorities;
- the actions that a vice-principal will take during the evaluation year to attain the goals;
- the leadership competencies and practices that will assist the vice-principal to attain the goals; and
- the methods by which a vice-principal's success in attaining the goals are to be measured.° § 30 Regulation 234/10

The annual growth plan includes each of the following:

- the leadership competencies and practices that will be the focus of the vice-principal's professional growth for that year;
- the professional growth activities that the vice-principal will undertake to assist him or her to develop the leadership competencies and practices identified under the previous bulleted item; and
- if the vice-principal has developed a performance plan, the professional growth activities that will assist him or her to attain the goals identified in the performance plan.° § 31 Regulation 234/10

The process prescribed for the appraisal of vice-principals is outlined in regulations.° § 32 Regulation 234/10 Three meetings are scheduled between a vice-principal and his or her principal. At the first meeting, the vice-principal's performance plan is developed and, if necessary, the annual growth plan for the year is reviewed and updated. At the second meeting, the progress of the vice-principal toward achieving the goals contained in his or her performance plan is reviewed, and other information relevant to the performance plan is discussed. At the third meeting, the results of the actions taken by the vice-principal to achieve the goals contained in his or her performance plan are reviewed, other information relevant to the performance plan is again discussed, and the vice-principal's annual growth plan for the year is reviewed and updated if necessary.

Vice-principals in Ontario receive either a satisfactory or unsatisfactory rating.° The rating is determined through a consideration of several factors related to the diligence, consistency, perseverance, and collegiality of his or her work toward the successful completion of goals identified in the performance plan. Furthermore, within the assessment the principal also considers the vice-principal's explanation and willingness to persevere if the goals were not successfully achieved within the appraisal timeframe.°

§ 33(1) Regulation 234/10

§ 33(2) Regulation 234/10

Following the three meetings between vice-principal and principal, a summative report on the performance appraisal is prepared. Herein, the principal includes the evaluation of the vice-principal, the performance rating of the vice-principal, and all necessary explanations underlying the principal's evaluation. Within 10 school days of receipt of the summative report, the vice-principal may request a meeting with the principal. Following this 10 day window, a copy of the summative report signed by both the principal and the vice-principal, a copy of the vice-principal's performance and growth plans for that year, and all other documents relied upon for the appraisal must be submitted to the board.°

§ 32 Regulation 234/10

4.6.2 *Unsatisfactory Ratings*

The consequence of an unsatisfactory rating in a vice-principal's performance appraisal is not imminently dire, although it would be cause for concern. Following receipt of the principal's summative report, the vice-principal who has received an unsatisfactory rating must be apprised of the reasons undergirding this conclusion. Furthermore, the principal will explain the areas in which the vice-principal's performance is lacking and the expectations for performance. The principal will seek input from the vice-principal on the manner in which the performance expectations might be achieved and will develop a written improvement plan for the vice-principal. Improvement plans signed by both the principal and the vice-principal are included in the summative report that is submitted to the director of education.°

§ 34 Regulation 234/10

A second performance appraisal is conducted by the principal at a time believed by the principal to be appropriately balanced when consideration is made of both (a) a reasonable time for the vice-principal to improve his or her performance, and (b) the best interests of the school.° The process related to the creation of a summative report found in section 4.6.1 above is repeated, but this time the rating is withheld for 40 to 80 days, unless otherwise decided by mutual agreement of the principal and the vice-principal.°

§ 34(7) Regulation 234/10

§§ 34(5), 34(6) Regulation 234/10

Should the vice-principal receive a second consecutive unsatisfactory performance rating, the vice-principal will be placed under review status° and any appropriate supervisory officer and the director will be informed in writing of that fact. The second summative report will include the reasons for which an unsatisfactory rating was made, the areas in which the performance remains lacking, the

see 4.6.3, below

expectations for performance, and the manner in which the vice-principal's performance has changed since the first review. Again, the principal will seek input from appropriate supervisory officers on the manner in which the performance expectations might be achieved and will develop a written improvement plan, in consultation with any appropriate supervisory officers the director of education, for the vice-principal. Second improvement plans signed by both the principal and the vice-principal are included in the summative report that is submitted to the appropriate supervisory officers and the director of education.°

§ 35 REGULATION 234/10

4.6.3 Review Status

The principal or supervisory officer, who regularly consults with the director of education and offers feedback and recommendations to the vice-principal for the purpose of improving the vice-principal's performance, monitors vice-principals placed under review. A third performance appraisal is conducted by the principal at a time believed by the principal to be appropriately balanced when consideration is made of both (a) a reasonable time for the vice-principal to improve his or her performance, and (b) the best interests of the school.° The process related to the creation of a summative report found in section 4.6.1 above is repeated, but this time the rating is provided 20 to 60 days following the date on which the vice-principal is informed of his or her review status, unless otherwise decided by mutual agreement of the principal or supervisory officer and the vice-principal.°

§ 36 REGULATION 234/10

§§ 36(4), 36(5) REGULATION 234/10

Should the principal or supervisory officer find the performance of the vice-principal under review to be satisfactory, the review status of the vice-principal will be removed and both the vice-principal and the director will receive a written statement to this effect.° The vice-principal will remain in his or her position, unless mutual agreement between the vice-principal and the board is otherwise found.°

§ 37(1) REGULATION 234/10

§§ 36(13), 37(8) REGULATION 234/10

4.6.4 Disciplinary Actions

The regulations stipulate that at any time up until 60 days following the date on which the vice-principal is informed of his or her review status, the principal and supervisory officer may jointly elect to suspend any action on a third performance appraisal and recommend in writing to the board that the vice-principal under review be reassigned, have his or her employment terminated, or take other appropriate actions.° Similar action may be taken following the completion of a third appraisal.° Any decision on action taken by the board—which may include a finding contrary to the conclusion drawn by the principal or supervisory officer with respect to satisfactory performance°—must be made within 60 days of the supervisory officer's recommendation to the board.°

§§ 36(7), 36(8) REGULATION 234/10

§§ 37(2), 37(3) REGULATION 234/10

§§ 36(11)(a), 36(13), 37(6)(a), 37(8) REGULATION 234/10

§§ 36(12), 37(7) REGULATION 234/10

While a process for the disciplining of vice-principals based upon performance appraisal is outlined above, this does not exclude a

§ 287.7 EA

board from the reassignment of duties, suspension, or termination of employment of a vice-principal in the absence of a performance appraisal,° so long as provisions for cause and natural justice are made.

4.7 REDUNDANCIES AND REASSIGNMENTS

§ 2(2) Regulation 90/98

§ 3(1) Regulation 90/98

§§ 4(1), 4(2) Regulation 90/98

Regulations provide processes to be followed by boards when principal or vice-principal positions are deemed redundant. Notice of redundancy status must be made 90 days in advance of a position becoming redundant.° Unless circumstances dictate otherwise, the board will assign a principal or vice-principal to another position for which they are qualified.° In cases where a principal or vice-principal is assigned to a position other than to teach, the regulations note that the reassigned principal or vice-principal will receive a principal or vice-principal's salary for one year.°

5.0 COLLECTIVE BARGAINING

Part 5.0 deals with collective barganing in Ontario. Collective agreements for teachers are officially negotiated at the school district level (see Part 7.0 for details about districts), through one or more official bargaining agents. Since 2004, however, a process by which local contracts arise suggests that a *de facto* province wide negotiation structure exists. Supervisory staff, principals, and vice-principals are not considered teachers for the purpose of collective agreements and contract bargaining. All terms and conditions of contracts between teachers and school boards remain in force for the duration of the contract and until a new or revised agreement is negotiated and concluded.

5

5.1 TEACHER BARGAINING UNITS, SCHOOL BOARDS, AND BARGAINING AGENTS

The majority of teachers in Ontario are, for contractual purposes, considered "Part X.1" teachers. The title reflects the part of the *Education Act* dealing with collective agreements that separates classroom teachers from teachers who occupy the position of supervisory officer, principal, vice-principal, or instructor in a teacher-training institution.° Only classroom teachers fall under the definition of "Part X.1" teacher, and therefore supervisory officers, principals, vice-principals, and others are not considered to be a part of any negotiated collective agreement between a school district and various teachers' unions. Simply put, "Part X.1" teachers' contracts are negotiated between unions—who represent teachers in Ontario—and school districts in which a union's membership is actively employed.

§ 277.1(1) EA

The *Education Act* prescribes° four teachers' unions in Ontario: (a) L'Association des enseignantes et des enseignants franco-ontariens, (b) the Elementary Teachers' Federation of Ontario, (c) the Ontario English Catholic Teachers' Association, and (d) the Ontario Secondary School Teachers' Federation. Though each calls itself either an association or federation, the *Education Act* highlights their status as trade unions for the purpose of bargaining,° and the *Education Act* considers each to be a teacher bargaining agent.

§§ 277.3(2), 277.4(3) EA

§ 277.13.1(2) EA; § 1 LABOUR RELATIONS ACT, 1995

§ 3(f) Labour Relations Act, 1995

Outside of those provisions within the *Education Act* that note the contrary, the *Labour Relations Act*, 1995 does not apply to teachers, supervisory officers, principals, or vice-principals in Ontario.°

§§ 1, 4(1) Teaching Profession Act, 1990

All four of the above mentioned teachers' unions are considered affiliates under the Ontario Teachers' Federation (OTF), and membership in both of these unions and the OTF are a requirement for employment by a school board as a teacher.°

Across the province, the circumstances underlying a teacher's contract (collective agreement) may differ depending upon two primary factors: (a) the teacher's specific employment conditions (in either an elementary or secondary school, and in either a full-/part-time or occasional position—the permutations of which are known as bargaining units) and (b) the type of school district in which the teacher is employed. The chart in *figure 5a* outlines 24 different types of teacher contract circumstances possible under the *Education Act*, 1990—but it is not necessarily the case that each resultant circumstance will be at play in any given negotiating year. To understand the chart, consider by way of example a teacher (a "Part X.1 teacher," as described above) who is employed to teach full-time in a secondary school in Windsor, within the Greater Essex County School District. First, the third column at the top of the chart, titled "Part X.1 Full-/Part-Time Secondary Teacher," is a bargaining unit and refers to the specific employment conditions. Next, because the Greater Essex County District School Board is an English language public school board, the first row on the left side of the chart, titled "English Language Public District School Board" reflects the type of school district in which the teacher is employed. The intersection of these two indicates the bargaining agent responsible for negotiating a collective agreement for our example teacher. Similarly, if an occasional teacher were hired to teach in École élémentaire publique L'Équinoxe in Pembroke, the contract would be negotiated by l'Association des enseignantes et des enseignants franco-ontariens—the intersection of "Part X.1 Occasional Elementary Teacher," for obvious reasons, and "French Language District School Board," because the school is within the Conseil des écoles publiques de l'Est de l'Ontario French language district school board.

5.2 CONTRACT NEGOTIATIONS

All collective agreements are legally binding upon the parties that originally negotiated them. Technically speaking, the negotiation of collective agreements is exclusively the responsibility of a bargaining agent (union) and a district school board. In other Canadian jurisdictions, this is known as local collective bargaining and is distinguished from provincial-level collective bargaining, which often involves a provincial teachers' federation representing the interests of teachers and a negotiating committee representing the interests of the school districts. Since 2004, a similar, but

Statute	School Board	Unit	Bargaining Agent
Education Act, 1990, §. 68	Exempt Land District School Board		l'Association des enseignantes et des enseignants franco-ontariens, the Elementary Teachers' Federation of Ontario, and the Ontario English Catholic Teachers' Association jointly
Education Act, 1990, §§. 59 - 67	District School Area Board	Non-French Language Instructional Unit	
		French Language Instructional Unit	l'Association des enseignantes et des enseignants franco-ontariens
Education Act, 1990, §§. 58.1 - 58.9	French Language District School Board		
	English Language Separate District School Board		Ontario English Catholic Teachers' Association
	English Language Public District School Board	Part X.1 Full-/Part-Time Elementary Teacher	Elementary Teachers' Federation of Ontario
		Part X.1 Occasional Elementary Teacher	
		Part X.1 Full-/Part-Time Secondary Teacher	Ontario Secondary School Teachers' Federation
		Part X.1 Occasional Secondary Teacher	
		Education Act, 1990, §§. 277.3 - 277.4	

Figure 5a. Possible Teaching Contract Circumstances in Ontario

unofficial, process has evolved in Ontario. Known as Provincial Discussion Tables, the provincial government has brought trustees' associations together with representatives of each union to engage in the settlement of key issues. The products of these negotiations are called Provincial Framework Agreements or Provincial Discussion Table Agreements. Following work at the provincial level, parties to local collective bargaining processes use the provincially negotiated results as the basis for local agreements.° The provincial government contemporaneously imposed a deadline of August 31 in any negotiation year for the signing of all local collective agreements.

Ontario Educational Services Corporation. (2012). *Good governance: A guide for trustees, school boards, directors of education and communities*. Toronto: the Author; Ontario English Catholic Teachers' Association. (2013). *Provincial discussion table task force*. Toronto, ON: the Author

§§ 277.11(1)(a), 277.11(2) EA

Collective agreements are negotiated every two or four years,° and typically include provisions for:

- teachers' salaries;
- positions of responsibility;
- staffing, vacancies, transfers, resignations, promotions, seniority, severance, and superannuation;
- professional development;
- teacher performance appraisals;
- personnel files;
- workload, non-teaching duties, staff meeting, and time-tabling;
- employee insurance, benefits, and leaves.

Because provincial legislation—principally the *Education Act* and any Regulations created under it—governs specific matters related to teacher qualifications;° the school year, holidays, and professional activity days;° and other more general administrative and operational functions of schools;° among others, these are not considered negotiable within the bargaining process.

Regulation 176/10

Regulation 304

Regulation 298

Collective agreements between bargaining units and district school boards are public documents. It is typical that a district school board will maintain a copy of current collective agreements on their website. Additionally, the Ontario Secondary School Teachers' Federation,° for example, maintains a document that summarizes collective agreements negotiated on behalf of their membership, organized by district school board.

OSSTF. (nd). *Where to teach in Ontario*. Toronto, ON: the Author. *retrieved May 2013 from http://www.osstf.on.ca/adx/aspx/adxGetMedia.aspx?DocID=3952*

District school boards are additionally responsible for the negotiation of collective agreements with non-teaching staff. These negotiations are governed by the Ontario *Labour Relations Act*, 1995.

5.3 SETTLEMENT OF DISPUTES

Both bargaining units and district school boards are obligated to uphold collective agreements they sign. The collective agreements themselves will contain procedures intended to support the settling of disputes encountered between bargaining units and district school boards; the grievance process is perhaps the most widely known, and often is engaged following a perceived breach of a clause in a collective agreement.

The Ontario *Labour Relations Act*, 1995, governs disputes that arise in the negotiation of collective agreements. Because all collective agreements expire on August 31 of the second or fourth year of their life,° parties to these agreements give notice of their intent to negotiate beginning by roughly June 1 of that year. Bargaining often begins within 15 days of this date and may involve the assistance of a mutually agreed upon mediator or a Minister of Labour appointed conciliation officer.° Bargaining may take several weeks, or even several months, and a collective agreement in place at the time bargaining begins will continue beyond August 31 until an agreement is struck.

§§ 277.11(1)(a), 277.11(2) EA

§§ 17 through 19, 59 Labour Relations Act, 1995

5.3.1 Conciliation Officers

It is the job of a conciliation officer to meet with each of the parties to a collective agreement and work with them to achieve agreement in a timely fashion. Within 14 days of his or her appointment, the conciliation officer must meet with both parties and report to the Minister of Labour as to the results of the endeavour. The timeframe for this report may be extended.° When the report of the conciliation officer indicates that a resolution to all points in dispute have been achieved, the Minister of Labour releases the conciliation report to the parties. Most collective agreements are settled in this fashion.°

Section 21 of the *Labour Relations Act*, 1995, holds that upon the failure of parties to agree following conciliation, the Minister of Labour may appoint a conciliation board to oversee the continued dispute resolution processes. To our knowledge at the time of writing, the appointment of a conciliation board has never happened. Rather, it has been the practice of Ministers of Labour to issue a report advising them that a conciliation board will not be appointed, and thus opens the door for parties to the negotiations to engage in legal employment sanctions, such as strikes (by teachers) or lockouts (by district school boards).

§ 20 Labour Relations Act, 1995

Ontario Educational Services Corporation. (2012). *Good governance: A guide for trustees, school boards, directors of education and communities*. Toronto: the Author.

5.3.2 Employment Sanctions

Rarely do collective agreement negotiations processes end in labour actions such as strikes (all types of withdrawal of services are considered strike actions) or lockouts—and unions or boards are not required to engage in such action merely because they are in a legal position do so. The Ontario Educational Services Corporation (OESC), in their 2012 report titled *Good Governance: A Guide for Trustees, School Boards, Directors of Education and Communities*, notes that each of the following must have occurred in advance of a strike or lockout action:

- one party has served the other with notice of intent to bargain;° (§ 59 Labour Relations Act, 1995)
- the collective agreement has expired;° (§ 46 Labour Relations Act, 1995)
- there has been conciliation conducted by the Ministry of Labour;° (§ 18 Labour Relations Act, 1995)
- fourteen days have elapsed since the Minister of Labour advised the parties that a conciliation board would not be appointed (that is, after the release of a "no-board report)" [*sic*];° and (§ 122 Labour Relations Act, 1995)
- a strike has been supported by a majority of the employees voting in a strike vote.° (§ 79 Labour Relations Act, 1995)

Strike votes require not more than a simple majority of members votes to pass, but must be taken no earlier than August 2 of any negotiation year (30-days prior to the expiration of an existing collective agreement).° (§ 79(3) Labour Relations Act, 1995) Participation in a legal strike is not considered grounds for termination by an employing board.° (§ 86 Labour Relations Act, 1995)

5.3.3 Back-to-Work Legislation

Section 57.2(2) of the *Education Act*, 1990, notes that the provincial government may enact so called back-to-work legislation where a strike or lockout, in the opinion of the Education Relations Commission—a body established to advise the Lieutenant Governor in Council on educational matters—"will place in jeopardy the successful completion of courses of study by the affected pupils." The passing and assent of such legislation has the affect of declaring a legal strike or lockout illegal, and thus forces schools to reopen and teachers back to work.

5.3.4 Bill 115, Putting Students First Act, 2012

Recent labour relations developments have had a significant impact on educators in Ontario. Amidst the ongoing contract negotiations with unions representing teachers and support staff since February, 2012, Bill 115 was given its first reading in the Legislative Assembly of Ontario on August 28, 2012, and received Royal Assent on September 11, 2012. The intention of this legislation was to ensure that school contracts fit the government's financial and policy priorities, and aims to prevent labour disruptions during 2013 and 2014. The Putting Students First Act was passed by the Legislative Assembly of Ontario as school boards, teachers, and support staff continued to engage in collective bargaining. The law allowed the provincial government to set rules that local school boards must adhere to when negotiating with local unions and to impose a collective agreement on the board, employee bargaining agent, and the employees of the board represented by the employee bargaining agent if negotiations are not completed by the end of 2012. This bill also limited the legality of teachers' unions and support staff going on strike. On December 31, 2012, Bill 115 came into effect, whereas the Minister of Education imposed two-year contracts on teachers and subsequently repealed the legislation once those contracts were in place (January 23, 2013). The Act established a restraint period during which the requirements and processes set out in the Act apply to boards, employees of boards, employee bargaining agents and collective agreements in the education sector. The restraint period is a two-year period that, for most employees, starts on September 1, 2012. The length of the period can be extended by regulation in certain circumstances.

This piece of legislation had several major implications for educators. Under the *Putting Students First Act*, the local collective agreements put in place were based on the terms of the negotiated agreement between the government and Ontario English Catholic Teachers' Association, and other memoranda of understanding signed before August 31, 2012. The terms of the two-year contracts included a wage freeze and regulations to establish and govern existing and new systems of sick leave credits and sick leave credit gratuities and provide for their termination.°

retrieved May 2013 from http://news.ontario.ca/edu/en/2013/01/new-agreements-for-teacher-support-staff-introduced--bill-115-to-be-repealed.html

6.0 ONTARIO'S PROVINCIAL SCHOOL SYSTEM

Part 6.0 presents background information on the major components of the public school system. The roles and contributions of these components to school activities are dealt with in Part 1.0 of this Guide.

6.1 MINISTRY OF EDUCATION AND THE MINISTER OF EDUCATION

6.1.1 *Ministry of Education*

The Ministry of Education and Training is a department of the Ontario government with numerous division, branches, and services through which it conducts formal work in the education sector throughout Ontario.° The vision of the Ministry is that

§ 2 EA

> Ontario students will receive the best publicly funded education in the world, measured by high levels of achievement and engagement for all students. Successful learning outcomes will give all students the skills, knowledge and opportunities to attain their potential, to pursue lifelong learning, and to contribute to a prosperous, cohesive society. (p. 4) °

Ministry of Education. (2011). *Results-based plan briefing book 2011/2012*. Toronto, ON: the Author. *retrieved May 2013 from http://www.edu.gov.on.ca/eng/about/annualreport/1112/EDUplan1112E.pdf*

The focus of the Ministry is embodied in their three goals for public education: "high level of student achievement; reduced gaps in student achievement; [and] high levels of public confidence in public education."° The Ministry of Education gives attention to early learning, child care, and the elementary and secondary education system.

Ministry of Education. (2013). *About the ministry*. Toronto, ON: the Author. *retrieved May 2013 from http://www.edu.gov.on.ca/eng/about*

To better understand the various functions of the Ministry of Education, it is helpful to explore the various units that constitute its divisions and branches. From time to time, the Ministry of Education changes its organizational descriptions. The Ministry organization chart° illustrates typical divisions and branches that have operated in and through the Ministry. An Assistant Deputy Minister oversees a division, and under each division are several branches—each staffed by a director and several other members of the civil service.

http://www.edu.gov.on.ca/eng/general/edu_chart.pdf

- **Community Services Information and Information Technology Cluster Division**

  The Community Services Information and Information Technology Cluster provides information management and information technology support as a shared service among several Ministries within the Government of Ontario.

- **Learning and Curriculum Division**

  The Learning and Curriculum Division is the principal elementary and secondary educational policy and program development division of the Ministry of Education. The Division focuses on supporting student learning through (a) the maintenance of challenging standards for in-school and lifelong academic community-based, and career achievement; and (b) the promotion of educational success for students within special education programs.

- **Elementary/Secondary Business and Finance Division**

  The focus of the Elementary/Secondary Business and Finance Division rests within the scope of policy and provision of Provincial Government funding for school boards. Additionally, the Division provides financial and operating grant management support services to schools.

- **Early Learning Division**

  The Early Learning Division is structured around branches dedicated to the success of child care quality assurance, child care licensing, and early learning initiatives of the Ministry of Education.

- **Instructional and Leadership Development Division**

  The Instructional and Leadership Development Division supports teaching, teachers, leadership growth and sustainability, and information practices in schools and school districts. The function of the Division has encompassed the design and oversight of several Ministry programs and services, including, but not limited to, the New Teacher Induction Program, the Teacher Performance Appraisal System, and a collection of other initiatives intended to support leadership and professional development, and data collection, analysis, and interpretation. Some of the Division's work offers assistance within inter-ministerial initiatives involving education more broadly understood.

- **French Language, Aboriginal Learning, and Research Division**

  Focusing on the needs of francophone and Aboriginal students in Ontario, the French Language, Aboriginal Learning, and Research Division holds a clarification and compliance function as a liaison between the Ministry and school boards. Additionally, the Division's Field Services Branch exists as a school board's gateway to general Ministry information and contact.

- **Corporate Management and Services Division**

  As the manager of the Ministry's internal resources, the Corporate Management and Services Division is responsible for administrative, financial, legal, human resources, and general planning initiatives. The Division works to ensure Ministerial compliance with Workplace Discrimination and Harassment Prevention policies, the *French Language Services* Act, 1990, and *Freedom of Information and Protection of Privacy Act*, 1990.

- **Student Achievement Division**

  The Student Achievement Division is composed of several branches that focus their attention on key initiatives in the areas of literacy and numeracy, general student success, and the Learning to 18 initiative.°

Ministry of Government Services. (2010). *Information access & privacy: Education*. Toronto, ON: the Author. *retrieved May 2013 from http://www.mgs.gov.on.ca/en/DOR/Listing/Unit/index.htm?unitId=UNT0002168*

6.1.2 Minister of Education

In Ontario, the Minister of Education is responsible for elementary and secondary education. The Minister is appointed by the Premier from the elected members of the Provincial Legislative Assembly to fulfill this important cabinet position. The Minister has both responsibilities and powers° that characterize the work of his or her position; some of these are listed below.

§§ 2 through 8 EA

The Minister:

- is to preside and have charge over the Ministry of Education.
- is responsible for the execution of the provisions of the *Education Act*, all regulations established by it, and all other statutes as assigned by the Lieutenant Governor in Council.
- may, subject to the approval of the Provincial Cabinet, order that a school or class be closed until a date specified; and otherwise establish procedures with respect to the closure of schools.
- may name all diplomas and certificates to be granted to pupils and set both the form and conditions for their granting.
- may prescribe both compulsory and optional courses of study to be taught in the primary, junior, intermediate, and senior grades.
- may issue curriculum documents and guidelines, and require that courses of study be developed by school boards from these.
- may permit school boards to establish course of study that are neither compulsory or optionally prescribed by the Minister.
- may issue policies, guidelines, and curriculum related to the establishment of junior kindergarten and kindergarten programs.
- may conduct reviews of public, separate, and private school

programming, and require public and private boards to supply information required for such review.

- may prescribe tests of pupil academic achievement, and make provisions for the administration, marking, and reporting of results.
- may establish policies and guidelines for school board trustees, directors of education, superintendents, supervisory officers, principals, and other educational officials.
- may establish procedures for the selection and approval of library books, reference books, and curricular and learning support materials.
- may prescribe the form for the registration of daily pupil attendance at school, and may issue guidelines respecting pupil records.
- may prescribe the conditions under which pupils are considered workers for *Workplace Safety and Insurance Act*, 1997, purposes.
- may permit school boards to hire a member of the teaching staff of a school, for not more than one year, who is not a member of the Ontario College of Teachers (OCT) if no member of the OCT is available to satisfy the human resource needs of the school board, or to similarly hire an unqualified individual into the position of early childhood educator; or withdraw any such permission.
- may grant to a school board permission to hire a teacher to teach a subject or hold a position where the teacher does not hold the certificate required for teaching the subject, for not more than one year; or withdraw any such permission.
- may accept, in lieu of any requirement otherwise prescribed, any experience or training that the Minister considers equivalent.
- may require employees of school boards to submit to medical examinations.
- may review and certify any training for teachers, designated early childhood educators, principals, supervisory officers, attendance counselors, and native counselors.
- may establish and administer correspondence courses.
- may establish and prescribe policies for the distribution of scholarships and other student awards.
- may establish guidelines and policies respecting topics for professional activity days.
- may require school boards to develop and implement policies related to equity and inclusiveness.
- may establish nutritional guidelines and standards for food and drink, or any ingredient thereof, provided on school premises or

in connection with school activities.

- may establish drug education policy frameworks and require school boards to establish policies based upon these.
- may collect personal information for the purposes of administering, planning, financing, managing risk, and researching or collecting statistics as required by the *Education Act* and Policies and Regulations established under the Act.
- shall ensure that appropriate educational programming and services are made available to all children with exceptionalities, without payment of fee by parents or guardians.

The Minister is responsible for administering the *Education Act* and for the provision of educational programs under the *Education Act*. He or she also advises the provincial cabinet on education matters (including the issuance of Education Regulations by Order in Council) and issues orders to ensure that the Act and Regulations are effectively administered.

Ministry of Education. (2011). *Results-based plan briefing book 2011/2012*. Toronto, ON: the Author. *retrieved May 2013 from http://www.edu.gov.on.ca/eng/about/annualreport/1112/EDUplan1112E.pdf*

The *Education Act* assigns the Minister of Education to his or her responsibilities. In addition, the Minister of Education is responsible (or shares responsibility with another Minister) for certain Ontario statutes, the most important of which° include:

- ***Education Act*, 1990** – regulating the junior kindergarten, kindergarten, primary, junior, intermediate, and senior educational programs;
- ***Day Nurseries Act*, 1990** – regulating the establishment, licensing, and operation of day nurseries;
- ***Early Childhood Educators Act*, 2007** – regulating the profession of early childhood educators;
- ***Education Quality and Accountability Office Act*, 1996** – establishing the office in its name that evaluates student achievement and the effectiveness of elementary and secondary programs;
- ***Ministry of Community and Social Services Act*, 1990** – provides funding and oversight of social programs;
- ***Ontario College of Teachers Act*, 1996** – establishes the independent regulatory body for the teaching profession in Ontario;
- ***Ontario Educational Communications Authority Act*, 1990** – establishes the educational broadcaster TVO, and provides the mandate to produce and deliver English-language distance education;
- ***Ontario French-language Educational Communications Authority Act*, 2008** – establishes a French-language analogue to the TVO, called TFO;

- ***Ontario School Trustees' Council Act*, 1980** – establishes the Ontario School Trustees' Council;
- ***Provincial Schools Negotiations Act*, 1990** – provides for a collective bargaining process for teachers at provincial schools for the deaf or blind;
- ***Sabrina's Law*, 2005** – requires schools to have policies respecting anaphylaxis;
- ***Teachers' Pension Act*, 1990** – an act respecting the Ontario Teachers' Pensions Plan Board and its governance and management of Ontario teachers' pensions;
- ***Teaching Profession Act*, 1990** – an act respecting the Ontario Teachers' Federation, and establishing the requirement for every teacher in Ontario to be a member.

6.2 APPOINTMENT OF MINISTRY OFFICIALS

The Lieutenant Governor in Council provides for the appointment of a Deputy Minister and other officials. Many ministry appointments to senior positions are made from staff already within the ministry or the government. It is not atypical for appointments to the positions of Deputy and even Assistant Deputy Ministers to be made on a change in government, from persons outside the public service who are known to share the new government's objectives.

The Minster of Education has a Parliamentary Assistant, who is him- or herself a member of the Legislative Assembly, and a Deputy Minister. As indicated above, there are several Division Directors who give leadership to the various branches of the Ministry of Education.

6.3 ADVISORY BODIES, COMMISSIONS, AND TRIBUNALS

§ 10 EA

The *Education Act*° provides for any required Advisory Body or Commission of Inquiry to advise the minister on matters related to education. Additionally, the Minister may establish Special Education Tribunals to adjudicate matters related to special education, and in particular appeals by parents of pupils with exceptionalities who are dissatisfied with the identification or placement of their children within the education system.

6.3.1 Education Relations Commission

§ 57.2 EA

The Education Relations Commission is established° to advise the provincial cabinet on matters related to teacher collective agreement negotiations, and specifically those occasions when the continuation of a teachers' strike or lockout would jeopardize the successful completion of a school year or course of study.

6.3.2 Languages of Instruction Commission

The membership of the Languages of Instruction Commission of Ontario (Commission des langues d'enseignement de l'Ontario) is appointed by the Provincial cabinet to investigate any matter related to instruction in the French language where French is the minority language for that school authority, or related to instruction in English where English is the minority language for that school authority. The Language of Instruction Commission of Ontario has five member, no fewer than two of which must speak English, and no fewer than two of which must speak French. The Commission reports to the Minister of Education.°

§§ 295 through 299 EA

6.4 LEGAL INSTRUMENTS OF THE MINISTER OF EDUCATION

6.4.1 Education Act Regulations

Regulations issued under the *Education Act* by orders in council are deemed part of the Act and have the force of law. Regulations are considered by legal experts as controlling, directing, and guiding principles to produce the less specific effects intended through the *Education Act* itself. Regulations must not be contrary in effect to the *Education Act* and not go further or outside the wide parameters of the Act. Provisions in Regulations must sustain all powers and duties stipulated by the *Education Act*.

7.0 SCHOOL DISTRICTS, BOARDS, AND AUTHORITIES

Part 7.0 deals with school districts, school boards, and school authorities and how they are established. Because the terminology employed can quickly become confused, it is helpful to keep in mind the following considerations.

- there are for principal types of school districts in Ontario:
  - » *English-language public* school districts;
  - » *French-language public* school districts;
  - » *English-language separate* school districts; and
  - » *French-language separate* school districts.
- any public or separate school district is a geographical area of land that encloses one or more schools;
- the boundaries of a public and separate school district are not necessarily coterminous and may overlap, cross, or envelope the other, and the same may be said of the boundaries of an English- and French-language school district;
- the boundaries of a public school district do not overlap, cross, or envelope another public school district, and the same may be said of two or more separate school districts, English-language school districts, and French-language school districts;
- each school district is governed by an elected *school board* or *board of education—public school boards* govern public school districts and *separate school boards* govern separate school districts, English boards govern English-language school districts and French boards govern French-language school districts;
- *school authority* is a generic name for any board that governs a school, school district, or school zone;

In the sections below, we describe the duties, powers, meetings, and legal status of the above mentioned bodies. Further, school closures are also considered.

7.1 SCHOOL DISTRICTS

According to section 58.1 of the Ontario *Education Act*, "The Lieutenant Governor in Council may make regulations providing for ... the establishment of areas of jurisdiction of district school boards." In this way, and in similar provisions noted within the same section, the Lieutenant Governor in Council holds the power create regulations governing the establishment, naming, amalgamation, merger, and dissolution of school districts in the province of Ontario. The Lieutenant Governor in Council may also establish geographical subdivisions of districts for the purpose of electing board of education representatives.°

§§ 58.1(2)(k)(ii), 58.1(2)(k)(iii) EA

Four types of school districts have been established by the provincial government in Ontario: English-language public school districts, French-language public school districts, English-language Roman Catholic separate school districts, and French-language Roman Catholic separate school districts.° Despite their name, "separate" school districts are "public" school districts by the commonplace meaning of *public*. Historically in Ontario—but contemporarily in Alberta and Saskatchewan—separate school districts were districts of the religious minority (whether Roman Catholic or Protestant, but only these) in a larger religious population (either Protestant or Roman Catholic), who would have been served by the public school district.° Since 1997, the Ontario public school districts have secularized, and separate school districts refer to those districts that integrate either Protestant or Roman Catholic religious practice into the provision of education. Currently, in all but one case in Ontario (the Protestant Separate School Board of the Town of Penetanguishene°), a separate school authority serves Roman Catholic interests. In 2012-2013, there were 31 English public school districts, 29 English Roman Catholic separate school districts, 8 French Roman Catholic separate school districts, and 4 French public school districts.°

§ 2(a) EA

§ 93 Constitution Act, 1867

§ 165 EA

Ministry of Education. (2012). *Legislative grants: 2012-2013*. Toronto, ON: the Author. *retrieved May 2013 from http://www.ontla.on.ca/library/repository/mon/26006/316609.pdf*

7.1.1 Establishment of a Separate School District

Historically, separate school authorities held the power to tax those properties owned by members of the population who shared the religious faith of the authority, and that lay in the geographic area of their district. Perhaps more simply put, Catholic separate boards could tax the property of Catholic citizens of their community where Protestants represented the religious majority, and Protestant separate boards could tax the property of Protestant citizens of their community where Roman Catholics represented the religious majority.° The public school authority taxed all other property in that area. In the 1800s and early 1900s, the vast majority of separate schools were elementary schools—very few operated secondary schools. The legacy of this anachronism, and the more recent addition of language rights under the *Charter of Rights and Freedoms*,° as well as the subsequent growth of secondary schooling and secularization of

§ 93 Constitution Act, 1867

§ 23 Constitution Act, 1982

the public school districts in 1997, has lead to some organizational diversity in publicly funded education in Ontario.

Religious minorities in Ontario (but only those that are Protestant or Roman Catholic°) retain their historical rights to establish separate school districts (known as a *separate school zone* when Roman Catholic and the *protestant separate school board of the town of <name of municipality>* when Protestant) and *separate school boards* where these do not already exist by virtue of section 2 in the *Education Act*. The establishment of a separate school district of this type, whether Protestant or Roman Catholic, may result from the petition of five members of five families of that minority faith.°

cf: § 93 CONSTITUTION ACT, 1867; ADLER V ONTARIO, 1996, 3 SCR 609

§§ 80, 158 EA

The petitioners must, in the case of a new Roman Catholic separate school zone:°

§ 80 EA

- call, by public notice, a meeting of local persons desiring a separate school zone;
- elect from their group a chair and secretary for the meeting;
- pass a motion determining the area of the separate school zone;
- elect board members;
- designate by name and residence all newly elected board members for the authority within their record of the meeting;
- ensure the record of their meeting and election of members is received and certified by the clerk(s) of the municipality(ies) in which the new authority will rest;
- ensure the record of their meeting and election of members is received and certified by the secretary of any board that has jurisdiction in all or part of the area in which the new authority will rest;
- submit to the Minister of Education and appropriate local property assessment commissioners the certifications noted above, along with a copy of the meeting record and the public notice calling the meeting.

Following completion of these steps, the Roman Catholic separate school zone is established with the named individuals as its school board members.

For Protestant petitioners, the process is much more simple. Thirty days following the submission (and receipt) of an application by five Protestant members of five Protestant families—living in a municipality where the teacher or teachers in the public school or schools are Roman Catholic—to the public school board, or municipal council in the absence of a school board, the Protestant separate school board for that municipality is established.°

§ 158 EA

Having said all that is above, the vast majority of schools in Ontario are under control of one of the English-language public school districts, French-language public school districts, English-language Roman Catholic separate school districts, or French-language Roman Catholic separate school districts described and established under section 2 of the *Education Act*.

7.2 SCHOOL BOARDS

§ 58.1(10) EA; Regulation 412/00
§ 80(2) EA
§§ 89, 165(1) EA

Each school district or school zone must have an elected school board, and the *Education Act* outlines the number of members to be elected for that purpose. A district school board must have no fewer than five but no more than 22 members,° Roman Catholic separate school zone boards have at least five members,° and Protestant separate school boards and rural separate school boards each have three members.°

§ 58.7 EA
§§ 58.8 through 58.9 EA; § 16 Assessment Act, 1990; Regulation 412/00
§§ 188, 226 EA

Each school board is required to have locally elected membership, in accordance with the manner that members of municipal councils are elected.° Because of the diversity of potential school boards that might exist in any given municipality, the law only permits voting by members of the public for one school board in their area. Electors of Roman Catholic separate school boards must be Roman Catholics and their property must be assessed such that they appear on the appropriate Roman Catholic separate school supporter list, and analogues are in place for electors of Protestant separate school boards and French-language school boards.° All owners of property not assessed under section 16 of the Ontario *Assessment Act*, 1990, are considered by default to be English-language public school board supporters and may elect (and be elected to) membership on the public school board in the area in which they reside. Under some circumstances, the Minister or the Lieutenant Governor in Council may appoint a member to a school board.° Members of a school board are also referred to as trustees.

A school board is a legal corporate body, which means that its duties and powers reside in the board as a whole rather than in the individual trustees. All decisions of the board must be made by formal resolution and a majority vote in favour at a legally constituted board meeting.

7.2.1 Members of a Board of Education

§ 209 EA

Persons who are elected (or appointed by the Minister) as members of a school board must make a prescribed declaration of office before the secretary of the board, or any other person authorized to administer an oath. The oath affirms the member's commitment to true, faithful, and impartial execution of the office to which they have been elected (or appointed), further affirms that the member will not succumb to bribery, and that the member bears loyalty to the Queen.° According to section 228, members of a school board may not continue to serve if they are convicted of an indictable offense or are absent, without authorization from the board, from three consecutive meetings.

Where school boards enter into agreements with First Nations for the purpose of providing education to First Nations students, the First Nation is entitled to have one representative appointed to that school board.° § 188 EA; Regulation 462/97

The Minister may make regulations to govern the election of student trustees to represent the interests of students on a district school board. However, student trustees are not considered members of the board, they are not entitled to move motions at a meeting of a board, nor are their votes binding upon the board. Student trustees are entitled to an honorarium for attendance; however, they are not permitted to attend certain closed meetings of a district school board.° § 55 EA

Where a board enters into any contracts, board members may not (beyond a few exceptions noted in applicable legislation) have any direct interests in those contracts, nor may they receive any direct profit, benefit, business, or office.° § 209 EA; Municipal Conflict of Interests Act, 1990

Section 218.1 of the *Education Act* prescribes the duties of a member of a school board, such that the member shall:

- carry out his or her responsibilities in a manner that assists the board in fulfilling its duties under this Act, the regulations and the guidelines issued under this Act, including but not limited to the board's duties ...;
- attend and participate in meetings of the board, including meetings of board committees of which he or she is a member;
- consult with parents, students and supporters of the board on the board's multi-year plan ...;
- bring concerns of parents, students and supporters of the board to the attention of the board;
- uphold the implementation of any board resolution after it is passed by the board;
- entrust the day to day management of the board to its staff through the board's director of education;
- maintain focus on student achievement and well-being; and
- comply with the board's code of conduct.

When a member of a school board is determined to be in breach of his or her board's code of conduct, the members of that board may: (a) censure the member in breach, (b) bar the member from attending all or part of a meeting of the board or a meeting of a committee of the board, or (c) bar the member from sitting on one or more committees of the board, for the period of time specified by the board.

7.2.2 Duties of Boards

In summary, the *Education Act* stipulates that school boards have prescribed duties and powers. It is the duty of the board to administer and manage the educational affairs of the school district or zone, in accordance with the *Education Act* and all regulations created under it. More specifically, according to section 169.1, boards must:

- promote student achievement and well-being;
- promote a positive school climate that is inclusive and accepting of all pupils;
- promote the prevention of bullying;
- ensure effective stewardship of the board's resources;
- deliver effective and appropriate education programs to its pupils;
- develop and maintain policies and organizational structures that promote the goals of the board and that encourage students to pursue their own educational goals;
- monitor and evaluate the effectiveness of policies developed by the board;
- develop and annually review a multi-year plan aimed at achieving the board's goals;
- monitor and evaluate the performance of the board's director of education.

The board must also prepare and submit reports on school operations required by the Minister and prescribe procedures to maintain satisfactory standards of comfort, safety, and sanitation for students and other facility users. The board defines and regulates all uses of school buildings, and must provide instruction and adequate accommodation to students who have the right to attend their schools and programming. The board is required to report children who are of compulsory age but who are not enrolled in any school. The board must provide textbooks and maintain insurance for school buildings, equipment, furnishings, and property of the district. A school board is obliged to participate in programs approved by the Minister for the education and training of teachers.°

§§ 14, 169.1 EA

7.2.3 Discretionary Powers of the School Board

A board has many discretionary powers to accompany their duties. These are primarily prescribed under section 171 of the *Education Act*, and include:

- employing the services of personnel, as necessary;
- entering into agreements with prescribed institutions, boards, municipalities, or other entities for purpose of ensuring quality and efficiency of services;
- establishing committees to provide advice on educational, financial, human resources, and property decisions, as necessary;
- determining the number and kind of schools in a school district,

and the provision of courses of instruction;

- operating and maintaining parks, playgrounds, and other recreational facilities (including gymnasia) both during and outside of the school year;
- operating cafeteria and milk programs;
- establishing and maintaining library facilities;
- paying the legal costs of members of the board or employees of the division;
- providing surgical treatment of children attending the school who suffer from minor physical defects.

Boards may invest funds, dispose of investments, dispose of or lease property.° They may grant leaves to employees (including maternity leaves), provide awards for the purposes of teachers and students attending post-secondary institutions. Subject to the approval of the Lieutenant Governor in Council, the Minister, and the regulations, boards may charge students fees.° Subject to certain conditions, a Minister° or a board may close a school.°

§§ 194, 241 EA

§ 11 EA

§ 66 EA

§ 171 EA

7.2.4 School Board Meetings

Every year, at their first meeting in December, school boards must select a chairperson and one vice-chair from among their trustees. If both the chair and the vice-chair are absent, the members present will elect a temporary chair. Subsequent to their first meeting, the board may meet at any time and place it believes to be expedient, and boards may, subject to the the regulations, meet via electronic communication technology. Special meetings of the board are called by the chair or in accordance with the board's own rules. A majority of members constitutes a quorum for conducting board business meetings, and the majority of votes decide questions at all board meetings; the chair may vote on all questions and any vote resulting in equal numbers of votes cast for and against is considered to have failed.°

§ 208 EA

"[M]eetings of a board and ... meetings of a committee of the board, including a committee of the whole board, shall be open to the public, and no person shall be excluded from a meeting that is open to the public except for improper conduct."° Notwithstanding the above statement, some meetings of a school board may be closed to the public if the content of the meeting will involve any of the following issues:

§ 207 EA

- the security of the property of the board;
- the disclosure of intimate, personal, or financial information in respect of a member of the board or committee, an employee or prospective employee of the board, or a pupil or his or her parent or guardian;

- the acquisition or disposal of a school site;
- decisions in respect of negotiations with employees of the board; or
- litigation affecting the board.

§ 191 EA

§ 191.2 EA

Board members may be remunerated for attending meetings of the school board, at a rate fixed by the board,° or for expenses members incur for travel and in support of the business of the board.°

7.2.5 School Closure

§ 66 EA

§ 171(1)(7) EA

Freuda-Kwarteng, E. (2005). School closures in Ontario: Who has the final say? *Canadian Journal of Educational Administration and Policy, 45*, 1–26.

A Minister of Education may close a school in a district school area if "there are for two consecutive years fewer than eight persons between the ages of five and fourteen years residing therein."° School boards may also elect to close a school "in accordance with policies established by the board from guidelines issued by the Minister."° Though commentary in academic literature suggests that provincial Regulations were in place regarding school closure processes,° at the time of printing, no Ontario Ministerial Regulation of this nature can be found through official Ministry of Education or Queen's Printer sources. However, in 2009, the Ministry provided a Pupil Accommodation Guideline that suggests school boards facing decisions on the future of a school ought to do so:

Ministry of Education. (2009). *Pupil Accommodation Review Guideline*. Toronto, ON: the Author. retrieved May 2013 from http://www.edu.gov.on.ca/eng/policyfunding/reviewGuide09.pdf

- with the involvement of the community to be affected;
- by ensuring that the community to be affected is well-informed of the decisions to be made, and the process to be followed; and
- by considering the important role played by a school in terms of the strength and health of the community.°

Ministry of Education. (2009). *Pupil Accommodation Review Guideline*. Toronto, ON: the Author. retrieved May 2013 from http://www.edu.gov.on.ca/eng/policyfunding/reviewGuide09.pdf

School boards must establish, follow, and publish online their own school closure policy, and ensure its compliance with the provincial Guideline. Planning and review documents detailing long-term enrolments are to be used to contextualize the review process. The Ministry encourages Boards to "focus on a group of schools within a school board's planning area rather than examine a single school" (p. 2 °).

The following steps are taken when a review process is followed:

Ministry of Education. (2009). *Pupil Accommodation Review Guideline*. Toronto, ON: the Author. retrieved May 2013 from http://www.edu.gov.on.ca/eng/policyfunding/reviewGuide09.pdf

1. The board will establish an Accommodation Review Committee (ARC)—including members of the community—and will draft reference criteria that delimit ARC discussions. Reference criteria may include "educational and accommodation criteria for examining schools under review and accommodation options." These might include a discussion of "grade configuration, school utilization, and program offerings"(p. 2 °).
2. The board will provide the ARC and the community affected with a School Information Profile document outlining how well the school(s) meet board objectives and reference criteria. The value

of the school to the students, school board, community, and local economy served will provide the foci of the data offered in the Profile.

3. The ARC will initiate the writing of an Accommodation Report to the board that may include accommodation options.
4. A period of community consultation and a minimum of four public meetings must follow. The time frame between the announcing of the review and the beginning of community consultation must be no more than 30 calendar days. The community consultation period must last for no less than 90 calendar days. The consultation will seek to ensure that the ARC receives feedback on its interim Report and accommodation options.
5. The ARC will finalize and submit its Accommodation Report to the board. At this time the Report becomes public.
6. Following the publication of the Report, the board has no fewer than 60 calendar days to consider the Report and vote on its recommendations.

Ministry of Education. (2009). *Pupil Accommodation Review Guideline*. Toronto, ON: the Author. retrieved May 2013 from http://www.edu.gov.on.ca/eng/policyfunding/reviewGuide09.pdf

7.2.6 *Income Tax on Remuneration, Honoraria, and Expense Allowances*

Under section 81(3) of the federal *Income Tax Act*, 1985, up to one half of a trustee's annual remuneration and expense allowance may be excluded from the trustee's income for purposes of calculating income tax.

7.3 LEGAL STATUS OF A SCHOOL BOARD

School boards exercise only those powers granted to them by the *Education Act*, 1990. These powers may be revoked or added to by the Legislative Assembly of Ontario. In this sense, school boards are not autonomous but derive their authority and power from the *Education Act* established by the Legislative Assembly. The Legislative Assembly derives its constituted authority through section 93 of the Canadian *Constitution Act*, 1876, which indicates that "In and for each Province and Legislature may exclusively make Law in relation to Education... ." Some of the functions assigned by the legislature to school boards are mandatory duties (the school board "shall"), some are discretionary powers (the school board "may"). The ways in which these functions are performed are at the individual school board's discretion, limited only by methods specified in the *Education Act*, other Acts of the province, and the regulations; by the requirements of the common law concerning natural justice and the duty to act fairly; and by the Canadian *Charter of Rights and Freedoms*.°

CONSTITUTION ACT, 1982

7.4 JOINT SERVICES OF SCHOOL BOARDS

§§ 8, 170, 171.1, 181 through 184, 187 through 190, 194, 196, 197, 249, 255, 257.11, 257.18, 259, 260.4, 260.5, 277.9, 284, 290, 291, 294, 312, 313 EA

A school board is permitted to make an agreement with any other board or boards, with an individual, municipal or conservation authority, corporation, hospital, university or college, Indian Band, the Minister of Education, the Government of Ontario, the Government of Canada, or a local authority in another province for the provision of services to students; for investment purposes; for acquisition or improvement to a school site and/or buildings; for employing teachers or other personnel for instruction, management, supervision, or maintenance, inside or outside the school division.°

7.5 SCHOOL COUNCILS AND PARENT INVOLVEMENT COMMITTEES

§ 2 Regulation 612/00

Section 170 of the *Education Act* states that "Every board shall … establish a school council for each school operated by the board, in accordance with the regulations; [and] [t]he Lieutenant Governor in Council may make regulations respecting school councils, including regulations relating to their establishment, composition and functions." The purpose of school councils is articulated in the opening sections of the Regulations: "through the active participation of parents, to improve pupil achievement and to enhance the accountability of the education system to parents," and further, "[a] school council's primary means of achieving its purpose is by making recommendations in accordance with this Regulation to the principal of the school and the board that established the council."°

§ 29 Regulation 612/00

§ 27 Regulation 612/00

Parent Involvement Committees are committees of school parents established under section 17.1 of the *Education Act*. Boards must establish a Parent Involvement Committee° "to support, encourage and enhance parent engagement at the board level in order to improve student achievement and well-being."°

The relationship between a school board and a school council is articulated in both the Regulations and certain sections of the *Education Act*. For example, sections 302 and 303 of the *Education Act* highlight the obligation boards have to consider the opinions of school councils with respect to the content of policies and guidelines established and reviewed by the board.

§ 28 Regulation 612/00

Parent Involvement Committees develop strategies that the board may use to improve communication with parents and general parent engagement.°

7.5.1 *Membership of School Councils*

§§ 3 through 5 Regulation 612/00

Every school council is comprised of elected and appointed members.°

- the number of elected parent members determined by the school council's own by-laws, or otherwise the number determined in the policy of the school board;
- the principal of the school;
- one elected teacher employed at the school (who is neither the principal nor the vice-principal of the school);
- one elected employee of the school (who is neither the principal, vice-principal, nor a teacher at the school);
- unless the school has been established for the purpose of adult education, if the school has one or more secondary grades, one student enrolled in the school who is appointed by the student council, if the school has a student council—otherwise, one elected student enrolled in the school;
- unless the school has been established for the purpose of adult education, if the school has no secondary grades, one student enrolled in the school who is appointed by the principal, if the principal determines, after consulting the other members of the school council, that the council should include a student representative;
- at least one, subject to the school council's own by-laws, community representative—generally speaking this cannot be an individual employed at the school or a member of the school board that established the school council—appointed by the other members of the council;
- one person appointed by an association that is a member of the Ontario Federation of Home and School Associations, the Ontario Association of Parents in Catholic Education or Parent Partenaires en Education, if established in respect of the school.

The Regulations require that parents must represent the majority of membership on a school council.

The Regulations determine terms of office. Each member of the school council holds office for one year and is eligible for re-election or reappointment.° Parents are disqualified from membership on the school council if he or she is employed at the school or if he or she is employed by the school board and has not taken "reasonable steps to inform people qualified to vote in the election of parent members of that employment."°

§ 6 Regulation 612/00

§ 6 Regulation 612/00

The election of members on a school council must take place during the first 30 days of a school year, and the community of school parents must be given notice of this date by the principal at least 14 days prior. Principals may post the notice in the school, or simply send the notice to each home with students.°

§ 4 Regulation 612/00

Every school council must make by-laws governing election procedures, the filling of vacancies, participation and conflict of

§ 15 Regulation 612/00
§ 16 Regulation 612/00

interest, and internal council conflict resolution.° Minutes and financial records must be kept accurate.°

7.5.2 *Meetings, Duties, and Responsibilities of School Councils*

The Regulations state that all school councils must meet at least four times during each school year. Meetings must be open to the public (parents are informed by the principal of scheduled meeting dates and times), may take place at the school, and half of the council's membership—such that more than the majority of members present are parents—constitutes quorum.°

§ 12 Regulation 612/00

The role of a school council is advisory. School boards are obligated to seek the opinions and views of members of school councils with regard to the establishment or amendment of board policies respecting:

- the conduct of persons in schools within the board's jurisdiction,
- appropriate dress for pupils in schools within the board's jurisdiction,
- the allocation of funding by the board to school councils,
- the fundraising activities of school councils,
- conflict resolution processes for internal school council disputes, and
- reimbursement by the board of expenses incurred by members and officers of school councils.°

§ 19 Regulation 612/00

Boards likewise seek the opinions and views of members of school councils with regard to:

- the development of implementation plans for new education initiatives that relate to pupil achievement or to the accountability of the education system to parents;
- board action plans for improvement, based on the Education Quality and Accountability Office's reports on the results of tests of pupils, and the communication of those plans to the public; and
- the process and criteria applicable to the selection and placement of principals and vice-principals.°

§ 19 Regulation 612/00

Generally speaking, a school council may make any recommendation to either the principal or the school board on any matter. Recommendations to a school board must be considered by the board, and a reply must be offered.°

§§ 20, 21 Regulation 612/00

School councils may engage in fundraising so long as the activities are in accord with policies of the board and funds raised are used for purposes aligned with board policies.°

§ 22 Regulation 612/00

It is the duty of every school council to "consult with parents of pupils enrolled in the school about matters under consideration by the council," and to annually report on its activities.° §§ 23, 24 Regulation 612/00

7.5.3 Membership and Constitution of Parent Involvement Committees

Every Parent Involvement Committee is comprised of elected and appointed members. ° §§ 33, 34 Regulation 612/00

- the number of appointed or elected parent members determined by the Parent Involvement Committee's own by-laws, and subject to the Regulations;
- the director of education of the school board;
- one member of the school board, appointed by the board;
- at least one, subject to the Parent Involvement Committee's own by-laws, community representative—this cannot be an employee or member of the board that established the school council

The Regulations determine terms of office. Some parent members of the Parent Involvement Committee hold office for one year, and others hold office for two. Each parent member is eligible for re-election.° § 37 Regulation 612/00

Every Parent Involvement Committee must make by-laws governing the conduct of the committee's affairs, the filling of vacancies, election of members, participation and conflict of interest, and internal council conflict resolution.° Minutes and financial records must be kept accurate.° § 43 Regulation 612/00 § 44 Regulation 612/00

7.5.4 Meetings, Duties, and Responsibilities of Parent Involvement Committees

The Regulations state that a Parent Involvement Committee must meet at least four times during each school year. Meetings must be open to the public (members are informed by the co-chairs of scheduled meeting dates and times), may take place at the school board office or other school board facilities, and half of the council's membership—such that more than the majority of members present are parents—plus the concurrent presence of the director of education and the board member, or their designates, constitutes quorum.° § 40 Regulation 612/00

The role of a Parent Involvement Committee is advisory. School boards and the Minister may seek the opinions and views of members with regard to improving student achievement and well-being. Recommendations to a school board must be considered, and a reply must be offered.° §§ 47, 48 Regulation 612/00

A Parent Involvement Committee may "solicit and take into consideration the advice of parents of pupils enrolled in schools of the

§§ 49, 50 Regulation 612/00

board with regard to matters under consideration by the committee," and must annually report on its activities.°

8.0 ADMINISTRATION OF SCHOOL DISTRICTS

Part 8.0 describes the critical role of school boards in Ontario education, as they govern school districts and the schools in these districts. School boards are called upon to ensure the effective administration of numerous responsibilities in school districts, mandated to maintain public trust. Board and administrative processes and structures are pre-determined by statute, regulations, policy, specific mandates, the practices of particular districts and the well-considered discretion that is required for deliberation and leadership where not otherwise prescribed.

8.1 DUTIES OF CHAIRPERSON

School districts are regions in Ontario wherein the elementary and secondary schools are overseen by one board. As indicated, all district school boards are governed by locally elected trustees (exceptions, however, are found in six school authorities located in hospitals, which have appointed rather than elected trustees). Each school board of trustees is responsible for ensuring the quality of learning and the safety of the school environment at each of the schools under its jurisdiction.° In addition, the publicly-funded district school boards are responsible for the provision of universally accessible education for all students, regardless of their ethnic, racial, or cultural backgrounds; social or economic status; gender; individual exceptionality; or religious preference.° Given these and other important entrustments, the school board exercises its responsibilities as a body and performs key leadership roles to ensure that its schools operate within the standards established by the Province, and that the programs and services remain responsive to the communities they serve (as indicated above).

retrieved May 2013 from http://www.schoolsincanada.com/School-Districts-in-Canada.cfm

Ontario Educational Services Corporation. (2012). *Good governance: A guide for trustees, school boards, directors of education and communities*. Toronto, ON: the Author, *retrieved May 2013 from http://www.opsba.org/files/GoodGovernance.pdf*

As one means for executing these responsibilities, the members of each board will annually elect, from among the elected trustees, a chairperson to preside over their meetings in a fashion consistent with board's procedures and practices. Working with the Director of Education, this Chairperson will establish the board agenda and will ensure that board members have the needed and requested material

Ontario Educational Services Corporation. (2012). *Good governance: A guide for trustees, school boards, directors of education and communities*. Toronto, ON: the Author, *retrieved May 2013 from http://www.opsba.org/files/GoodGovernance.pdf*

to inform their discussions and decisions. Typically the designated Chairperson is also the spokesperson for the board and provides, with the board, focused leadership on mission, vision, and effective governance of board matters.°

8.2 EXECUTIVE OFFICERS OF THE BOARD OF EDUCATION

In order to fulfill its responsibilities, every board of education must appoint a director, board secretary-treasurer (or secretary and treasurer or superintendent of administration, and any other official, assistant or support personnel for proper and efficient administration of the school district). The duties of these persons are prescribed by the board, except where described in the *Education Act*.

8.2.1 Director of Education

Ontario Educational Services Corporation. (2012). *Good governance: A guide for trustees, school boards, directors of education and communities*. Toronto, ON: the Author, *retrieved May 2013 from http://www.opsba.org/files/GoodGovernance.pdf*

§ 283.1(1) EA

The Director of Education is appointed as the Chief Executive Officer and Chief Education Officer (CEO) of the school board with powers and duties prescribed, first by the *Education Act* and then also by the position-holder's employing board. As the only employee who reports directly to the board, this person also serves the secretariat role for the board. Through the Director of Education, a school board holds all of its schools and employed personnel accountable for school district performance, based on expectations set at both the provincial and board levels. School board staff report either directly or indirectly to the director of education.° The director is responsible for: advising the board on operational matters; implementing board policies; managing all facets of school board operations; ensuring that the board's multi-year plan establishes the board's priorities and identifies the resources that will be used to achieve them; implementing, and monitoring the implementation of, the multi-year strategic plan (MYSP), reporting on this to the board, as well as reviewing it annually with the board; ensuring that the MYSP includes board expectations for the achievement of goals at the end of each of the three years; bringing to the board's attention any act or omission by the board that could violate or has violated the *Education Act* or any of its policies, guidelines or regulations. If the board does not respond in a satisfactory manner, the Director is required to report the act or omission to the Deputy Minister of Education;° and reaching a mutual understanding with board concerning the performance outcomes expected for the exercise of this role. Essentially, all Supervisory education officer in Ontario are responsible to the Minister of Education (ensure that ministry policies are carried out by school boards) and to their employing school board (where they perform the duties assigned to them).

8.2.2 Board Treasurer and Board Secretary

The *Education Act* requires each board to appoint a treasurer. If the board has no more than five members, the treasurer may be a board member.° The treasurer is authorized to receive and account for all board money and to account for all papers and money in the possession, power or control of the board. The *Education Act* states that the Director of Education must act as the Secretary of the Board. As Secretary, the Director of Education makes sure there are records of the minutes of meetings, that reports requested by the provincial Ministry of Education are forwarded, and that all members are notified of board meetings. The Secretary also calls any special meetings requested by a majority of board members.° All correspondence addressed to the Secretary and Director of Education (when in his or her capacity as secretary), must be shared with the board. If the secretary is absent, the chair of the meeting may appoint a member or anyone else as temporary secretary to record the minutes for that meeting.°

§ 170(1) EA

§ 198(1) EA

§ 208(10) EA

8.2.3 Superintendent of Education

Supervisory officers, often called superintendents, are appointed to lead and supervise schools and programs. Boards must notify the Minister when a supervisory officer is appointed.° Superintendents are accountable to the Director of Education and work with school principals and staff, in accordance to ministry and board policy. Superintendents report to the board through the Director of Education.° These school district supervisory officers are assigned to implement Ministry of Education and board policy and to provide supervisory oversight to the educational personnel and programs in district schools. These leaders ensure that performance appraisals are conducted and that the schools are accountable for student achievement school. They also ensure that buildings are maintained according to ministry and board policy and, for example, report to the medical officer of health where a school building or school property poses health concerns.°

Regulation 309

§ 286(1) EA

§ 286(1) EA

8.3 QUALIFICATIONS OF SENIOR EDUCATIONAL LEADERS

Supervisory officers must meet certain standards to be hired and engaged in their important work. Members of The Ontario College of Teachers who have at least five years of successful classroom teaching experience, hold an acceptable post-secondary degree and have a master's degree° are eligible for the Supervisory Officer's Qualification program.° Supervisory officers employed by school boards must hold supervisory officer's qualifications and have either principal's qualifications or two years experience in administrative roles in education. Of course, supervisory officers are expected to possess the knowledge, skills and attitudes needed to function effectively and proactively in an increasingly complex environment. Their ongoing professional learning must reflect these needs. There is a Supervisory Officer's Qualification Program (or SOQP) consisting

§ 35 Regulation 176/10

retrieved May 2013 from http://www.oct.ca/~/media/PDF/Supervisory%20Qualification/EN/2011%20SOQP%20Guide%20EN%20ACCESSIBLE%20WEB.ashx

of four instructional modules (each of at least 50 hours of instruction; and one module consisting of at least 50 hours of practical experience in the workplace).

8.4 SENIOR EDUCATIONAL LEADER ORGANIZATIONS

Senior supervisory officers belong to one or more of the following organizations, depending on which education system they serve:

The Council of Ontario Directors of Education (CODE) is the professional association representing the Chief Executive Officers of the seventy-two District School Boards in Ontario. This association is the common public voice of Senior School District Administrators working with Government and various associations.°

retrieved May 2013 from http://www.ontariodirectors.ca

The Ontario Association of School Business Officials (OASBO) consists of professionals who are committed to collaborative development, sharing and promotion of leading business practices in education.°

retrieved May 2013 from https://www.oasbo.org

The Ontario Catholic School Business Officials Association (OCSBOA) works with partners in Catholic education to foster their members' professional development and networking, promote effective best management practices, and support Gospel values in service of Catholic education.°

retrieved May 2013 from http://www.ocsboa.ca

The Ontario Public Supervisory Officers' Association (OPSOA) is a professional organization that represents approximately 300 superintendents and directors of education from the thirty-one English language Public District School Boards of Ontario.°

retrieved May 2013 from http://www.opsoa.org

The Ontario Catholic Supervisory Officers' Association (OCSOA) is the professional organization of Catholic Supervisory Officers. This association dedicates itself to furthering the interests of Catholic education and to promoting the professional development and welfare of its members.°

retrieved May 2013 from http://www.ocsoa.ca

Association des gestionnaires en éducation franco-ontarienne (AGEFO) is a professional organization of non-union managers involved with French education in Ontario, with a French-language school board, or with an affiliated organization. L'AGEFO seeks to promote the professional development of its members and the importance of their contributions in achieving the educational mission of the boards of the French language in Ontario.°

retrieved May 2013 from http://www.agefo.ca

9.0 THE BASICS OF SCHOOL DISTRICT BUDGETS

This part provides an overview of how education is financed in the Province of Ontario by giving a brief description of annual operating budgets, revenues and expenditures, capital budgets, and auditing and reporting to the Minister.

One of the most significant responsibilities of school boards to set annual operating budgets. While the Ministry of Education provides the grants used to support school districts, it is the responsibility of board members and their executives to work with the funds provided. They must work in accordance with statutory requirements, and develop a budget that best suits the programs and services offered in their school districts, and regulated by the *Education Act*.

Understanding how school districts finance education in their jurisdictions can be a daunting and confusing task, but the basics are quite simple. There are two types of budgets prepared by school boards:

1. An annual operating budget for such expenses as teacher and staff salaries, instructional materials, equipment and supplies, heat, light, student transportation.
2. A capital budget will reflect plans for such expenses as building or renovating schools, operating buses, completing renovations, and purchasing long-term equipment.

Both of these types of budgets will indicate how much will be spent and on what priorities (expenses) and where the money will come from (so that expenses are balanced with revenue).

9.1 FINANCES IN THE *EDUCATION ACT*

In the *Education Act*,° the financing of education in Ontario is outlines in general terms under various subject areas:

§§ 230 through 257 EA

- **General (Division A):** Sections 230 through 257.4 (grants, borrowing and investments)
- **Education Taxes (Division B):** Sections 257.5 through

257.14 (property taxes, when funds are allocated, powers of municipalities)

- **Taxes Set by Board (Division C):** Sections 257.15 through 257.29
- **Supervision of Boards' Financial Affairs (Division D):** Sections 257.30 through 257.52
- **Education Development Charges (Division E):** Sections 257.53 through 257.105.

Rather than follow the above sequence, this Guide will provide a general overview of school district operations with respect to operating budgets and capital budgets.

Financing education in Ontario is a shared responsibility, mainly between the Provincial government and school boards. Ontario school boards are allocated funds based on student enrolment and the learning requirements of students in each board district.° This is done with a funding formula. Property taxes are collected in school district communities and these funds are supplemented to the amounts established by funding formula.

REGULATION 155/09

Boards receive base line funding for general recognized costs such as salaries, instructional materials, and equipment. Funds are also designated for particular student needs (i.e., English-as-Alternative-Language or Special Education programming, for example). Of course, some funds are used to build new schools (capital projects) and others used to maintain, improve or renovate facilities or grounds. In turn, school boards have the responsibility to decide the amount of this funding that is required by each school. Schools have some discretion to spend allocated funds, according to plans and priorities established by Province, board and the school itself. School boards are required to develop a balanced budget within the funding allocated to them by the Ministry of Education. This means that they must not spend more than they receive.°

Ontario Educational Services Corporation. (2012). *Good governance: A guide for trustees, school boards, directors of education and communities*. Toronto, ON: the Author, *retrieved May 2013 from http://www.opsba.org/files/GoodGovernance.pdf*

9.2 ANNUAL OPERATING BUDGETS

Each fiscal year, school boards must prepare and adopt estimates of its revenues and expenses for the fiscal year.° The fiscal year for school boards is September 1 to August 31, which coincides with the school operational year. These estimates will include program objectives and anticipated revenue and expenditures for the next fiscal year, including: costs for administrative services, instruction, equipment, supplies, plant operations, student transportation, fees and payments to other boards or agencies, debt retirement, and contributions to capital requirements. In a 1996 Supreme Court of Canada ruling, Catholic district school boards must bear the cost of (a) infusing Catholicity through the programs and curriculum, (b) developing faith of students, and (c) Religious Education and Family

§ 232(1) EA

Life Education programs.°

Generally, boards usually hold public consultations on budgets in March. After holding public consultations to seek the viewpoints of interested parties, including school councils and the board's parent involvement committee, the board of education budgets are formed as finalized estimates and then adopted during open meetings.

Ontario Educational Services Corporation. (2012). *Good governance: A guide for trustees, school boards, directors of education and communities*. Toronto, ON: the Author, *retrieved May 2013 from http://www.opsba.org/files/GoodGovernance.pdf*

Budgets cannot be finalized until the government announces the Grants for Student Needs (GSN) for the year ahead. This announcement usually occurs towards the end of March each year.

9.2.1 Revenues

Since 1998, the provincial government has had full control of property tax revenues and has assumed the previous authority of school boards to levy local property taxes. All *real* property that is liable to assessment and taxation under the *Assessment Act* is taxable for school purposes.° Authority is given to the Lieutenant Governor in Council (Provincial Cabinet) to make regulations governing the making of grants, from money appropriated by the Legislature for educational purposes.° The Government uses a formulae-based funding approach to determine the revenue each board receives. This funding is known as the Grants for Student Needs (GSN):

§ 257.6(1) EA

§ 234(1) EA

> A board's total Grants for Student Needs allocation is determined by: the formulas in the Pupil Foundation Grant; the School Foundation Grant; thirteen special purpose grants and allocations; and, funding for Interest Expense and for Non-Permanently Financed Capital Debt. These grants are intended to provide a total amount of revenue based on the specific needs of a board and its students.(p. 75 °)

Ontario Educational Services Corporation. (2012). *Good governance: A guide for trustees, school boards, directors of education and communities*. Toronto, ON: the Author, *retrieved May 2013 from http://www.opsba.org/files/GoodGovernance.pdf*

This funding formula aims to distribute funds equitably among all school boards across the Province. The calculation of the grant funds school board efforts to maintain schools and build new ones where they are needed. The school boards are entrusted with the translation of Provincial vision and standards for education.

The measure of enrolment for purposes of calculating funding for school boards is the Average Daily Enrolment (ADE) of pupils; wherein boards report the full-time equivalent enrolment in each district school as of October 31st and March 31st (it is the average of these two count dates that determines full-time equivalents. The cost of educating students varies according to a number of factors. These variables include type of students (special education, English as Second Language), age of students and geographic circumstances (rural, remote, poor).

The grant payable by the Province to the school boards uses the following formula: (A + B) - (C + D + E) + F, where

- "A" is total amount of grant allocation for recognized expenses to which board is entitled;

- "B" is amount of the board's adjustment for declining enrolment;
- "C" is amount of the board's tax revenue;
- "D" is amount of board's total fees revenue for pupils;
- "E" is amount of board's expenses due to strike or lock-out affecting operations;
- "F" is the total amount of grant allocations related to special education entitlements.

To provide a concrete example of revenues to boards, the example of the 2013-14 grant allocations are illustrative. A total amount of 20.8 billion dollars was projected for Ontario boards (of which 9.6 billion was pupil foundation grant, 2.5 billion was for special education grants and 2.3 billion was for school facility operations and renewal grants).

Using, a current-value assessment system, the Government sets a uniform tax rate for the education portion of property taxes for all residential properties to support the education system. The rates set for business property taxes vary by municipality but is set by Government. Municipalities collect the education portion of property taxes for the school boards in their communities on behalf of the Province. As indicated, the Ministry of Education, using the funding formula, will determine each board's overall allocation using the funding formula.° It is also possible for a school board to pass bylaws to help pay for new school sites, where there is a need for new real estate developments to increase capacity within the board's jurisdiction.°

Ontario Educational Services Corporation. (2012). *Good governance: A guide for trustees, school boards, directors of education and communities*. Toronto, ON: the Author, *retrieved May 2013 from http://www.opsba.org/files/GoodGovernance.pdf*

§§ 257.53 through 257.105 EA; Regulation 20/98

9.2.2 Expenditures

Ontario educates approximately two million students in 5000 schools. Budget estimates for boards of education include all costs associated with educating students. As indicated, boards are responsible to ensure that estimated expenditures do not exceed its estimated revenue.° Boards must ensure that local priorities are met (thus the need for some flexibility and discretion) within the constraints and standards set forth by the Government (i.e., achievement of class size targets). Boards are accountable to both local constituents and the Province through various consultative and reporting mechanisms. They must achieve balanced budgets (this is a specific legal obligation in the *Education Act*) and limit spending on administration and governance to what the allocation provides. In other words, school boards may not spend more than 15% of their budget on administration.° In addition, money held in a reserve fund can not be expended, pledged or applied to any purpose other that for the purposes that it was established for, without Minister of Education approval.° Planning is vital for school boards to properly manage educational resources.

§ 231(2) EA

retrieved May 2013 from http://www.guideduparentsolidaire.ca/Media/Content/files/French%20Catholic%20School/FCS_Ch21R.pdf

§ 231(6) EA

Effective stewardship of a board's allocated responses require due diligence on the part of the board and its executives. A variety of approaches are used to manage expenditures across the Province. In some cases, the budget is centralized with the district office exercising discretion in the determination of school-level budgets. On the other hand, there are some boards where school principals exercise, with their staff and community some limited site-based management of budgets, through management committees or the school councils.° Boards are allowed to enter into agreements with other boards to provide for administrative or instructional purposes, student transportation or services of teachers or other personnel.°

retrieved May 2013 from http://www.guideduparentsolidaire.ca/Media/Content/files/French%20Catholic%20School/FCS_Ch21R.pdf

§ 181(1) EA

There are expenses that are common to school boards and their schools. These are costs that are recognized as legitimate expenses to deliver accountable, quality education. These common cost are a part of the calculations to determine the school division grants. There is a basic per pupil range of costs, which account for student special needs and actual costs (including: transportation, administration, instruction, and so forth).

9.3 CAPITAL BUDGETS

A capital budget is a plan used to reflect a school district's long term investments such as school buildings, replacement roofs, renovation or reuse of facilities. Capital projects are longer term, capacity building investments that are considered worth pursuing but apart of from operating budget. The age of schools, the educational needs of certain types of initiatives, fluctuating enrolments, and technological advances contribute to the importance of change-ready financial planning on the part of Government and boards. Capital programs enable boards to accommodate their students. The New Pupil Places funding provides boards who have enrolment growth to construct new schools or additions. Under this funding model, the long-term capital debt from construction is supported by the increases in revenue boards receive as enrolment increases.° School board carry out capital projects with ministry approvals and the Ministry of Education provides majority of funding of the capital projects.°

Ontario Educational Services Corporation. (2012). *Good governance: A guide for trustees, school boards, directors of education and communities*. Toronto, ON: the Author, *retrieved May 2013 from http://www.opsba.org/files/GoodGovernance.pdf*

retrieved May 2013 from http://www.fin.gov.on.ca/en/reformcommission/chapters/ch6.html

A board may decide to erect a school building on land that is leased by the board where the term of the lease, the school site and the plans of the school building are approved by the Minister.° It is permissible for a board to gain the approval of the Minister of Education to "add to, alter or improve a school building that is acquired by the board under a lease."°

§ 195(5) EA

§ 195(6) EA

Ontario school boards are able to borrow money through Ontario School Boards Financing Corporation (OSBFC). The OSBFC is a non-profit corporation providing efficient and highly flexible access to the debt capital markets while minimizing the costs.° It is also

retrieved May 2013 from http://www.msc.gov.mb.ca/legal_docs/orders/ontario.html

§§ 193 through 196 EA

§ 194(1) EA

possible for a board to sell, lease, or otherwise dispose of a property° that is no longer required for school purposes, with the approval of the Lieutenant Governor in Council.°

9.4 AUDITS AND REPORTING TO THE MINISTER

The Ministry of Education in Ontario has a number of conditions attached to its funding of school board. For example, funds allocated to teaching in the classroom must be targeted to the classroom; funds allocated to Special Education must be targeted to these programs; funds allocated to school construction and repairs must be used solely for these purposes; and the board must not spend more than what is allowed for administration and the management of the schools and the board. It is Director of Education's responsibility to ensure that the board spends funds appropriately and the board monitors their Director of Education to ensure that their policies are implemented according to directives.

Ontario Educational Services Corporation. (2012). *Good governance: A guide for trustees, school boards, directors of education and communities*. Toronto, ON: the Author, *retrieved May 2013 from http://www.opsba.org/files/GoodGovernance.pdf*

§§ 252(1), 252(2) EA

In addition, every district school board in the Province is required to establish an audit committee. The audit committee is composed of both trustees and non-trustee members appointed by the school board. The purpose of board audit committees is to provide oversight of the school board's financial reporting, controls, and risk management. This mechanism facilitates financial transparency and accountability. The internal audit committee examines the efficacy of operations, the reliability of financial reporting. This is a decentralized approach to safeguarding assets, deterring, and investigating fraud. Internal auditors report to the audit committee during the fiscal year in order to help the school boards achieve their stated objectives. Trustee and non-trustee committee members the school board to objectively assess the performance of their organization, its management and its auditors.° Within a month after receiving the auditor's report on the board's financial statements, the financial statements and the auditor's report is made public (as prescribed).°

The Minister of Education may also appoint an investigator (auditor) to investigate the financial affairs of a school board under certain circumstances, including: where financial statements indicate that the board has operated with a deficit, where there has been a failure to pay any debentures or where there has been a default on debts or other financial liabilities, or where the Minister has reason to be concerned about a board's financial integrity or capacity. The Minister of Education has the authority to issue orders, directions, and decisions relating to the affairs of the board, and even to assume complete control over all the board's affairs.

10.0 FRANCOPHONE EDUCATION IN ONTARIO

10.1 OVERVIEW OF FRANCOPHONE EDUCATION

Ontario's Francophone community has long cherished its cultural and linguistic heritage and the inculcation of that culture and its values of family, faith, and community to its youth through education in the French language. It was no surprise for the legislative assembly of Ontario to declare in the *French Language Services Act* that the French language was an official language of education in Ontario. Today, within Ontario's French-language school system, which is one of the four categories of publicly funded Ontario school systems, there are 12 French-language school boards, with a total of 425 French-language schools. In these schools, the curriculum is taught exclusively in French—with exception given to English language courses. Their mandate is "to protect, enhance, and transmit the French language and culture."°

retrieved May 2013 from http://www.edu.gov.on.ca/eng/amenagement

In English-language schools, the importance of the French language is acknowledged both through several options offered to students and certain requirements related to graduation.

This part provides information regarding: (a) the History of French Language Education in Ontario; (b) the Structure of Francophone education in Ontario; (c) French instruction within English-Language schools; and (d) a conclusion with respect to the current state of Ontario's Francophone system of education.

10.2 THE HISTORY OF FRENCH-LANGUAGE EDUCATION IN ONTARIO

The history of Francophone education began in 1786 with the establishment of a French-Catholic elementary school in the Windsor area, and reached a point in Upper Canada such that by 1840 that there were parallel publicly supported Catholic (French) and Protestant

(English) school systems. Within short order, the political climate in Upper Canada changed and, in 1855, English became a compulsory subject in all Ontario schools. Five years later, the English language was declared Ontario's sole language of instruction in schools (except where numbers warranted otherwise). In 1910, as a response to the discriminatory actions of the Ontario government, the Franco-Ontarian community was constituted.

Barber, M. (n.d.) Ontario Schools Question. *The Canadian Encyclopedia. retrieved May 2013 from http://www.thecanadianencyclopedia.com/index.cfm?PgNm=TCE&Params=A1ARTA0005945*

The anti-French forces in Ontario responded in 1912, led by the Ontario Premier, James Whitney. Their action was based on the recommendation of the *Merchant-Scott-Côté Report*, and was embodied, most specifically, in "Regulation 17."° Regulation 17 restricted the use of the French language in Ontario schools to the first two years of elementary school. The following year, in 1913, the French language was only allowed to be studied for one hour per day. Thus began what came to be known as the Ontario School Question and ensuing litigation on the part of French language advocates seeking to have Regulation 17 declared *ultra vires* (or beyond the power of the Ontario government, given protections for denominational education rights under section 93 of the constitution—as it was then known, the *British North America Act*, 1867). While the Ontario government never fully implemented Regulation 17, a 1917 court challenge to the Judicial Committee of the Privy Council confirmed its constitutionality. Thus, section 93 of the *British North America Act* was held by the highest court to protect denominational (religious) rights, but not language rights.

Barber, M. (n.d.) Ontario Schools Question. *The Canadian Encyclopedia. retrieved May 2013 from http://www.thecanadianencyclopedia.com/index.cfm?PgNm=TCE&Params=A1ARTA0005945*

In 1927, the Provincial government, under Premier Fergson, repealed Regulation 17. The result gave the determination of whether or not French might be used in schools to a "departmental committee"—a policy that "encouraged improved bilingual teaching, including recognition of the University of Ottawa Normal School, and produced higher retention rates for Franco-Ontarian students."°

By 1968, the fear over Québec separation caused reflection in the Ontario government with respect to the treatment of the province's French speaking minority. In that same year, the *Education Act* was amended giving Franco-Ontarians the right to have French-language elementary and secondary schools. This recognition of the importance and relevance of the French language to Ontario, as well as both its French and non-French speaking population, had grown become clear by 1972. In 1972, the Council on French-Language Schools (Conseil supérieur de l'éducation des écoles de langue française) was created, followed shortly thereafter by the Ontario Languages of Instruction Commission. In 1977, the first "appointment of an Assistant Deputy Minister responsible for French-language education" was made.°

retrieved May 2013 from http://www.ofa.gov.on.ca/en/flsa-history.html

Over the 30 years that followed, the discriminatory nature of many of Ontario's past laws on education—*vis-à-vis* the French language—were repealed and replaced with more culturally sensitive policies and legislation. It has been hoped that policies and legislation might provide the bases of enriched education for all Ontarian youth through the encouragement of the use of the French language in Ontario schools. Milestones include:°

Historical overview of French-Language Services in Ontario. retrieved May 2013 from http://www.ofa.gov.on.ca/en/flsa-history.html

- in 1984, the right to receive education in French at elementary and secondary levels;
- in 1986, the governance of French schools and instructional units provided to the Francophone community;
- the establishment of the Cousineau Commission (the French-Language Education Governance Advisory Group) to recommend "criteria for the governance of French-language education in Ontario"the re-establishment of the Council on Franco-Ontarian Education (CEFO); and
- "Creation of the Advisory Committee on Francophone Affairs (ACFA) to advise the Minister of Colleges and Universities on the issue of French-language postsecondary studies (July 1991).

In 1997, twelve French-language school boards (4 public and 8 separate) were created with funding equivalent to that of English-language school boards.° Throughout the period between 2004 and 2006, funding equal to $30 million was allocated by the Ontario Government to the province's 12 French-language district school boards as a first step in the implementation of the province's French-Language Education Strategy.

Historical overview of French-Language Services in Ontario. retrieved May 2013 from http://www.ofa.gov.on.ca/en/flsa-history.html

10.3 THE KEY POLICY

A key policy for French-language education in Ontario arrived with the launching of the Politique d'aménagement linguistique 2004. The policy's purpose was to "help promote French language and culture, improve student achievement and self-esteem and help keep young Franco-Ontarians in French-language schools." The *Aménagement Linguistique Policy* of 2005° "sets out the guidelines for aménagement linguistique interventions both for the Ministry of Education and for Ontario's French-language school boards." Under this policy, the Ontario government intends to continue its fostering of the French language; it has established "a permanent Elementary and Secondary French-Language Education Task Force to advise the Minister of Education on unique Francophone matters such as promoting French culture, reducing assimilation and helping to retain Francophone students."°

Ministry of Education. (2005). *Aménagement Linguistique Policy.* Toronto, ON: the Author. *retrieved May 2013 from http://www.edu.gov.on.ca/eng/document/policy/linguistique/linguistique.pdf*

Historical overview of French-Language Services in Ontario. retrieved May 2013 from http://www.ofa.gov.on.ca/en/flsa-history.html

10.4 THE FEDERAL GOVERNMENT

The Federal Government has assisted Ontario in its desire to assist French language instruction by entering into the "Provincial-Federal Funding Agreement for French-Language Education and French-as-a-Second-Language Instruction."° The Agreement provides $301

Historical overview of French-Language Services in Ontario. retrieved May 2013 from http://www.ofa.gov.on.ca/en/flsa-history.html

million of federal funding over four years for minority and second-language instruction at the elementary, secondary, and post-secondary levels, as well as an additional $30 million in recognition of the fact that Ontario has the largest minority French-language community in the country.

10.5 STRUCTURES OF FRANCOPHONE EDUCATION IN ONTARIO

10.5.1 French - Language Schools

In Ontario, there are four publicly funded school systems: the French public system, the French Catholic system, the English public system and the English Catholic system. The French public system and the French Catholic system are referred to as the *French-language schools systems* and comprise 12 French-language school boards, which incorporate approximately 425 French-language schools. In these schools, all subjects are taught in French and the mandate from the Ontario Government extends "to protect, enhance and transmit the French language and culture." More particularly, each of the two public French school systems articulates its purposes as follows:

- **French Catholic School System:** A [French] Catholic district school board expresses its *raison d'être* through the Christian faith and the values taught by the Catholic Church and draws on the teachings of this faith in its activities. It offers religious instruction that helps students live their Catholic faith more fully. A Catholic board promotes close cooperation among its schools, parishes, the clergy, educators, and parents.
- **French Public School System:** A [French] public district school board expresses the human, moral, and democratic values of Canadian society. It respects the religious antecedents of all students enrolled in the board. Cooperation among the board, its schools, and the wider community fosters knowledge and appreciation of diversity in a spirit of harmony, tolerance, and compassion.°

Ministry of Education. (2005). *Aménagement Linguistique Policy.* Toronto, ON: the Author. *retrieved May 2013 from http://www.edu.gov.on.ca/eng/document/policy/linguistique/linguistique.pdf*

The French-Language schools are qualitatively different from their English counterparts in Ontario. As the Ontario government states,

> The uniqueness of French-language schools lies in the fact that their mission is not only to educate their students but also to protect, enhance, and transmit the language and culture of the community they serve. Protecting, enhancing, and transmitting the language and culture are an explicit part of their mandate… .In implementing this mandate, French-language schools offer a quality education that meets the needs of every one of their students, while simultaneously providing a social setting, a meeting ground, and a forum for exchange and collaboration with parents and the francophone community, as well as a resource for the community and all

its stakeholders. (p. 7 °)

Ministry of Education. (2005). *Aménagement Linguistique Policy.* Toronto, ON: the Author. *retrieved May 2013 from http://www.edu.gov.on.ca/eng/document/policy/linguistique/linguistique.pdf*

10.5.2 Admission to French Language Schools

Ontario's youth may be admitted to its French Language schools either (a) as entitled to do so under section 23 of the *Canadian Charter of Rights and Freedoms* as a rights holder or (b) by qualifying under section 293 of the *Education Act.*

§ 23 Constitution Act, 1982

The *Charter*° states that Canadian citizens,

> (a) whose first language learned and still understood is that of the English or French linguistic minority population of the province in which they reside, or
>
> (b) who have received their primary school instruction in Canada in English or French and reside in a province where the language in which they received that instruction is the language of the English or French linguistic minority population of the province,
>
> have the right to have their children receive primary and secondary school instruction in that language in that province.

The *Charter* goes on to comment upon continuity of language instruction and "where numbers warrant"—but the Ontario *Education Act*, under section 1 states,

> 1. (1) "French-speaking person" means a child of a person who has the right under subsection 23 (1) or (2), without regard to subsection 23 (3), of the Canadian *Charter of Rights and Freedoms* to have his or her children receive their primary and secondary school instruction in the French language in Ontario; ("francophone")

And further provides this definition:

> "French-language rights holder" means a person who has the right under subsection 23 (1) or (2), without regard to subsection 23 (3), of the Canadian *Charter of Rights and Freedoms* to have his or her children receive their primary and secondary school instruction in the French language in Ontario; ("titulaire des droits liés au français") .

Given the above, it is clear that,

- A parent or guardian who lives in Ontario, is a Canadian citizen and meets at least one of the following criteria is a rights holder:
  - » His/her native language is French, that is, the first language learned and still understood; or
  - » He or she has received his or her education at the elementary level in a French-language education institution in Canada ; or
  - » He or she is the parent (guardian) of a child who has received or receives his/her education at the elementary or secondary

level in a French-language education institution in Canada.

Students who are unable to meet the above criteria, may still apply to attend a French Language school. Under section 293 of the *Education Act*,

> 293. (1) A French-language district school board, on the request of the parent of a pupil who is not a French-speaking person, or of a person who has lawful custody of a pupil who is not a French-speaking person, or of a pupil who is an adult and is not a French-speaking person, may admit the pupil to a school of the board if the admission is approved by majority vote of an admissions committee appointed by the board and composed of:
>
> (a) the principal of the school to which admission is requested;
>
> (b) a teacher of the board; and
>
> (c) a supervisory officer employed by the board.
>
> (2) A school authority that operates a French-language instructional unit, on the request of the parent of a pupil who is not a French-speaking person, or of a person who has lawful custody of a pupil who is not a French-speaking person, or of a pupil who is an adult and is not a French-speaking person, may admit the pupil to the French-language instructional unit if the admission is approved by majority vote of an admissions committee appointed by the school authority and composed of,
>
> (a) the principal of the school to which admission is requested;
>
> (b) a teacher who uses the French language in instruction in the school; and
>
> (c) a French-speaking supervisory officer

Where school authority has no French-speaking supervisory officer

> (3) Where a school authority does not employ a French-speaking supervisory officer, it shall arrange for a French-speaking supervisory officer employed by another board or by the Minister to serve as a member of the admissions committee.

Indeed, the Ontario government has stated that

> French-language schools welcome newcomers who speak neither of Canada's official languages. Special measures are implemented by school boards to assist both the learner and his or her family to better integrate into the community and ensure that the student meets with success at school.°

retrieved May 2013 from http://www.edu.gov.on.ca/eng/amenagement/parent.html

10.5.3 Curriculum

Students in French-language schools learn from the same Ontario curriculum as their counterparts in the English-language school systems. The only difference is that students in French-language schools learn the curriculum in French, and in a French cultural setting. English taught in French-language schools from elementary school to Grade 12 follows the same curriculum as the one delivered in English-language schools.°

retrieved May 2013 from http://www.edu.gov.on.ca/eng/amenagement/parent.html

10.5.4 Funding

It is noteworthy that in 1997 the Ontario government created four public and eight Catholic French-Language school boards and provided the same funding to them as for the English-language school boards. Moreover, between 2004 and 2006, the province allocated $30 million in funding to Ontario's 12 French-language school boards.

10.6 THE FRENCH LANGUAGE IN ENGLISH LANGUAGE SCHOOLS

Under the *French Language Services Act*, the French language is an official language of education in Ontario. Ontario's students are required to study the French language, although several options are available to complete that task. Specifically, it is a requirement that every student study French from Grades 4 to 8 and earn a minimum of one secondary credit in French in order to qualify to receive the Ontario Secondary School Diploma.

10.6.1 Programs

There are three programs offered to Ontario's English Language school students: Core French, Extended French, and French Immersion. Core French is a single academic subject that attempts to "develop a basic usable command of the language."

In Extended French, the language is studied as an academic subject but is also the language of instruction for one additional academic subject—e.g., mathematics. In this program, at least one quarter of the overall instruction is in French.

The French Immersion program moves beyond the extension program where along with French as an academic subject, three or more academic courses are taught in French. Overall, half of the instruction in this program is in French.

The Government of Ontario seeks through these programs to develop the students' skills and knowledge of the French language but also to "help students develop an appreciation of the language and French culture in Canada and the world."°

retrieved May 2013 from http://www.edu.gov.on.ca/eng/amenagement/FLS.html

10.6.2 Curriculum

The Curricula for The Ontario Curriculum: French As a Second Language, 2001: Extended French, Grades 4-8; French Immersion, Grades 1-8 are available on-line from the Ontario Government °

retrieved May 2013 from http://www.edu.gov.on.ca/eng/curriculum/elementary/fsl.html

11.0 ABORIGINAL (FIRST NATIONS, MÉTIS, AND INUIT) EDUCATION IN ONTARIO

11.1 DEFINING THE ISSUES AND TERMINOLOGY

This part describes key documents, trends and organizational patterns for provision of educational services to First Nations, Métis, and Inuit persons in Ontario.

Given that the Province has made a sincere and sustained effort to redress the injustices of the past to Aboriginal peoples with respect to the education of Aboriginal youth, what is the current state of Aboriginal education in Canada? John Irvin of the *National Post* (October 19, 2010) reports,

> The statistics are not encouraging: The proportion of people on reserve who have completed high school has not increased in the past decade and the gap between natives and non-natives is growing. The 2006 census suggested that 46% of young native males and 39% of young native women did not finish high school—compared to 16% and 11% respectively for non-natives. Obviously, this has consequences for employment prospects, but the impact on Canadian society extends well beyond lost talent. For example, U.S. studies suggest a high school diploma reduces the prospect an individual will commit violent or property crime, with one academic suggesting that each additional high school graduate saves the public nearly US$3,000 as a result of the reduction in crime.
>
> Everyone involved in native education acknowledges aboriginal students receive less government funding per head than non-native students in provincial schools—even if they can't agree how much less. Two years ago, Indian Affairs gave me some internal statistics that suggested it spent an average of $6,916 per student in 2006/07. This compared with a national average of $8,165 for non-natives in 2004/05, according to Statistics Canada. This gap has likely widened since then, since native education spending has been pegged

> at increases of 2% a year, while many provincial governments have ramped up spending.

If Irvin is correct, there is much yet to be done in Ontario to assist Aboriginal youth in their education. Therefore, it is noteworthy that the Ontario government is making a sincere attempt to work with Aboriginal peoples in improving the educational plight of Aboriginal students in the province.

retrieved May 2013 from http://www.edu.gov.on.ca/eng/aboriginal/fnmiFramework.pdf

Several further definitions of terminology and issues are below drawn from Appendix D of the *Ontario First Nation, Métis and Inuit Education Policy Framework*:°

- **Aboriginal peoples.** The descendants of the original inhabitants of North America. Section 35(2) of the *Constitution Act*, 1982, states:

  > In this Act, 'Aboriginal peoples of Canada' includes the Indian, Inuit, and Métis peoples of Canada." These separate groups have unique heritages, languages, cultural practices, and spiritual beliefs. Their common link is their indigenous ancestry.

- **Aboriginal rights.** Rights held by some Aboriginal peoples as a result of their ancestors' use and occupancy of traditional territories before contact with Europeans or before British sovereignty in Canada. Aboriginal rights vary from group to group, depending on what customs, practices, and traditions were integral to the distinctive culture of the group.
- **Band.** Defined by the *Indian Act*, in part, as "a body of Indians ... for whose use and benefit in common, lands ... have been set apart." Each band has its own governing band council, usually consisting of a chief and several councillors. The members of the band usually share common values, traditions, and practices rooted in their language and ancestral heritage. Today, many bands prefer to be known as First Nations.
- **First Nation.** A term that came into common usage in the 1970s to replace the word "Indian," which many found offensive. The term "First Nation" has been adopted to replace the word "band" in the names of communities.
- **First Nation Education Authority.** A First Nation Education Authority is comparable to a board of education. Most First Nations have an Education Authority, which is responsible for administering education for the community. It is responsible for hiring teachers and principals working in the community school(s), determines the curriculum to be used in the school(s), and negotiates tuition agreements with local provincially funded school boards when students have to leave the First Nation community to continue their elementary and/or secondary education.
- **Indian.** A term that may have different meanings depending on

context. Under the *Indian Act*, it means "a person who pursuant to this Act is registered as an Indian or is entitled to be registered as an Indian." A number of terms include the word "Indian," such as "Status Indian," "Non-status Indian," and "Treaty Indian." Status Indians are those who are registered as Indians under the *Indian Act*, although some would include those who, although not registered, are entitled to be registered. Non-status Indians are those who lost their status or whose ancestors were never registered or lost their status under former or current provisions of the *Indian Act*. Treaty Indians are those members of a community whose ancestors signed a treaty with the Crown and as a result are entitled to treaty benefits. The term "Indian" was first used by Christopher Columbus in 1492, believing he had reached India.

- ***Indian Act.*** Federal legislation that regulates Indians and reserves and sets out certain federal government powers and responsibilities towards First Nations and their reserved lands. The first *Indian Act* was passed in 1876, although there were a number of pre- and post-Confederation enactments with respect to Indians and reserves prior to 1876. Since then, the act has undergone numerous amendments, revisions, and re-enactments. [Aboriginal Affairs and Northern Development Canada] administers the act.
- **Inuit.** Aboriginal people in northern Canada, living mainly in Nunavut, the Northwest Territories, northern Quebec, and Labrador. Ontario has a very small Inuit population. The Inuit are not covered by the *Indian Act*. The federal government has entered into several major land claim settlements with the Inuit.
- **Métis people.** People of mixed First Nation and European ancestry. The Métis history and culture draws on diverse ancestral origins, such as Scottish, Irish, French, Ojibwe, and Cree.
- **Reserve.** Lands set aside by the federal government for the use and benefit of a specific band or First Nation. The Indian Act provides that this land cannot be owned by individual band or First Nation members.
- **Traditional lands.** Lands used and occupied by First Nations before European contact or the assertion of British sovereignty.
- **Treaty.** A formal agreement between the Crown and Aboriginal peoples.
- **Treaty rights.** Rights specified in a treaty. Rights to hunt and fish in traditional territory and to use and occupy reserves are typical treaty rights. This concept can have different meanings depending on the context and perspective of the user.

11.2 BACKGROUND EDUCATION

In the United States of America, the Indian nations were defeated in wars that were often motivated by the acquisition of land or raw materials, were very bloody, and were often illegal even under the laws of the United States. The end result were proud but militarily defeated peoples uprooted from their historical lands and relegated to patches of land in disparate parts of that nation. In Canada, the situation regarding First Nations was decidedly different. Near the birth of the nation, First Nations peoples joined the Canadian colonists in defending the nation against American invaders and later were courted by the Canadian government into treaties to secure government control over western lands that it feared would otherwise be overrun by Americans. Notwithstanding this relationship, the Canadian government later was to wage war against a legitimate Métis government in Manitoba and hang its leader, Louis Riel, a former member of the Parliament of Canada, for insurrection in what was certainly a suspect political trial.

Further mistreatment of First Nations occurred in British Columbia where native lands were simply taken from native peoples without any treaty settlements being entered into by provincial authorities. Outrages continued as evidenced by the unequal treatment of Aboriginal veterans of the Canadian Armed Services who after serving the country in war were not eligible for the same veteran's benefits as white veterans. Of course, the most outrageous action by the Canadian Government was the attempt to assimilate Aboriginal children (First Nations, Inuit, and Métis) into white society through the creation of the Residential School System.

The Aboriginal people of Canada suffered for generations in what has been described by some as cultural genocide both through that system of residential education, race-based discriminatory laws, and by the neglect of Aboriginal families relegated to ghettos of poverty and despair in urban areas and on reserves.

It is fair to say that in Canada, generations of Aboriginal children have suffered greatly due to the inherently racist nature of North American society and government policies. Not only did such policies hamper their pedagogical development, self-esteem, and well being, but actually caused a menacing harm that would prove to last for generations. The lack of attention to the educational needs of Aboriginal children has had a deep and lasting negative impact on their education—as evidenced by the fact that educational outcomes for aboriginal youth have lagged far behind the rest of the Canadian population.° Certainly, as the Ontario Ministry of Education has noted, historically teachers have failed to be aware to the learning styles particular to the cultures of the First Nations and have lacked any resources for situating learning within the context of the First Nations' cultures. Clearly a change in the understanding of education and First Nations was necessary as stated in the *Report of the Royal Commission on Aboriginal Peoples, Volume 3 - Gathering Strength*, 1966,

National Indian Brotherhood. (1972). *Indian Control of Indian Education*. Ottawa, ON: the Author; Special Committee of the House of Commons on Indian Self-Government. (1983). *The Penner Report*. Ottawa, ON: the Author; Royal Commission on Aboriginal Peoples. (1996). *Final Report*. Ottawa, ON: the Author; Nault Working Group. (2003). *Report on First Nations Education*. Ottawa, ON: the Author

> Throughout history, Aboriginal parents and community

> teachers have expressed the will and aspirations of the Aboriginal community concerning the education of their children. They want education to prepare the children to participate fully in the economic life of their communities and in Canadian society. But this is only part of their vision ... education must develop children and youth as Aboriginal citizens, linguistically and culturally competent to assume the responsibilities of their nations. Youth that emerge from school must be grounded in a strong, positive Aboriginal identity. Consistent with Aboriginal traditions, education must develop the whole child, intellectually, spiritually, emotionally, and physically. (pp. 433-434) °

Royal Commission on Aboriginal Peoples. (1996). *Report of the Royal Commission on Aboriginal Peoples, Volume 3, Gathering Strength*. Ottawa, ON: Canada Communications Group.

Perhaps in recognition of and a response to the legacy of harm and neglect there has been a sincere attempt by Canada's provincial governments to address the educational plight of Aboriginal children. Indeed, in September 2004,

> the Council of Ministers of Education, Canada, identified Aboriginal education as a priority issue. Ministers acknowledged the need to find new and varied ways of working together to improve the outcomes of First Nation, Métis, and Inuit students across both the elementary/ secondary and post secondary education systems. (p. 25 °)

Ministry of Education. (2007). *Ontario First Nation, Métis and Inuit Education Policy Framework*. Toronto, ON: the Author. *retrieved May 2013 from http://www.edu.gov.on.ca/eng/ aboriginal/fnmiFramework.pdf*

Before moving on to the particulars of that Policy, which articulates the intention and direction of the province of Ontario with respect to First Nations education, it would be helpful to provide the legal basis for Aboriginal education under Canada's constitutional documents and federal statutes.

11.3 THE *CONSTITUTION ACT*, 1867 *

Section 91, subsection 24 of the *Constitution Act*, 1867 gives the government of Canada the exclusive right to make laws for "Indians, and Lands reserved for the Indians". At the time of Confederation, aboriginal rights recognized by the *Royal Proclamation of 1763* had not been extinguished for many Indians and Indian lands, most of which were outside the jurisdiction of any province. The assumption of this responsibility by the federal government was logical and probably necessary. Nevertheless, this provision is unusual in the division of powers because it names a class of persons rather than a function. As such it operates at cross purposes to much of the rest of the constitution. For example, the federal government is responsible for Indians, and the provinces are responsible for education, health, and child welfare, but who is responsible for the education, health, and child welfare of Indians? The answers are neither simple nor

* Note: Sections 11.3 through 11.5—and their subsections—were previously published by Dr. Larry Bezeau, then a faculty member of the University of New Brunswick, in *Educational Administration for Canadian Teachers*. It is with his permission that these sections have been reproduced. One ought to note that the perhaps antiquated terminology used by Bezeau is, in fact, the legal terminology still used today in much federal legislation.

consistent across functions.

The word "Indian" is not defined in the *Constitution Act*, 1867, and the only judicial decision concerning the constitutional definition of Indian determined, in 1939, that it includes Eskimos, now called Inuit ("Reference as to ..."). The need for such a determination resulted from the extension in 1912 of the boundaries of the province of Quebec into previously federal territory such that some Inuit came, for the first time, within the boundaries of a province. According to the Supreme Court of Canada, the correct definition of Indian for constitutional purposes is dictated by the usage of the word in Canada and England around 1867. The court did an exhaustive analysis of documents of that period. These included official reports, censuses of North America, letters, draft legislation, and dictionaries. They also compared English documents with French translations. The court rejected the definitional separation of Indians and Eskimos appearing in dictionaries after 1867 and in common use at the time of the decision in favour of the earlier construction of the word. Although we do not know exactly how Indian is defined in the *Constitution Act*, 1867, we may, in the absence of other judicial decisions, refer to its common meaning around the time of Confederation. Surprisingly, one question the courts have never answered, because they have never been asked, is whether the Métis, descendants of Indians and French settlers, are Indians for the purposes of this act. Sanders concludes, using essentially the same reasoning that the Supreme Court of Canada used for the Inuit, that the Métis are constitutional Indians and that to argue otherwise is "contrary to early practice and disruptive of well established patterns of Indian policy." (p. 421 °). Subsection 24 of section 91 is worded in such a way that it operates as two headings, one for Indians and the other for Indian lands. Cases concerning one frequently have no applicability to the other. For the purposes of education, it sometimes matters whether an Indian is on Indian land, but the many court decisions regarding the land question have little relevance to education.

Sanders, DE. (1981). Aboriginal Peoples and the Constitution. *Alberta Law Review*. *19*(3), 410–427.

11.4 THE *CONSTITUTION ACT*, 1982

The *Constitution Act*, 1982 contains three sections with provisions for the aboriginal peoples of Canada. The first section is in the "Canadian *Charter of Rights and Freedoms*," while the other two are outside the *Charter* in a separate part of the Act that deals specifically with aboriginal peoples. These provisions would appear to be most logical in the reverse order and are so dealt with below.

Part II of the *Constitution Act*, 1982 is entitled "Rights of the Aboriginal Peoples of Canada" and contains sections 35 and 35.1.

> 35. (1) The existing aboriginal and treaty rights of the aboriginal peoples of Canada are hereby recognized and affirmed.
>
> (2) In this Act, "aboriginal peoples of Canada" includes the

Indian, Inuit and Métis peoples of Canada.

(3) For greater certainty, in subsection (1) "treaty rights" includes rights that now exist by way of land claims agreements or may be so acquired.

(4) Notwithstanding any other provision of this Act, the aboriginal and treaty rights referred to in subsection (1) are guaranteed equally to male and female persons.

Subsections 1 and 2 above constitute the original section; subsections 3 and 4 were added by a constitutional amendment approved in 1983. The second subsection in Part II (35.1), also added as part of the 1983 amendments, commits Canadian governments to hold a constitutional conference before amending section 91(24) of the *Constitution Act*, 1867 and to invite aboriginal representatives to participate in the discussion of that item.

Potential jurisdictional problems created for aboriginal Canadians by the non-discrimination clauses of the "Canadian *Charter of Rights and Freedoms*" have been avoided by a specific exempting provision contained in the *Charter*. Any legislation dealing with a specific class of persons is likely to be discriminatory, either unfavourable to persons excluded from the class or unfavourable to the class itself. Court challenges are likely from persons inside or outside the class depending on the legislation being challenged. Section 25 of the *Charter* deals with this problem.

25. The guarantee in this *Charter* of certain rights and freedoms shall not be construed so as to abrogate or derogate from any aboriginal, treaty or other rights or freedoms that pertain to the aboriginal peoples of Canada including

(a) any rights or freedoms that have been recognized by the Royal Proclamation of October 7, 1763; and

(b) any rights or freedoms that now exist by way of land claims agreements or may be so acquired.

Legislation that is favourable to aboriginal Canadians and that is covered by the rights and freedoms specified in section 25 cannot be challenged under the *Charter*. As part of the 1983 amendments, paragraph (b) was altered to ensure that both existing and future rights and freedoms would be protected.

11.5 GENERAL PROVISIONS OF THE INDIAN ACT

The day-to-day relationship between the Indians and the government of Canada is controlled by the *Indian Act*, an act of the Parliament of Canada that is administered by the Department of Indian Affairs and Northern Development [now Aboriginal Affairs and Northern Development Canada]. It is important to note that the present *Indian Act* does not cover all Indians as constitutionally defined but may purport to cover some persons who would not meet the constitutional definition of Indian.

11.5.1 Definition of Indian

In practice, federal responsibility for Indian education has been based on the *Indian Act* definition of Indian, which has changed over the years. The Parliament of Canada is free to define "Indian" in its own legislation. But such a definition should not include persons who are excluded by the constitutional definition since, in the area of education, Parliament does not have the right to make laws for these persons.

Section 2 of the present *Indian Act* defines an "Indian" as a "person who pursuant to this Act is registered as an Indian or is entitled to be registered as an Indian." Such a person is sometimes called a "status Indian." Section 4.(1) of the *Indian Act* excludes Inuit from the definition of Indian. A complex set of provisions describes entitlement to registration and the registration procedures. During the 1980s, major changes were made to the rules governing Indian registration, primarily to eliminate gender discrimination. One consequence was a decrease in the number of unregistered Indians and a corresponding increase in the number of registered Indians.

Registration of Indians in its full complexity is a topic well beyond the scope of this book. However, it is worth noting that although Indian status is largely inherited it is quite possible for a registered or status Indian to have no Indian ethnicity or ancestry. Furthermore, a status Indian need not be a Canadian citizen. Finally, the Métis are not Indians under the *Indian Act* in practice they are a provincial responsibility in education and other functions assigned to the provinces.

11.5.2 Jurisdictional Provisions

Under section 4(2) of the *Indian Act*, the federal cabinet may determine that the provisions of the *Indian Act*, except those concerning Indian registration and land surrenders, do not apply to named groups of Indians. This has been used to allow some bands a greater measure of self-government than would otherwise be possible. The move toward aboriginal self-government and exemption from the *Indian Act* has been especially strong in northern Québec and British Columbia. Exempted Indian bands have their own provisions for education.

The basis for resolving potential conflicts between federal and provincial legislation that either implicitly or explicitly concerns Indians is an important one. Powers have been divided between the two levels primarily by function, and the question that must be answered with respect to Indians is which level assumes responsibility for those functions assigned to the provinces. This includes such important functions as education, child welfare, health, civil rights, and municipal institutions. Even in areas where provincial laws govern, the federal government often finances the services provided for Indians.

Section 88 of the *Indian Act*, reproduced below, is an attempt to resolve this difficult jurisdictional question.

> 88. Subject to the terms of any treaty and any other Act of the Parliament of Canada, all laws of general application from time to time in force in any province are applicable to and in respect of Indians in the province, except to the extent that such laws are inconsistent with this Act or any order, rule, regulation or by-law made thereunder, and except to the extent that those laws make provision for any matter for which provision is made by or under this Act.

Provincial laws of general application that do not conflict with an Indian treaty apply to Indians in the absence of specific federal legislation for Indians covering the same matter. Indians must abide by provincial law in matters of motor vehicle registration and child welfare, for example, because of the absence of any federal law making provision in these areas for Indians. With respect to Indians, provincial law gives way to treaties and federal law.

11.6 EDUCATIONAL CLAUSES IN THE INDIAN ACT

The *Indian Act* consists of 152 section on topics such as administration, Indian register, band lists, reserves, special reserves, management of money, election of chiefs and band councils legal rights, and schools. Sections 114 to 122 contain the most relevant educational provisions of the Act and are listed as:

- section 114(1) deals with agreements with provinces and territories. It says "The Governor in Council may authorize the Minister, in accordance with this Act, to enter into agreements on behalf of Her Majesty for the education in accordance with this Act of Indian children, with a. the government of a province; the Commissioner of the Yukon Territory; the Commissioner of the North-West Territories; the Commissioner of Nunavut; a public or separate school board; and a religious or charitable organization." "The Minister , may, in accordance with this Act, establish, operate and maintain schools for Indian children."°

§ 114(2) INDIAN ACT, 1985

- section 115 allows the minister to make regulations on standards for buildings, equipment, teaching, education, inspection and discipline in connection with schools; provide for transportation; enter into agreements with religious organizations for the support and maintenance of children and apply moneys "to or on behalf of a child who is attending a residential school to the maintenance of that child at the school."
- with respect to attendance, every Indian child who has attained

§ 116(1) Indian Act, 1985

the age of seven years is to attend school.° The Act stipulates that "the Minister may require an Indian who has attained the age of six years of age to attend school; require an Indian who becomes sixteen years of age during the school term to continue to attend school until the end of that term; and require an Indian who becomes sixteen years of age to attend school for such further period as the Minister considers advisable, but no Indian shall be required to attend school after he [or she][becomes eighteen years of age."°

§ 116(2) Indian Act, 1985

- an Indian child may not be required to attend school by reason of sickness or unavoidable cause reported to principal; with permission of superintendent, in order to assist in husbandry or urgent and necessary household duties (period not exceeding six weeks); where under efficient instruction at home; or where student is unable to attend because of insufficient accommodation in the school.°

§ 117 Indian Act, 1985

- section 119 provides for the appointment of truant officers, with powers of a peace officer, to ensure that students attend school as required by their age.
- a truant officer may be a member of the Royal Canadian Mounted Police, an appointed special constable or a school teacher and a chief of the band, when authorized by the superintendent.°

§ 122 Indian Act, 1985

- section 118 provides for students whose parents are either Protestant or Roman catholic to not be assigned to a school conducted by a different faith group than the parent. The Act stipulates that only with the written permission of the parent shall a student be assigned to a school conducted under Roman Catholic auspices where the parent is Protestant, or a school conducted under Protestant auspices, where parent is Roman Catholic.
- where the majority of band members belong to one religious denomination, the school is to be taught by a teacher of that denomination. Where the majority of members are not of the same religious denomination, then a meeting of electors shall determine by majority vote shall determined the specific religious denomination of the person to be the teacher of the day school.°

§ 120 Indian Act, 1985

- with the approval of the Minister and under regulation, a Protestant or Roman Catholic ministry may have a separate day school or day school classroom on reserve unless numbers do not warrant.°

§ 121 Indian Act, 1985

11.7 BAND OPERATED SCHOOLS

Canada's federal government has the constitutional responsibility for the funding of First Nations students living on reserves. As First Nations move toward self-government, bands have now established and operate their own schools on reserves, thus replacing the control and operation of reserve schools formerly established and operated by the Department of Indian Affairs. First Nations schools are not subject to provincial jurisdiction and hence they need not follow the provincial curriculum, however, the norm is that these school utilize the provincial curriculum and hire provincially certified teachers to teach in the First Nations schools.

11.7.1 Band Operated Schools in Ontario

The Ontario government recognizes five cohorts of Aboriginal students in Ontario and provides the following statistics which provides a background for recent developments in Ontario's journey in Aboriginal education.

Outlined within Appendix A of the document titled *Ontario First Nation, Métis, and Inuit Education Policy Framework*,° there are five cohorts of Aboriginal students in Ontario, as follows:

retrieved May 2013 from http://www.edu.gov.on.ca/eng/aboriginal/fnmiFramework.pdf

1. First Nation students who live in First Nation communities and attend federally funded elementary or secondary schools in First Nation communities.
    - » The estimated number of students is 20,100 (according to the *2001 Census*).
    - » Elementary and secondary education of these students is the responsibility of the local First Nation Education Authority, the band council, or the federal government.
    - » Funding for the education of these students is provided by the federal government.
    - » Secondary schools in First Nation communities register with the Ministry of Education as private schools in order to offer credit courses leading to the Ontario Secondary School Diploma. In 2005, there were 34 First Nation secondary schools.
    - » The Ministry of Education provides professional development opportunities for teachers and principals in First Nation schools on a fee for-service basis.
2. First Nation students who live in First Nation communities but attend provincially funded elementary or secondary schools under a tuition agreement.
    - » The number of students is 5,212 (according to the Ministry of Education October Report [2004/05])
    - » Some First Nations provide education programming up to Grade 6, others up to Grade 8. Most students must leave their communities to continue their education in provincially funded schools.
    - » A tuition agreement between a First Nation or the federal

government and a school board covers the cost of education provided by the school board.

3. First Nation students who live in the jurisdiction of school boards and attend provincially funded elementary or secondary schools.
   - » The estimated number of students is 18,300 (2001 Census)
   - » Education funding for these students is provided by the Ministry of Education under the Grants for Student Needs (GSN), and the students are treated like all other students of the board.
4. Métis students attend provincially funded elementary or secondary schools.
   - » The estimated number of students is 26,200 (2001 Census)
   - » Education funding for these students is provided by the Ministry of Education under the Grants for Student Needs (GSN), and the students are treated like all other students of the board.
5. Inuit students attend provincially funded elementary or secondary schools.
   - » The estimated number of students is 600 (2001 Census)
   - » Education funding for these students is provided by the Ministry of Education under the Grants for Student Needs (GSN), and the students are treated like all other students of the board:

11.8 RECENT ONTARIO HISTORY

retrieved May 2013 from http://www.ontario.ca/aboriginal/new-approach-aboriginal-affairs

In June of 2005, the Government of Ontario released Ontario's *New Approach to Aboriginal Affairs*.° That approach sought to remedy the challenges in First Nations communities and to stress the importance of education of First Nations youth. In particular, four areas were stressed:

- working with Aboriginal communities and organizations and school boards to develop an Aboriginal Education Policy Framework;
- fostering good relationships between First Nations and school boards;
- establishing clear roles and responsibilities, including those that pertain to the federal government's relationship with First Nations;
- working with the federal government to improve the learning environment and educational outcomes of First Nation students on reserve.

In January of 2007, the Ontario Government released the Ontario First Nation, Métis and Inuit Education Policy Framework,° which was stated as "the foundation for delivering quality education to First Nations, Métis and Inuit students in provincially funded schools in Ontario."° That document noted that an "estimated 50,312 Aboriginal [note: the term Aboriginal includes First Nation, Métis, and Inuit peoples.] students ... attended provincially funded elementary and secondary schools in Ontario (18,300 First Nations, 26,200 Métis, and 600 Inuit students who live in the jurisdictions of school boards, and 5,212 living in First Nations communities but served under a tuition agreement)." The Policy Framework is guided by four principles: excellence and accountability; equity and respect for diversity; inclusiveness, cooperation, and shared responsibility; and respect for constitutional and treaty rights. The goals of the Policy Framework are threefold: to achieve a high level of student achievement; to reduce gaps in student achievement between Aboriginal students and the rest of the province's students, and to engender a high level of public confidence.

retrieved May 2013 from http://www.edu.gov.on.ca/eng/aboriginal/fnmiFramework.pdf

retrieved May 2013 from http://www.edu.gov.on.ca/eng/aboriginal/policy.html

Under each Policy Goal, the province established policy measures of success, and specific strategies to attain the goals. It stated further that it is crucial to Ontario's Aboriginal Education Strategy° and is one of six documents that, on recent inquiry, a representative of the Ministry has suggested are the foundation of the Strategy. The documents are:

retrieved May 2013 from http://www.edu.gov.on.ca/eng/aboriginal

- *Sound Foundations for the Road Ahead*;
- *Background: Aboriginal Education in Ontario*;
- *First Nation, Métis and Inuit Education Policy Framework*;
- *Aboriginal Student Self-Identification*;
- *Curriculum: Native Studies and Native Languages*; and
- *Aboriginal Perspectives: The Teacher's Toolkit*.

One document, *Aboriginal Student Self-Identification*, sought to delineate a process that would allow aboriginal students to self-identify in a respectful and confidential manner so that the Ministry could have some benchmarks for how many aboriginal youth were in the public school systems. The Ontario Native Studies and Native Languages curriculum is offered both to Native students and non-Native students in order to provide information and to raise the knowledge and consciousness of Ontario's youth to "Aboriginal peoples cultures, histories, contributions and perspectives." The curriculum on Native languages is intensive as are the resources for that area.° *The Teachers' Toolkit* " is a new collection of electronic resources from the Ministry of Education to help elementary and secondary teachers bring Aboriginal perspectives into their classrooms."° It provides both teaching ideas and strategies for classroom use.

retrieved May 2013 from http://www.edu.gov.on.ca/eng/curriculum/elementary/nativelang.html

retrieved May 2013 from http://www.edu.gov.on.ca/eng/aboriginal/Guide_Toolkit2009.pdf

retrieved May 2013 from http://www.aboriginalaffairs.gov.on.ca/english/about/about.asp

It should also be noted that in June 2007, "the stand-alone Ministry of Aboriginal Affairs was created to replace the Ontario Secretariat of Aboriginal Affairs"[°] with a wide mandate one part of which was to "promote collaboration and coordination across ministries on Aboriginal policy and programs" which has implications for the education of First Nations students in Ontario.

retrieved May 2013 from http://www.edu.gov.on.ca/eng/aboriginal/RoadAhead.html

In the fall of 2009, "Sound Foundations for the Road Ahead: Progress Report on Implementation of the Ontario First Nation, Métis, and Inuit Education Policy Framework" provided "an overview of the steps the ministry, school boards, schools, and community partners have taken to implement the strategies outlined in the framework and to support First Nation, Métis, and Inuit student success."[°] Funding for aboriginal education had increased from three million to twenty-eight million dollars in four years and enrolment in Native studies and language courses had dramatically increased since 2005 along with more favourable relations between school boards and First Nations.

12.0 PRIVATE SCHOOLS

This part provides an overview of the provisions for the registration, types, funding, staffing, administration and inspection of private schools in Ontario.

Private or independent schools educate a significant number of Ontario's youth. There are approximately 130,000 students in Ontario's 1000 registered private schools, and they are not publicly funded. One of the main reasons for choosing private schools in Ontario is disappointment with the public system.°

retrieved May 2013 from http://www.cisontario.ca/uploaded/Resources_for_Families/UWO_Study.pdf

There are a number of umbrella organizations serving independent schools in Ontario and each school determines which association will best serve its needs. There is no single body that represents all independent schools. Examples of such organizations include the Ontario Federation of Independent Schools° and the Conference of Independent Schools of Ontario.°

retrieved May 2013 from http://www.ofis.ca

retrieved May 2013 from http://www.cisontario.ca

12.1 THE DEFINITION OF A PRIVATE SCHOOL

According to the *Education Act*, a private school ("école privée") is deemed as any educational institution that is partially or entirely funded by sources other than the government, and that students of appropriate age attend for instruction between 9:00 to 16:00 on a typical school day.

12.1.1 The Establishment of a Private School

All private schools that wish to operate in Ontario are obliged to complete and submit to the Ministry a Notice of Intention to Operate a Private School.° Operators of private schools in Ontario are required to notify the Ministry of Education annually of their intention to operate. It is illegal to operate an unregistered private school. Anyone who does so is guilty of an offense and liable to a fine of not more than $50 for every day of school's operation.

§ 16.1 EA

12.2 TYPES OF PRIVATE SCHOOLS

The following classification of private schools is an unofficial one, but it is useful. The various types are not mutually exclusive; it is possible for a school to fit more than one category, and not all schools fit the system well.

- **Nursery Schools and Kindergartens**

  Nursery schools and kindergartens offer instruction to preschool children. In Ontario, many private kindergartens and nursery schools take children at an earlier age than the public system.

- **Single Philosophy**

  Some schools are based on a single philosophy or method of education. These include Waldorf schools based on the philosophy of Rudolf Steiner and schools that follow the teachings of Maria Montessori. If the philosophy is a religious one, the school may be classified as religious or denominational.

- **Specialty**

  Specialty schools offer a regular academic program with extra emphasis on an academic or non-academic subject. There are specialty schools in the plastic and performing arts, for example. There are schools that specialize in ballet. Some schools offer an outdoor or wilderness component that encourages resourcefulness and self-reliance in students. Not all specialty schools are private.

- **Religious or Denominational**

  Religious or denominational schools come in a variety of distinct types, not always Christian. Christian schools representing several denominations, usually fundamentalist Protestant, have increased greatly in number in recent years. Although Roman Catholicism is a Christian denomination, the term "Christian school" is usually reserved for fundamentalist Protestant schools. Other denominations, including the Anglicans and the United Church, have private schools, some of which would be regarded as elite. Non-Christian religious schools include Jewish or Hebrew schools, and Islamic schools.

- **Elite**

  The traditional view of a private school is that of an elite school. Many private schools position themselves as having longstanding traditions and a history dating back many decades. They are frequently residential and usually expensive. In the past, most were single-sex schools, but in recent years many have become co-educational.

- **Military**

  Military schools at the secondary level are much more common in the United States than in Canada. They are usually residential and sometimes all male. Their curriculum includes academic subjects combined with military training, both offered in an atmosphere of military discipline. Some of these could be classified as elite.

- **Catch-up**

  Catch-up schools take children who are having difficulty in public schools and provide remedial help with a view to re-inserting them into the public school system. They tend to emphasize the diagnosis of learning difficulties followed by tailor-made programs and tutoring. The category of catch-up schools overlaps with that of special-education schools.

- **Preparatory/University Preparatory**

  Preparatory schools typically offer challenging academic programs designed to help students prepare for application to university. Many are non-residential and may offer AP or IB programs or other specialized approaches to education. An example of such school is Leahurst College in Kingston.°

  retrieved May 2013 from http://www.leahurstcollege.ca/

- **Other**

  Other types of private schools include heritage language and immersion schools. A heritage language is a language associated with one's ancestry or culture such as Ukrainian, Greek, Italian, or German. English and French, being official languages, are excluded from this category. Some private schools cater to foreign students who wish to finish secondary school here to make it easier for them to enter Canadian universities. Finally there are private schools that are residential and provide around-the-clock supervision of children but which do not otherwise seem to differ much from public schools.

12.3 PRIVATE SCHOOL CURRICULUM

Private elementary schools are not obliged to use the Ontario curriculum.° Therefore, the ministry does not conduct inspections of private elementary schools. Secondary schools are also not obliged to use the Ontario curriculum. However, because the Ministry will not issue the Ontario Secondary School Diploma to a student who does not have academic credits from courses which have approved by the Ministry, some private secondary schools choose to offer credits towards the Ontario Secondary School Diploma. Private secondary schools are authorized to grant credits only after a Ministry inspection and this authority may be revoked following an inspection. The credit granting status of a school is noted on the Ministry's website.°

retrieved May 2013 from http://www.edu.gov.on.ca/eng/general/elemsec/privsch/

retrieved May 2013 from http://www.edu.gov.on.ca/eng/general/elemsec/privsch/

12.4 TEACHERS IN PRIVATE SCHOOLS

Teachers in Ontario's private schools need not by certified by the Ontario College of Teachers. Those teachers who teach in private schools and who are also certified are listed on the Ontario College of Teachers' website. If a private school operator wants a school's teacher's teaching performance to be assessed for certification purposes, such a request can be made to the Ministry asking that the Minister of Education inspect a teacher's performance as she or he "requires the recommendation of a supervisory officer for certification purposes."°

§ 168 EA

12.5 THE ROLE OF THE MINISTRY OF EDUCATION

The Ministry of Education has an overseer's role in the province's private schools. In particular, it demands that the schools keep accurate records on a variety of matters and that the schools provide that data regularly to the Ministry. It may also inspect the school at the request of the operator for specific purposes. Lastly, the Ministry may invoke its statutory right to inspect any school as stated below.

12.5.1 *Record Keeping*

The Ministry keeps a publicly accessible record of information on all private schools which includes "general information about each school, such as religious affiliation, the availability of residential facilities, and, more importantly, whether or not the school offers credits towards the Ontario Secondary School Diploma (OSSD)." This information is gleamed from the annual statistical reports which each private school must provide to the Ministry. In particular, the Minister may require that "the principal, headmaster, headmistress or person in charge of a private school" provide "information regarding enrollment, staff, courses of study and other information as and when required by the Minister."° Failure to comply with such a Ministerial requirement is guilty of an offence under the *Education Act* and liable for a fine of a maximum of $200.00.°

§ 16.5 EA

§ 16.5 EA

12.5.2 *Requested Ministry Inspection*

A private school operator may ask for an inspection of the school with regard to "the standard of instruction in the subjects leading to the Ontario secondary school diploma, the secondary school graduation diploma, and to the secondary school honour graduation diploma, and the Ministry may determine and charge a fee for such inspection."° The Ministry inspects only the standard of instruction, but not premises, health and safety practices or matters relating to staffing. °

§ 16(7)EA

retrieved May 2013 from http://www.edu.gov.on.ca/eng/general/elemsec/privsch/

12.5.3 *Directed Ministry Inspection*

Although the Ministry does not normally inspect private elementary schools nor private secondary schools that do not offer credits towards the Ontario Secondary School Diploma, it may direct an inspection by a supervisory officer and if obstructed, the party obstructing is liable for a fine of no more than $500.00.° The relevant section reads,

§ 16(6) EA

> 16 (6) The Minister may direct one or more supervisory officers to inspect a private school, in which case each such supervisory officer may enter the school at all reasonable hours and conduct an inspection of the school and any records or documents relating thereto, and every person who prevents or obstructs or attempts to prevent or obstruct any such entry or inspection is guilty of an offence and on conviction is liable to a fine of not more than $500.

12.6 PARENTS' DUE DILIGENCE IN THE SELECTION OF A PRIVATE SCHOOL

The Ontario Ministry of Education has provided a check list of items which parents considering sending their child of children to a private school might consider.° It constitutes a due diligence list for parents and is worth restating here. The Ministry states,

retrieved May 2013 from http://www.edu.gov.on.ca/eng/general/elemsec/privsch/

When thinking about entering into a contract with a private school, consumers may want to consider, among others, the following issues. Does the school:

- conduct criminal reference checks on staff?
- use the Ontario curriculum?
- employ teachers who are members of the Ontario College of Teachers?
- administer Education Quality and Accountability Act testing?
- publish its admissions policy?
- enter into contracts with parents regarding fees, refunds and other policies?
- have a procedure for resolving complaints by parents and pupils?
- publish the number of years it has been in operation?
- have liability insurance in respect of accidents involving pupils?

13.0 HOME SCHOOLING

This part details home schooling provision, registration obligations, parental rights and responsibilities, school boards responsibilities, and monitoring authority in Ontario.

Although home schooling involves the removal of the child from the public schools, it does not result in the placement of the child in an institutional setting. Instead the child is educated at home, usually by one or both parents. Parents who teach their children at home take advantage of the "efficient instruction elsewhere" clauses or special home-schooling clauses found in provincial school legislation. Normally, an educator acting on behalf of the province or a local school board determines whether the instruction is efficient. If it is not, the children can be forced to return to the public schools if they are within the age of compulsory attendance.

In contrast to private schooling, most home schooling takes place at the lower grade levels. Many parents who teach their children at home while they are at the elementary level find that their homes lack the specialized facilities available in secondary schools for science and technology teaching. Most parents lack sufficient knowledge of advanced subject specialties to provide adequate high school instruction. Another problem faced by home-schoolers, not exclusively at the secondary level, is the lack of opportunity for the child to socialize with children of the same age.

There are many reasons given by parents for schooling their children at home. Dissatisfaction with the public schools is a common theme, but some parents find them too rigid and others too flexible, some too secular and others too religious. Some cite not enough discipline in public schools and others too much. Some parents want their children to avoid sex education, and others, allergenic substances. Some see the public schools as condoning the use of drugs and do not wish to expose their children to this temptation. Some parents use travel as a teaching tool while home schooling, a method not as readily available to the public schools.

There are approximately 20,000 home schooled students in Ontario.° They are not, if between the age of six and sixteen, exempt from

retrieved May 2013 from http://www.ofis.ca/

receiving an education, as required under section 21(1) of the *Education Act*. However, pursuant to 21(2)(a) if "the child is receiving satisfactory instruction at home or elsewhere," she or he is exempt from attending the public school system. Notwithstanding that exemption the Ministry of Education maintains a strong interest in their pedagogical development. That interest is articulated in Policy/Program Memorandum No. 131 (hereafter, in this section, "the Policy"). The Ministry states,

> This memorandum provides direction to school boards ... and schools concerning policies related to home schooling and the excusing of children from school who are receiving home schooling. School boards should bring this memorandum to the attention of parents ... who are providing home schooling.

13.1 PARENTS' RESPONSIBILITY

The responsibility of parents who wish to home school their child or children begins with the submission of an annual letter entitled "Notification of intent to provide home schooling" to the local school board, saying that "we understand our responsibility under the *Education Act* to provide satisfactory instruction for our school-age child(ren) and do hereby declare our intent to do so."° An example of the content and format of that letter is provided for in Appendix B to the Policy. Noteworthy is that Ministry of Education does not require that children who are home schooled follow the Ontario curriculum.

POLICY/PROGRAM MEMORANDUM NO. 131, "HOME SCHOOLING"

13.1.1 Parental Access to School Board Resources

Home-schooling parents who have given notification to their local school board may download "curriculum policy documents and curriculum support material" from the Ministry website,° and support services from the Ministry of Health and Long-Term Care under the local community care access centres. A parent may also enrol a child in a course through the Independent Learning Center provided that the school board is informed of the patents intent to have their child be home schooled. An administration fee must be paid by parents for this service. Home schooling parents may also avail themselves of student testing services—at no cost, provided by the local school board. The Ministry's Policy says:

retrieved May 2013 from http://www.edu.gov.on.ca

> Parents providing home schooling may wish their child(ren) to participate in assessments for students in Grades 3, 6, and 9, and/or the Ontario Secondary School Literacy Test (normally given to students in Grade 10), all of which are administered by the Education Quality and Accountability Office (EQAO). These parents must contact the school board by September 30 (or another date specified by the school board) of the year in which the assessments/tests are being conducted for information about the dates, times, and locations. Parents who wish their children to participate in

any of these assessments/tests will not be charged a fee either by the board or by the EQAO.

13.2 SCHOOL BOARD RESPONSIBILITY

Under the Policy, the Board will accept the Notification on the face of it and not investigate unless it has "reasonable grounds" to believe that satisfactory instruction is not being provided.° The Board will send a letter to home schooling parents that states that it understands that the parents are providing satisfactory instruction and offering testing for Grades 3, 6, and 9 and/or the Ontario Secondary School Literacy Test that is normally provided in Grade 10. A copy of the Policy will also be provided to those parents.°

Policy/Program Memorandum No. 131, "Home Schooling"

for a sample letter from a board, see: Policy/Program Memorandum No. 131, "Home Schooling"

13.2.1 Partial Enrolment

In the event that a home schooled student attends a school part-time, the school board will receive a prorated per-pupil grant "according to the amount of time the student is in attendance at the school." Although a home schooled student may not be enrolled as a full-time day student, if she or he is receiving some instruction in the school that shall be noted in the appropriate school register.

13.2.2 Home Schooled Student Entering Public Secondary Schooling

Home schooled students, other than mature students, who seek to be enrolled in secondary school will be admitted according to their equivalent grade level as per the Ontario Secondary Schools, Grades 9 to 12: Program and Diploma Requirements, 1999 (OSS).°

retrieved May 2013 from http://www.edu.gov.on.ca/eng/document/curricul/secondary/oss/oss.pdf

13.2.3 School Board Investigation

The Grounds

As with all interpretation of statutes or policies it is difficult to say what in particular might constitute "reasonable." The Ministry provides examples of what would constitute "reasonable grounds" for a school board investigation of a home schooling situation:°

Policy/Program Memorandum No. 131, "Home Schooling"

- refusal of a parent to notify the board in writing of the intent to provide home schooling
- a credible report of concern by a third party with respect to the instruction being provided in the home
- evidence that the child was removed from attendance at school because of ongoing conflicts with the school, not for the purpose of home schooling

- a history of absenteeism by the child prior to the parent's notifying the board of the intent to provide home schooling

The Procedure

POLICY/PROGRAM MEMORANDUM No. 131, "HOME SCHOOLING"

The school board may have one of its officials meet with the family or ask the family for a written report on its home schooling to the board. There are three primary issues in these cases: (a) is there a plan for the education of the child, (b) do the plans "ensure literacy and numeracy at developmentally appropriate levels" and (c) are there " plans for assessing the child's achievement."°

The Questions

Although sample questions that may be asked by a board representative of the home-schooling parents are on the Ministry website that provides the Policy, they are significant enough to be repeated in this Guide. They are as follows:

» If the board chooses to have a board official meet with the family, the following questions and requests may be used as a guide for the discussion: Do you have an instructional plan, regularly planned instructional time, and a daily work schedule? Please provide details.

» What subjects are you teaching?

» What do you expect to accomplish with your child in English, mathematics, and other subjects this year?

» Is your instructional program based on the Ontario curriculum or on a different curriculum?

» If you follow the Ontario curriculum, which documents do you use?

» If you do not use Ontario curriculum documents, please describe the curriculum documents you do use.

» Please describe the typical kinds of activities that you provide for your child in the subjects you are teaching. Please provide samples of your child's work in each subject area.

» What types of materials do you use to assist you in accomplishing your plans (e.g., encyclopaedias, textbooks, magazines, newspapers, television programs, materials on the Internet, computer programs)?

» Please describe the techniques you use to assess your child's learning.

» Do you use community resources to support your instruction? If so, which ones?

» Do you network with other parents who provide home

schooling? How?

» Please feel free to provide any other information that would help the board determine whether instruction is satisfactory.

If the board requests a written response from the home schooling parents, the form entitled "Appendix D Sample of Form for Gathering Information in an Investigation" is sent to the Parents to be completed and returned to the school board.°

POLICY/PROGRAM MEMORANDUM NO. 131, "HOME SCHOOLING"

13.3 THE PROVINCIAL SCHOOL ATTENDANCE COUNSELLOR

13.3.1 The Request

In the event that neither of the above approaches result in a satisfactory resolution of the issues, the board may act under sections 24(2) or 30 of the *Education Act* to request that an inquiry be commenced by the Provincial School Attendance Counsellor.° However, the Policy is directive in that before a board may make such a request it must ensure that it has:

POLICY/PROGRAM MEMORANDUM NO. 131, "HOME SCHOOLING"

- taken appropriate steps to determine whether the child is receiving satisfactory instruction;
- retained documentation of its communication with the parents, including copies of written communication, notes on telephone calls and other verbal communication, a record of the types of communication (e.g., telephone call, registered letter), and a record of the number of attempts to communicate;
- retained documentation on the nature of the information and material provided by the parent in response to the board's investigation;
- prepared a factual summary of its investigation, including a conclusion, which will be forwarded to the Provincial School Attendance Counsellor.°

POLICY/PROGRAM MEMORANDUM NO. 131, "HOME SCHOOLING"

> If the inquiry determines that the child is not receiving satisfactory instruction and the Provincial School Attendance Counsellor orders that the child attend school, the school board must determine the appropriate action to be taken.°

POLICY/PROGRAM MEMORANDUM NO. 131, "HOME SCHOOLING"

Home schooling is a well regulated aspect of Ontario's system for the education of its youth. Parents are supported by the Province through the provision of various opportunities to enrich students' knowledge and to be appropriately and voluntarily assessed in their educative growth by the province. The Ministry retains jurisdiction over all of Ontario's students and their education through the actions of local school boards and ensures that every child in Ontario will have the opportunity for satisfactory instruction.

14.0 STUDENT SAFETY, HEALTH, AND WELFARE

This part presents an overview of the topics on student safety, positive and accepting school climate, student health and wellbeing, and protection of student against negligence and abuse.

14.1 SAFE SCHOOLS LEGISLATION

Safety is a fundamental part of our education system, as a safe school environment enables learning and teaching in a school climate that fosters responsibility, respect and academic excellence. The Ontario's Safe Schools legislation includes a number of coordinated initiatives to ensure that schools are safe, inclusive, and accepting. Historical and recent developments in safe schools legislation are presented below in a chronological order.

14.1.1 Bill 81, The Safe Schools Act, 2001

As the beginning of 21st century was marked by the perceptions of the increased violence in schools, it became common knowledge in Canada in general (and in Ontario in particular) that the state of public schools was in trouble. In order to address this social problem, policy-makers sought urgent solutions, enabling Bill 81 to be passed in 2001 becoming the Safe Schools Act. Bill 81 was put forth in year 2000 particularly to amend Section 23 of the *Education Act* that previously limited the authority to suspend students to school principals and the authority to expel students belonged to school boards. The bill was passed in 2001 under a conservative government and named the *Safe Schools Act*, 2001. In order to address the public school safety and discipline concerns in Ontario's public schools, the Act contained a code of conduct that list specific infractions that would warrant mandatory student suspensions, expulsions from a particular school or school board, and full expulsions (expulsion from all public school boards in the province). This Act also included police-school board protocol that was to be arranged between each school board and the police. Under this Act, school boards were allowed to add more infractions to their board policies for which suspensions and expulsions are either mandatory or discretionary.

14.1.2 Zero Tolerance Policies

Daniel, Y., & Bondy, K. (2008). Safe Schools and Zero tolerance: Policy, program and practice in Ontario. *Canadian Journal of Educational Administration and Policy, 70.*

The Code of Conduct provisions introduced the concept referred to as "zero tolerance" into the Ontario school system. Despite the existence of empirical data from the United Kingdom, the U.S. and other Canadian provinces (e.g., Nova Scotia) that noted several shortcomings of zero-tolerance policies, Ontario nevertheless introduced a "zero tolerance" type policy as a political solution to educational issue.°Although, policymakers in Ontario were careful not to employ the phrase "zero tolerance" in policy documents, individual school boards used the phrase in its policies.

The phrase "zero tolerance," first coined in U.S. national policy to stomp out the social problem of illegal drug use and trafficking, aims at asserting authority. "Zero tolerance" policies are based on the assumption that individuals act and misbehave in a rational manner and if it is made impossible (zero likeliness) for transgressors to get away with the transgression, they will not do it. Because of their root in a criminal justice system, "zero tolerance" policies and philosophies in schools strengthened the similarities between schools and prisons. In the educational context, "zero tolerance" means intolerance of violence in schools by imposing some consequences for action. "Zero tolerance" had become a hot and debated issue among academics and practitioners. While the proponents argue that zero-tolerance policies rid schools of dangerous students and, in so doing, create safer spaces for others at school, opponents state that there is no evidence that schools that use "zero tolerance" procedures are safer. In recent years, there has been growing criticism of zero tolerance policies in schools, mainly because of the excesses to which such policies lead (see an example of such criticism by using the link in the area below). One of the main lines of argument against "zero tolerance" policies in Ontario was that true zero tolerance policies have no discretion. The black and white approach to violence doesn't take into account the context or needs of the student. Ontario legislation responded to these criticisms by including mitigating factors (however, because mitigating factors are embedded in the legislation, which do give principals discretion in dealing with the behaviour, zero is not really a zero anymore: one can't have mitigating factors and true zero tolerance). Despite mitigating factors, Ontario schools have witnessed a significant increase of suspensions and expulsions. The number of expelled students increased from 106 in 2000-2001 to 1,909 in 2003-2004. The number of suspensions also increased overtime. 152,626 students were suspended in 2003-2004, but in actuality 229,394 suspensions were issued that year. Therefore, multiple suspensions were given to individuals. Male students accounted for 77% of suspended students, and students with exceptionalities accounted for an alarming 18%.

Under the *Safe Schools Act*, the Ministry required school boards to implement the policies, guidelines, and procedures in accordance with the Act, but it did not require school boards to establish courses and services for suspended and expelled students. Therefore, students who were suspended and expelled became the sole responsibility of their families and communities, with the school providing no support. This meant that these students' human right to public education was denied during the time they were away from school.

Criticisms of "zero tolerance" approach and other consequences of implementing the *Safe Schools Act* were brought to the attention of Ontario Human Rights Commission (OHRC) by parents, educators, and community organizations. Just before the Act was reviewed by the Ministry of Education (Safe Schools Action Team) five years after it was implemented, the OHRC adamantly requested that the Ministry gather race-based and gender-based data to ensure that their review was thorough and addressed the concerns raised by the public.

14.1.3 Bill 212, Progressive Discipline and School Safety Act, 2007

The *Safe Schools Act* was reviewed at the end of 2005 – beginning of 2006, and Bill 212, an act to amend the *Education Act* in respect of student behaviour, discipline, and safety was passed in June 2007. It has been renamed the *Progressive Discipline and School Safety Act*, 2007. Its provisions took effect on February 1, 2008. Bill 212 amends, but does not completely repeal, the "safe school" provisions of Bill 81. While the philosophy of Bill 81 was grounded in a "zero tolerance" approach to student discipline and led to a regime of strict discipline on the part of most school boards, Bill 212 was prepared in response to a complaint launched by the Ontario Human Rights Commission regarding the unfair treatment through the "zero tolerance" approach to student discipline of racialized students and students with disabilities claiming that "safe schools" provision of the *Education Act* and the Ministry's and school board's (TDSB) policies on discipline had a disproportionately negative impact on pupils from racialized communities and pupils with disabilities and was therefore discriminatory." The term progressive discipline was the key ingredient to the amended Act which is intended to move away from notions of zero-tolerance. In fact, under this new Act, school boards are now required to remove the zero-tolerance phrase from all policy documents.

Progressive Discipline emphasizes a move away from punitive measures that isolate students who exhibit inappropriate behaviour, towards a supportive new approach that corrects and counsels. Progressive discipline is notable in that it is flexible, involves parents and support professionals. In this way it is a policy that aligns more closely with the *Youth Criminal Justice Act* than the zero tolerance

"A case of excessive force?"

In R v. Godin (1996, New Brunswick Queen's Bench), two grade five boys accused their teacher of striking them in the face in class and in the corridor when trying to break up a fight between them. The teacher had, in fact, used his hands to turn the boys' heads around to force them to pay attention to him after the fight. The boys' parents complained to the police, and the teacher was charged and convicted. He was given a conditional discharge but appealed the conviction.

The New Brunswick Court of Queen's Bench acquitted the teacher on all counts. It held that the teacher had a duty to teach and maintain control and was entitled to use reasonable force to stop the fighting and disruptive behaviour. In fact, failure to do so would have been dereliction of duty and a possible cause for negligence.

The test applied to determine whether a teacher is justified in using section 43 [of the Criminal Code] as a defense is as follows:

- Did the student commit a breach of school discipline that justified the use of force?
- Alternately, was the teacher's belief that the discipline was justified founded on reasonable and probable grounds.
- Was the teacher's belief that discipline was justified ill-founded, but completely honest and genuine.
- Was the use of force "by way of correction?"
- Was the force used reasonable under the circumstances and not of the kind to cause serious or permanent injury to the student?

"Corporal Punishment: Conviction Overturned" *EduLaw for Canadian Schools, 7*(10), June 1996

approach could. Main changes included:

- Extending the right to discipline to include actions that are off school property where the activity has a negative impact on school climate;
- Adding "bullying" to the list of infractions;
- Removing full expulsion and the power of principals to expel and the power of teachers to suspend;
- Revising the committee of the board that would hear suspension appeals or hold expulsion hearings to at least three members of the board;
- Revising the time frame that a board must hear and determine a suspension appeal to 15 school days;
- Replacing the mandatory suspension model with a more discretionary model;
- Superintendent must be consulted for a suspension of 11 or more days;
- Removing the process of senior board personnel to review a suspension appeal;
- 16 or 17 year olds may be party to an expulsion or suspension appeal hearing where they have withdrawn from parental control;
- Requiring programs for suspended and expelled students;

- Expelled students remain students of the board so long as they are in attendance in an expulsion program provided by the board;
- In considering whether to suspend a student the principal is required to take into account any mitigating factors or other factors set out in the legislation.

One of the major changes was the alternative suspension program. It was required to be based on restorative practices; to follow a wellness model rather than a deficit model – building strengths and capacities in suspended students; to focus on social and emotional skill development in the following areas: conflict resolution, anger management, critical thinking and problem solving, communication skills, and resiliency factors; to include home school delivery via modified day; to provide the support of a half-time Child and Youth Worker; and other progressive discipline initiatives. The rules for suspensions and expulsions of students were specified in Regulation 472/07, which specified a due process for disciplinary action.

14.1.4 Bill 157, Keeping Our Kids Safe at School Act, 2010

Education Amendment Act (Keeping Our Kids Safe at School) or as it is better known as Bill 157, was passed in June, 2009 by the Ontario government particularly in response to the vagueness in understandings of what constituted violence and safety in schools across school boards. This legislation amends Part XIII (Behaviour, Discipline, and Safety) of the *Education Act.* Bill 157 targeted codes of conducts which have now been modified in the following areas, (a) duty to respond, (b) duty to report, (c) supports for students, and (d) delegation of the principal's authority. Bill 157 came into force on February 1, 2010 and Ontario is the first province in Canada to enforce legislation of this kind.

The Bill requires board employees who become aware that a pupil may have engaged in an activity listed in subsection 306 (1) or 310 (1) of the Act (e.g., violent incidents, such as bullying) to report on the matter to the principal. All respondents must respond in a safe manner that protects the personal safety of the respondent and the safety of others. If it is unsafe to respond, it is important to report verbally to the principal as soon as possible. It also requires a principal who believes that a pupil has been harmed as a result of an incident to notify the parents or guardians of the students involved in the incident. This legislation also requires school staff who observe a pupil behaving in a way that is likely to have a negative impact on the school climate to respond in accordance with policies and guidelines, i.e., intervene and address inappropriate, disrespectful behaviour among students. Changes in the responsibility to report behaviours and incidents include all school board employees, cafeteria staff, and community-school liaison officers who become aware of a student who may have engaged in an activity for which suspension or expulsion must be considered. They must report in writing to the principal the details of the activity, no later than the end of the school day.

All reports regarding incidents that violate sections 306 (activities leading to suspension) or 310 (activities leading to expulsion) of the *Education Act* must be done in writing. It is common that all school board employees have access to the Intranet to communicate with their colleagues in their board and can complete the reporting through the Safe Schools Progressive Discipline Application. All other reporting should be done through the main office of the school. Principals are now also required to contact the parents or guardians of students who were victims of acts carried out by other students who were suspended or expelled as a result. However, under Bill 157, principals are prohibited from contacting the parents or guardians of victims if there is a chance that the victims will suffer further harm at home. Additionally, principals require written consent from students who are 18 years old to disclose information to their parents or guardians.

14.1.5 Bill 13, Accepting Schools Act, 2012

On June 5, 2012, Bill 13, the *Accepting Schools Act*, was passed, amending the *Education Act*. These amendments came in effect on September 1, 2012. Bill 13 requires school boards to prevent and address inappropriate and disrespectful behaviour among students in schools. These behaviours include bullying, discrimination and harassment. The new law makes it clear that these behaviours are unacceptable in our schools. It promotes respect and understanding for all students regardless of race, gender, sexual orientation, disability or any other factor. It requires school boards and schools to have policies in place on progressive discipline, bullying prevention and intervention, and on equity and inclusive education. It outlines tougher consequences for students who bully others (suspending and considering expulsion (an important provision of this bill) if the student has already been suspended for bullying and the student's presence in the school creates an unacceptable risk to the safety of others, or the bullying was motivated by bias, prejudice or hate). The *Education Act* already requires supports for suspended and expelled students if students are expelled or on long-term suspension (more than five school days), they will receive academic/non-academic support through a suspension/expulsion program. Students who are suspended for up to five school days will receive a homework package. The school boards are required to provide training and information to teachers and other school staff on an annual basis about bullying prevention and promoting positive school climates, and include goals around positive school climate and bullying prevention in their multi-year plans and make these plans available to the public.

It also outlines new principals' duties to investigate all reports submitted by board employees, and to notify parents of students who have engaged in behaviour for which they can be suspended or expelled and that harmed another student. Similar notification provisions exist for parents of students who have been affected by bullying or harmed. Bill 13 also requires schools to provide support for students who want to lead activities or organizations that promote positive school climate. It also expanded responsibility for organizations using school property to follow the relevant Provincial Code of Conduct and the requirement to add "to prevent bullying" to board Codes of Conduct.

14.2 POSITIVE SCHOOL CLIMATE

The *Education Act*° stipulates that schools in Ontario are to be safe, inclusive and accepting of all students. According to PPM 128, a school should be a place that promotes responsibility, respect, civility, and academic excellence in a safe learning and teaching environment.° A positive school climate exists when all members of the school community feel safe, included, and accepted, and actively promote positive behaviours and interactions. Building and sustaining a positive school climate is a complex challenge requiring evidence-informed solutions and a whole-school approach, which involves all members of the school community.

§ 300 EA

POLICY/PROGRAM MEMORANDUM NO. 128, "PROVINCIAL CODE OF CONDUCT AND SCHOOL BOARD CODES OF CONDUCT"

This goal can be achieved by encouraging a positive school climate and preventing inappropriate behaviour, such as bullying, sexual assault, gender-based violence, and incidents based on homophobia, transphobia, or biphobia. In order to provide students with a safe learning environment, mechanisms are to be in place to address inappropriate pupil behaviour and promote early intervention; to provide support to pupils who are impacted by inappropriate behaviour of other pupils; and to establish disciplinary approaches that promote positive behaviour and use measures that include appropriate consequences and supports for pupils to address inappropriate behaviour.

All students, parents, teachers and other school staff have the right to be safe, and to feel safe, in their school community. With this right comes the responsibility to contribute to a positive school climate. School boards are charged with adopting and implementing "measures to promote the safety of the board's students and staff."° They are responsible for developing and implementing safe schools policies and programs that actively involve parents and families, they are also expected to work with community agencies and local organizations to develop protocols for facilitating referrals and to provide services and support for students and their parents and families. Boards and schools therefore are required to focus on prevention and early intervention as the key to maintaining a positive school environment in which students can learn and teachers can teach.

§ 11(6)(f) EA

Promoting a Positive School Climate: A Resource for Schools, *retrieved May 2013 from http://www.edu.gov.on.ca/eng/parents/ResourceDocEng.pdf*

There are many dimensions of student welfare, including the social, physical, and emotional aspects of a student's life. School personnel and policy-makers are increasingly taking this fact into account in the provision of services to students and in the ways that schools are organized. A number of elements were identified by the Ministry of Education as those that promote a positive school climate:°

- **Student Voice.** Schools give students the opportunity to provide input on matters related to their learning and school environment. Students are given various opportunities to lead and/or contribute to school activities. Student perspectives are taken into account in the decision-making process, and students are encouraged to be involved at all levels.
- **Parent Engagement.** Schools provide parents with opportunities to learn about, support and actively engage in their children's experience at school.
- **Community Partnerships.** Schools engage community groups to work with the school in a mutually beneficial way to support students and/or parents.
- **Learning Environment.** Schools provide students with a wide range of opportunities and ways to learn and to practise and demonstrate their learning. Students learn about the diversity of their world and come to understand the importance of learning.
- **Social-Emotional Environment.** Schools promote fairness, equity, respect for all, and a sense of belonging and connectedness. They create a safe and caring environment for all.
- **Physical Environment.** The school environment, inside and outside the building, is welcoming and makes the school a safe place that is conducive to learning.

Policy/Program Memorandum No. 145, "Progressive Discipline and Promoting Positive Student Behaviour"

According to PPM 145,° schools are required to conduct anonymous school climate surveys of their students every two years and to share the results with their safe schools teams.

14.2.1 *Code of Conduct*

§ 301(1) EA

The *Education Act* states that "the Minister may establish a code of conduct governing the behaviour of all persons in schools."° In 2000, the Minister of Education issued the Code of Conduct, setting out regulations to be followed by school boards to ensure a standardized systematic way of addressing safety and discipline issues. As a policy of the Minister, the Code of Conduct was applicable on school premises, school buses, and at school events. The subsequent revisions in 2007 and 2012 reflected the major safe school legislation changes. The current revision of the provincial Code of Conduct (as outlined in PPM 128)° reflects Bill 13 amendments to the *Education Act* that pertain to the promotion of a safe, inclusive, and accepting school climate. The provincial Code of Conduct sets clear provincial

Policy/Program Memorandum No. 128, "Provincial Code of Conduct and School Board Codes of Conduct"

standards of behaviour that apply to students whether they are on school property, on school buses, at school-related events or activities, or in other circumstances that could have an impact on the school climate. They also apply to all individuals involved in the publicly funded school system – principals, teachers, other school staff, parents, volunteers, and community groups. Standards of behaviour include respect, civility, responsible citizenship, and safety.°

Parents' Guide to the Ontario Code of Conduct, 2008, *retrieved May 2013 from http://www.edu.gov.on.ca/eng/safeschools/code.pdf*

The following are the purposes of this provincial code of conduct:°

§ 301(2) EA

1. To ensure that all members of the school community, especially people in positions of authority, are treated with respect and dignity.
2. To promote responsible citizenship by encouraging appropriate participation in the civic life of the school community.
3. To maintain an environment where conflict and difference can be addressed in a manner characterized by respect and civility.
4. To encourage the use of non-violent means to resolve conflict.
5. To promote the safety of people in the schools.
6. To discourage the use of alcohol and illegal drugs.
7. To prevent bullying in schools.

Every school board is responsible for bringing the code of conduct to the attention of students, parents and guardians and others who may be present in schools under the jurisdiction of the board.° They are to develop their own codes of conduct, whereas the standards of behaviour in school board codes of conduct must be consistent with the requirements outlined in the provincial code of conduct.

§ 301(3) EA

14.2.2 Equity and Inclusive Education

With the purpose of reducing discrimination and embracing diversity in schools, the Ontario Equity and Inclusive Education Strategy was launched in 2009. This strategy is designed to promote fundamental human rights as described in the Ontario Human Rights Code and the Canadian *Charter of Rights and Freedoms*, as well as standards outlined in the provincial Code of Conduct. The strategy aims to ensure that all students, parents, and other members of the school community are welcomed and respected; and, that every student is supported and inspired to succeed in a culture of high expectations for learning.° The strategy aims to help better identify and remove discriminatory biases and systemic barriers to student achievement — related to racism, sexism, homophobia and other forms of discrimination — that may prevent some students from reaching their full potential. It is based on three goals: shared and committed leadership; equity and inclusive education policies and practices; and, accountability and transparency.

Realizing the Promise of Diversity: Ontario's Equity and Inclusive Education Strategy, 2009, *retrieved May 2013 from http://www.edu.gov.on.ca/eng/policyfunding/equity.pdf*

All school boards are required to review and/or develop, implement

POLICY/PROGRAM MEMORANDUM NO. 119, "DEVELOPING AND IMPLEMENTING EQUITY AND INCLUSIVE EDUCATION POLICIES IN ONTARIO SCHOOLS"

Equity and Inclusive Education in Ontario Schools: Guidelines for Policy Development and Implementation, 2009, *retrieved May 2013 from http://www.edu.gov.on.ca/eng/policyfunding/inclusiveguide.pdf*

and monitor an equity and inclusive education policy as per requirements outlined in PPM No. 119,° in the policy document *Realizing the Promise of Diversity: Ontario's Equity and Inclusive Education Strategy*, and in the document *Equity and Inclusive Education in Ontario Schools: Guidelines for Policy Development and Implementation*. School boards are required to embed the principles of equity and inclusive education in all aspects of their operations, including policy development, programming, and practices related to research, curriculum resources, instruction, and assessment.°

School board policies must be comprehensive and must cover the prohibited grounds of discrimination set out in the Ontario Human Rights Code on any of the following grounds: race, colour, ancestry, place of origin, citizenship, ethnic origin, disability, creed (includes religion), sex, sexual orientation, age, family status, and marital status. Boards may also address related issues resulting from the intersection of the dimensions of diversity that can also act as a systemic barrier to student learning.

School boards and schools are expected to use inclusive curriculum and assessment practices and effective instructional strategies that reflect the diverse needs of all students and the learning pathways that they are taking. Schools must provide students and staff with authentic and relevant opportunities to learn about diverse histories, cultures, and perspectives and to enable students and other school community members to see themselves represented in the curriculum, resources, programs, and culture of the school. Students should be able to feel engaged in and empowered by what they are learning, supported by teachers and staff, and welcomed in their learning environment.

14.3 POSITIVE STUDENT BEHAVIOUR, DUTIES, AND DISCIPLINE

14.3.1 *Duties of Students*

§ 23(1) REGULATION 298

Together with the rights that students have to access and benefit from educational services, they also have duties concerning their attendance and deportment.° Students are required to:

- exercise diligence in studies;
- exercise self-discipline;
- accept discipline as would be exercised by a kind, firm, and judicious parent;
- attend classes punctually and regularly;
- be courteous to fellow pupils and obedient and courteous to teachers;

- be clean in person and habits;
- take the required tests and examinations; and
- show respect for school property.

Students are accountable for their conduct to the school principal while on the school premises, on out-of-school activities that are part of the school program, and while travelling on a school bus or on a bus under contract to a board.

14.3.2 Bullying and Harassment

Under the *Education Act*, there are clear legal responsibilities for school boards, principals and teachers to provide a safe, orderly school environment. For their part, students are responsible for observing approved standards of deportment, courtesy and respect for the rights of others. Despite the law, harassment and bullying have been a fact of life in some school environments, but in recent years there has been an effort to make those behaviors unacceptable in schools and elsewhere. And courts have become involved ruling that school boards will be held responsible for bullying when it is allowed to continue without administrative actions to prohibit it or address it when it arises.

The Criminal Code of Canada provides guidance where bullying is severe enough to be considered criminal harassment. Section 264(1) of the Criminal Code states that "no person shall….engage in conduct that causes the other person reasonably, and in all circumstances, to fear for their safety or the safety of anyone known to them." Conduct that is prohibited consists of:

- repeatedly following from place to place the other person;
- repeatedly communicating with, directly or indirectly, the other person;
- besetting or watching the dwelling-house or place where the other person resides, works, or carries on business or happens to be;
- engaging in threatening conduct directed at the other person or any member of their family.

Growing awareness of bullying, and initiatives such as the "safe schools" movement have resulted in provincial and school board policies and specific processes both practical and reactive, to deal with instances of bullying, intimidation and harassment.

Bullying can be seen to mean a number of different actions, but all are based on common factors: a power imbalance, a repetition of incidents, an intent to harm, and victim distress. The *Education Act*° defines bullying as a form of repeated, persistent, and aggressive behaviour directed at an individual or individuals that is intended to cause (or should be known to cause) fear and distress and/or harm to another person's body, feelings, self-esteem, or reputation. § 1(1) EA

Bullying occurs in a context where there is a real or perceived power imbalance between the pupil and the individual based on factors such as size, strength, age, intelligence, peer group power, economic status, social status, religion, ethnic origin, sexual orientation, family circumstances, gender, gender identity, gender expression, race, disability or the receipt of special education. Bullying can be physical (e.g., hitting, pushing, slapping, tripping, damaging property), verbal (e.g., name calling, mocking, insults, threats, and sexist, racist, homophobic, or transphobic comments), or social/psychological (e.g., excluding the victim, spreading rumors, ignoring, humiliating). Harm to the victims of bullying may be physical, mental, emotional, and psychological. Bullying may occur in the school or during school activities, or outside the school through the use of any physical, verbal, electronic, written, or other means.

14.3.3 Technology-mediated Issues in Schools and Cyberbullying

In the past two decades a revolution in communication technology has had a profound effect on society and a concurrent impact on education and schools. The advent of the internet, and of numerous electronic communications devices have affected, to varying degrees teaching and learning, and relationships between students and between students and teachers. Although mostly positive in nature, the impact of technological change has necessitated revisions in laws, policies and procedures to address any negative consequences.

Cyberbullying involves the use of communication technology to support deliberate, repeated, and hostile behavior intended to harm others. Cyberbullying is most often aimed at students but it can also be used to attack the reputation of teachers, administrators, or others. Cyberbullying, like other forms of bullying, is about power and control, but it is somewhat different in that it can be conducted more anonymously and away from direct supervision, especially when carried out on home computers or other devices outside school.

§ 1(1.0.0.1) EA

Cyber-bullying occurs through the use of technology (spreading images and video, hurtful comments through social networking such as Facebook, Twitter, and YouTube, emails, cell phone text and multimedia messages, instant messaging, defamatory web logs (blogs)). It may also include:°

- creating a web page or a blog in which the creator assumes the identity of another person;
- impersonating another person as the author of content or messages posted on the internet; and
- communicating material electronically to more than one individual or posting material on a website that may be accessed by one or more individuals.

The law does provide guidance, assistance, and protection in addressing problems arising from technological changes. As noted above, cyberbullying has been recently added into the definition of bullying in the *Education Act*. Other legislation addresses this issue through interpretation of broad principles rather than through laws aimed at specific devices. Ontario's *Libel and Slander Act*,° for example, addresses the matter of defamatory printed or broadcasted words (libel) or spoken works (slander). While the Act specifically refers to malicious publication in newspapers, the principle is thought to apply broadly to other forms of "publishing" including by electronic means. Furthermore, reference to "words" also includes pictures, visual images, gestures, and other methods of signifying meaning.

LIBEL AND SLANDER ACT, 1990

The *Criminal Code of Canada* prohibits "defaming libel" material published without justification that would likely injure the reputation of a person or expose that person to hatred, contempt or ridicule, or is designed to insult the person.° The Code specifically refers to newspapers, magazines or periodicals containing public news but legal challenges have been initiated which would include the electronic media as well. The *Criminal Code* does refer to "electro-magnetic, acoustic, mechanical or other device[s]" but the focus of that reference is to issues related to the invasion of privacy such as in the interception of computer transmissions.°

§ 297 CRIMINAL CODE OF CANADA, 1985

§ 183 CRIMINAL CODE OF CANADA, 1985

14.3.4 Bullying Prevention and Intervention

According to PPM 144, school boards are required to develop and implement policies on bullying prevention and intervention. °Every board must establish a bullying prevention and intervention plan for the schools of the board, and must require that all schools implement the board's plan.° When establishing their plan, boards must solicit the views of students, teachers, principals, and other staff of the board, volunteers working in the schools, parents of the students, school councils, and the local community.°

POLICY/PROGRAM MEMORANDUM NO. 144, "BULLYING PREVENTION AND INTERVENTION"

§ 303.3(1) EA

§ 303.3(3) EA

Board policies must include a comprehensive strategy to address incidents of bullying, including appropriate and timely responses. Provisions must include programs, interventions, and other supports for students who have been bullied, students who have observed incidents of bullying, and students who have engaged in bullying.° The programs, intervention, and other supports should be curriculum-linked and consistent with a progressive discipline approach and may be provided by social workers, psychologists, or other professionals who have training in similar fields, as determined by the board. Each school in Ontario must have a safe schools team working to promote a safer and more welcoming learning environment. Teams include the school principal, a teacher, a student (where appropriate), a parent and a member from the broader community. School boards should provide opportunities for all students to participate in equity and inclusive education, bullying prevention, and leadership initiatives within their own school. Boards must review their bullying prevention

§ 170(1)(7.2) EA

and intervention plan at least once every two years.

School boards may address the issue of cyber-bullying in various ways, from specific policies and procedures to proactive educational programs designed to impress upon students that cyber-bullying like all other forms of bullying is unacceptable. School boards may develop policies and procedures to govern the use of communications technologies in school. One commonly used procedure it to employ blocking software and filters on in-school computer systems to prevent access to inappropriate websites which, for some, include social networking sites such as Facebook and YouTube. Another approach is related to "cell-phone use" policies. While some school boards have developed explicit "no-cell-after-the-bell" policies, others do not have such policies, and it is left up to the school to adopt it if it so wishes. In the absence of board or school policies, teachers may set explicit limits in their class.

Bullying Awareness and Prevention Week

Ontario has designated the week beginning on the third Sunday of November as Bullying Awareness and Prevention Week to help promote safe schools and a positive learning environment. Safe Schools Teams usually plan creative activities or launch initiatives that heighten awareness of bullying and its impact on the school community. By conducting Bullying Awareness and Prevention Week activities, schools are promoting positive change in student achievement and well-being.

Policy/Program Memorandum No. 145, "Progressive Discipline and Promoting Positive Student Behaviour"

14.3.5 Progressive Discipline

As outlined in PPM 145,° progressive discipline is a whole-school approach that utilizes a continuum of prevention programs, interventions, supports, and consequences to address inappropriate student behaviour and to build upon strategies that promote and foster positive behaviours. When inappropriate behaviour occurs, the application of disciplinary measures shifts from punitive to corrective and supportive approaches. Schools are required to utilize a range of interventions, supports, and consequences that are developmentally and socio-emotionally appropriate and include learning opportunities for reinforcing positive behaviour while helping students to make better choices.

Drawing upon evidence-informed practices that promote positive student behaviour, school boards are required to develop and implement a board policy on progressive discipline that supports positive student behaviour. School boards must require that all their schools develop and implement a school-wide progressive discipline plan. Boards are expected to establish performance indicators for monitoring, reviewing, and evaluating the effectiveness of board policies and procedures related to progressive discipline in consultation with teachers, school staff, students, parents, school councils, and community service providers. In revising their policies and guidelines on progressive discipline, boards have the flexibility to take into account local needs and circumstances, such as geographical considerations, demographics, cultural considerations, and availability of board and community supports and resources.

14.3.6 *Suspensions and Expulsions*

Suspensions and expulsions are disciplinary actions against students who engaged in activities at school, at a school-related activity, or in any other circumstances where the student's behaviour has a negative impact on the school climate.

Suspension means temporary removal of student from school for a specific period of time. Suspensions may be short-term (up to 5 school days) or long-term (up to 20 school days). Students cannot take part in school activities or events while suspended. Only the principal of the school has the authority to suspend students. Upon the receipt of report about the incident, the principal determines what disciplinary action is required. Some situations will require the principal to consider suspension; in more serious incidents, the principal will automatically suspend students and consider whether to recommend expulsion.

If the incident leads to suspension, the principal is required to inform the aggressor's parents within 24 hours of the incident, followed by the written notice detailing the reason for and the duration of the suspension, as well as the appeal process.

According to the *Education Act*,° a principal may consider suspension for the following reasons: § 306(1) EA

- Uttering a threat to inflict serious bodily harm on another person;
- Possessing alcohol or illegal drugs;
- Being under the influence of alcohol;
- Swearing at a teacher or at another person in a position of authority;
- Committing an act of vandalism that causes extensive damage to school property at the pupil's school or to property located on the premises of the pupil's school;
- Bullying;
- Any other activity for which a principal may suspend a student under a policy of the board.

When considering suspension for the above reasons, the principal must consider the mitigating and other factors concerning the individual student:

- The student's age;

- The student's history, (for example, disciplinary history; whether progressive discipline has already been tried; or personal history such as a recent trauma in the student's life);
- Whether the student can control his/her behaviour;
- Whether the student can understand the possible consequences of his/her behaviour;
- Whether the student's presence in the school creates an unacceptable risk to anyone else;
- Whether the behaviour is related to harassment because of the student's race, ethnic origin, religion, disability, gender, sexual orientation or any other type of harassment;
- How the discipline will affect the student's ongoing education.

For special needs students who have an Individual Education Plan, the principal will also consider:

- Whether the behaviour was a manifestation of a disability identified in the student's plan;
- Whether appropriate accommodation has been provided;
- Whether suspension is likely to aggravate or worsen the student's behaviour or conduct.

Policy/Program Memorandum No. 141, "School Board Programs for Students on Long-Term Suspension"

Students who are suspended from school have opportunities to continue learning and to help them stay on track with their education. Students who are suspended for one to five school days are expected to receive a homework package. According to PPM 141,° a Student Action Plan (SAP) must be developed for every student on a long-term suspension who makes a commitment to attend the board program for suspended students. Students who are suspended for six to 10 school days must be offered an academic program that will help them keep learning. Students who are suspended for 11 to 20 school days must be offered an academic program, as well as supports to promote positive behaviour. All suspensions can be appealed to the school board.

§ 310(1) EA

Expulsion means a removal of student from school for an indefinite period of time. Students are suspended while expulsion is being considered by the school board. Only school boards can expel students upon the recommendation of the principal. Students must be immediately suspended and expulsion considered if they have engaged in any of the following behaviours:°

- Possessing a weapon, including possessing a firearm.
- Using a weapon to cause or to threaten bodily harm to another person.
- Committing physical assault on another person that causes bodily harm requiring treatment by a medical practitioner.

- Committing sexual assault.
- Trafficking in weapons or in illegal drugs.
- Committing robbery.
- Giving alcohol to a minor.
- Bullying, if,
    - » the pupil has previously been suspended for engaging in bullying, and
    - » the pupil's continuing presence in the school creates an unacceptable risk to the safety of another person.
- Any of the activities leading to possible suspension° if they are motivated by bias, prejudice or hate based on race, national or ethnic origin, language, colour, religion, sex, age, mental or physical disability, sexual orientation, gender identity, gender expression, or any other similar factor. § 306(1) EA

In the process of investigation and before recommending to the school board that a student be expelled, the principal must consider the following mitigating and other factors:

- The student's age
- The student's history (for example, disciplinary history; whether progressive discipline has already been tried; or personal history such as a recent trauma in the student's life)
- Whether the student can control his/her behaviour
- Whether the student can understand the possible consequences of his/her behaviour
- Whether the student's presence in the school creates an unacceptable risk to anyone else's safety
- Whether the behaviour is related to harassment because of the student's race, ethnic origin, religion, disability, gender, sexual orientation or any other type of harassment
- How the discipline will impact the student's ongoing education.
- If students have special education needs and have an Individual Education Plan, the principal will also consider:
    - » Whether the behaviour was a manifestation of a disability identified in the student's plan
    - » Whether appropriate accommodation has been provided
    - » Whether expulsion is likely to aggravate or worsen the student's behaviour or conduct.

If students have special education needs and have an Individual Education Plan, the principal must also consider:

- Whether the behaviour was a manifestation of a disability identified in the student's plan
- Whether appropriate accommodation has been provided
- Whether expulsion is likely to aggravate or worsen the student's behaviour or conduct.

Policy/Program Memorandum No. 142, "School Board Programs for Expelled Students"

The school board will decide whether students are expelled from their own school or from all schools of the board. Expelled students who are expelled from all schools in their board cannot go to school or take part in school activities or events. According to PPM 142,° if students are expelled only from their school, they will be assigned to another school in the board and provided with supports and resources (e.g., anger-management counselling). If students are expelled from all schools in the board, the board must offer them academic and additional supports to promote positive behaviour in a program for expelled students. A Student Action Plan (SAP) must be developed along with the re-entry plan to assist with the student's return and integration into the school. When students complete the program, they can return to their original school or a school in a different school board. All expulsions can be appealed to a tribunal.

14.3.7 *Reporting and Responding to Incidents*

Because a positive school climate is essential for students to succeed in school, all stakeholders – staff, students, parents, community agencies – have an important role in making schools safer by reporting and responding to incidents that have a negative impact on the school climate.

§ 300.2 EA

All school board employees have a duty to report in writing to their principal any incident that must be considered for suspension or expulsion.° Employees included in this list are vice principals; teachers and educational assistants; all non-teaching staff, such as those involved in social work, child and youth work; psychology and other related disciplines; administrative and custodial staff; and school bus drivers.

§ 300.4 EA

§ 5 Regulation 412/09

§ 300.2(2) EA

All staff who work directly with students must respond to incidents that will have a negative impact on the school climate.° These could include instances of inappropriate and disrespectful behaviour among students, including racist, sexist, and/or homophobic comments, graffiti or vandalism. Employees included in this list are principals and vice principals, teachers, educational assistants and other non-teaching staff, such as those involved in social work, child and youth work, psychology and other related disciplines. Board employees are not required to respond to the incidents if responding would, in their opinion, cause immediate physical harm to themselves, a student, or any other person.° In these cases they are expected to report the incident to the principal as soon as it is safe to do so.°

14.4 DISCIPLINE AND USE OF FORCE

If effective work in a school is to be carried on, a measure of good order must be maintained. According to common law (or commonly accepted principles that have accumulated over an extended period of time as a result of precedent and tradition), every parent, or person standing in the place of a parent, shall behave toward children in their care as would a wise, kind, firm, and judicious parent. Case law (or the law of precedence from various legal cases) specifies that courts must ask themselves three questions in dealing with the use of force toward pupils:

- Was the teacher acting within the scope of their authority?
- Was there cause for force?
- Was the force used reasonable under the circumstances?

Statutory law (or the law established by act of legislature), provides the following guidelines in:

- The *Education Act* (duties of pupils/teachers);
- The *Charter of Rights and Freedoms* (freedom from cruel and unusual punishment; right to safety of person);
- The *Criminal Code* (particularly sections 27, 30, 34, 37, 38, 43)

Education Act stipulates that acceptance of discipline by a student does not include or authorize corporal punishment.° The Criminal Code of Canada provides the basis for immediate action in the context of violent confrontations. Section 27 of the Code indicates that individuals are permitted to use reasonable force to prevent the commission of an offence that would likely cause immediate or serious injury to a person or property. Section 30 indicates that individuals who witness a breach of the peace are empowered to do a number of things including the use of force to prevent a continuation of the breach and to detain the perpetrator for the purpose of delivering him or her to a peace officer. Section 34 entitles an individual the justification for the use of necessary force to defend him or herself against an unprovoked assault. Section 37 provides that an individual is justified in using necessary force to prevent an assault against him-herself or someone under his or her protection. Section 38 suggests that people may use reasonable force in the defense of personal property. In the case of any violent confrontation, a teacher, school administrator, or any school personnel is given justification for the use of force.

§ 23(2) Regulation 298

According to Section 43, every school teacher, parent, or person standing in the place of a parent is justified in using force by way of correction toward a pupil or child, as the case may be, who is under his care, if the force does not exceed what is reasonable under the circumstances.° *Prosser on Torts* (1941) said:

§ 43 Criminal Code of Canada, 1985

> A parent or one who stands in place of a parent, may use reasonable force, including corporal punishment, for discipline and control. A school teacher has the same authority. It is sometimes said that the parent, by sending the child to school, has delegated his discipline to the teacher; but since many children go to public schools under compulsion of law, and the child may well be punished over the objection of the parent, a sounder reason is the necessity for maintaining order in and about school.

Note that in section 43, the special defense available to teachers, parents and others who stand "in the place of a parent" (often referred to by the Latin phrase "*in loco parentis*"), only applies if force is used for the purpose of correction, if the force used does not exceed what is reasonable under the circumstances, and if the student involved is under the care of the teacher involved. The defense in section 43 would not apply if, for example, the judge found that the teacher used force for the purpose of revenge or to humiliate the pupil. It also would not apply if the teacher used more force than was reasonable.

CANADIAN FOUNDATION FOR CHILDREN, YOUTH AND THE LAW V CANADA (ATTORNEY GENERAL), 2004 SCC 4

In 2004, the Supreme Court of Canada° offered some degree of clarity related to the interpretation of section 43 within the context of the Constitution (specifically, the question before the court was, is section 43 constitutional given section 7 of the *Charter of Rights and Freedoms*?); the result offered additional instruction for teachers and other personnel in Canadian schools. In its ruling, the majority of the Court's nine justices concluded that section 43 does not infringe a child's right to security of the person or equality, and similarly it does not constitute a defense of cruel or unusual punishment. Importantly, the ruling retained the delimitation that section 43 only applies as a defence for parents, guardians, and school teachers, and further delimited the interpretation of the section to educative circumstances.

Highlighted in the 2004 Supreme Court ruling are two central concepts: (a) "by way of correction," and (b) "reasonable under the circumstances." Correction entails the assumption that force used by these select individuals against a child must be corrective—sober, reasoned, and directly addressing an undesirable behaviour, with the intent to restrain, control, or express disapproval. Such correction may only be employed when the child has the developmental capacity to understand and benefit from its use—thus, it is not defensible to exert corrective force against children under the age of two years, nor against children with mental incapacities or disabilities. The reference to reasonability under a given set of circumstances assumes that the force will be transitory and trifling, neither harms nor degrades the child, and is proportional to the error or misbehaviour. As an analogue to the earlier mentioned question of age appropriateness, reasonable also implies that the force ought not be used against young adults, given its likelihood to precipitate aggressive or antisocial responses. In the context of schools, reasonable means that the force must not be corporal punishment, but does permit teachers to forcibly remove or constrain unruly students in pursuit of compliance with given instructions. More broadly, the force must not involve objects (rulers, sticks, belts, and the like) and may never be directed at the head.°

Barnett, J. (2008), *The "spanking" law: Section 43 of the Criminal Code*. Ottawa, ON: Parliament of Canada, Law and Governance Division. Retrieved May 2013 from http://www.parl.gc.ca/content/lop/researchpublications/prb0510-e.htm

14.4.1 "No Touch" Policy

Virtually all school jurisdictions in Canada have long since forbidden the use of corporal punishment (e.g., "the strap"). Many school boards may develop and implement "no touch" policies; that is, policies that forbid teachers from touching pupils in any circumstances. As there is no uniform requirements for school boards to establish such policies, each school board's policy may vary in their guidelines.

14.4.2 Assault

Educators may be charged with the criminal offence of assault when the use of force becomes unreasonable. A person commits assault when:°

§ 265(1) Criminal Code of Canada, 1985

- without consent of another person, applies force intentionally to that other person, directly or indirectly;
- attempts or threatens, by an act or gesture, to apply force to another person on reasonable grounds; or
- while openly wearing or carrying a weapon or an imitation thereof, he accosts or impedes another person or begs.

Section 266 speculates that everyone one who commits an assault is guilty of an indictable offence and liable to imprisonment for a term of not exceeding five years or an offence punishable by summary conviction. The person who, in committing an assault, carries, uses or threatens to use a weapon or an imitation thereof, or causes bodily harm to the complainant, is guilty of an indictable offence and liable to imprisonment for a term not exceeding ten years.° Section 268 outlines that person is guilty of an aggravated assault who wounds, maims, disfigures or endangers the life of the complainant and is liable to imprisonment for a term not exceeding fourteen years. Whoever unlawfully causes bodily harm to any person is guilty of an indictable offence and liable to imprisonment for a term not exceeding ten years.°

§ 267 Criminal Code of Canada, 1985

§ 269 Criminal Code of Canada, 1985

14.5 LOCAL POLICE/ SCHOOL BOARD PROTOCOLS

Police play a vital role in supporting and enhancing the efforts of schools and their communities to make schools safe places in which to learn and work. In addition to responding to and investigating school-related incidents, police are essential partners in the prevention of crime and violence in schools. It is the policy direction of the Ministry of Education and the Ministry of Community Safety and Correctional Services that school boards and police services establish and follow a police/school board protocol to ensure a shared understanding of the respective roles, procedures, and decision-making authority of the two parties in preserving and promoting school safety.

Provincial Model for a Local Police/School Board Protocol, 2011, *retrieved May 2013 from http://www.edu.gov.on.ca/eng/document/brochure/protocol/locprote.pdf*

The Provincial Model for a Local Police/School Board Protocol° identifies 22 elements that must be included in such protocols, and sets out requirements for related procedures, such as procedures for reporting to police, search and seizure procedures, detainment and arrest, supports for victims, investigating incidents involving suspension or expulsion during the police investigations of those incidents, and contacting parents when students are to be interviewed by police. The document also sets out provincial policy for developing and maintaining lock-down procedures for elementary and secondary schools. When developing local police/school board protocols, school boards and police services must consider all relevant federal and provincial legislation.

Policy/Program Memorandum No. 120, "Reporting Violent Incidents to the Ministry of Education"

According to PPM No. 120,° school boards are required to provide annual reports to the Ministry of Education (using the Ontario School Information System [OnSIS]) about all violent incidents that occur on school premises during school-run programs, whether they were committed by a student of the school or by any other person. Boards must also collect and analyze data on the nature of violent incidents to support the development of board policies and to inform board and school improvement plans.

14.6 SEARCH AND SEIZURE

Under both the common law and The *Education Act*, students are subject to the general discipline of the school. School authorities (principals) have the responsibility for the supervision of the school and the well-being and good order of the students in their control. Therefore, school authorities have the right to conduct searches of students, their lockers, belongings and desks and seize the retrieved evidence.

The legality of a search depends simply upon reasonableness in all of the circumstances.

Determining reasonableness is a two-step process:

- whether the action was justified at its inception; and
- whether the search actually conducted was reasonably related in scope to the circumstances which justify the interference in the first place.

The search must not be excessively intrusive. Principals have a discretion in minor offences whether or not to call in parents and involve the police. Police must notify the principal before conducting searches on school premises (under some exigent circumstances, police may execute a search without a warrant and without notice to the principal).

Section 8 of the Canadian *Charter of Rights and Freedoms* guarantees that Canadians are to be secure against unreasonable search and seizure. What does that guarantee mean in the context of the administration of schools?

R v JMG (1987), 54 CR (3D) 380 (ONT. CA)

In a case R *v* JMG,° the leading authority in Canada regarding the right to conduct searches and make seizures in schools, the Ontario Court of Appeal upheld: "Society has an interest in the maintenance of proper educational environment which involve being able to enforce school discipline efficiently and effectively." The court held the search of a student for drugs to be a logical extension of normal discipline procedures to which students submit when they attend school.

To Search or not to Search?

The vice-principal of a junior high school was told by students that a 13 year old student was selling drugs and would have some in his possession at a school dance later that evening.

At the dance, the vice-principal located the student and escorted him to his office where he telephoned the police. A police officer arrived, spoke briefly with the vice-principal outside the office. When the two then enter office, the police officer introduced himself and sat down. The vice principal searched the student and found a small amount of marijuana in the student's sock. The police officer then took control of the investigation and the student was charged with possession of a controlled substance.

At trial the judge ruled that the vice-principal had acted as an agent of the police, as established by precedents in an earlier case. As such, evidence of any crime discovered during the course of a search may be used only if the search was carried out under the proper authority of a search warrant, which had not been done. The evidence against M.J.M. was dismissed. The decision was overturned on appeal by the Nova Scotia Court of Appeal and that decision was appealed to the Supreme Court of Canada.

The Supreme Court of Canada held that the Canadian ***Charter of Rights and Freedoms*** did apply to school boards, but it agreed with the Nova Scotia Court of Appeal that educators had a compelling interest in maintaining a safe educational environment and that students had a lower expectation of privacy while in school. In effect, the Supreme Court ruled that school authorities did have the right to search a student.

In so doing, the Supreme Court provided guidance to school authorities in the matter of search and seizure, stating that,

- a warrant is not essential in order to conduct a search of a student;
- the school authority must have reasonable grounds to believe there has been a breach of school regulations or discipline and that a search of a student would reveal evidence of that breach;
- school authorities are in the best position to assess information given to them to justify a search;
- reasonable grounds might include: credible information from one student; information from more than one student; a teacher's or principal's own observations; or any combination of the above; and
- the search itself must be carried out in a reasonable manner. It should be conducted in a sensitive manner and be minimally intrusive.

Educational Law Reporter, 10(37)

R v. M(MR) [1998] 3 SCR 393

The other case, R *v* M(MR),° decided by the Supreme Court of Canada, illustrates many of the issues at hand.

This case, and others, have noted that while a search conducted by a school administrator is similar to that of a police investigation, the analogy is incomplete. Courts have ruled that the expectation of privacy in a school environment where there are reasonable grounds for believing a criminal activity has occurred is lower that outside the school. Moreover, courts have noted that society has an interest in maintaining proper order and discipline in schools. Since school administrators are given the responsibility of ensuring discipline, they should be given latitude in doing so, provided of course that they have "reasonable" grounds for doing so and conduct themselves in a "reasonable" manner.

Parents and others want to ensure that schools are free of weapons, alcohol and illegal drugs, as well as from gang-related activities.

R v AM [2008] 1 SCR 569

In an important judgment made in April 2008, the Supreme Court of Canada further clarified expectations of privacy for students.° The case involved student, AM, who was charged with possession of drugs for the purpose of trafficking when marijuana and "magic mushrooms" were found in his backpack during a warrant less, random search of an Ontario school by police using a "sniffer dog." Although the principal had given permission for the search, at the trial in 2002, the judge ruled that the search was "unreasonable" under section 8 of the *Charter of Rights and Freedoms*. He excluded the evidence obtained during the search and acquitted the student. The Crown appealed and lost the appeal. Eventually the case was heard by the Supreme Court which supported the lower courts findings that the search contravened section 8 of the *Charter* since the dog sniff amounts to a search. They thus upheld the student's acquittal.

In their ruling the justices noted that "teenagers have little expectation of privacy from the searching eyes and fingers of parents," but expect the content of their backpacks kept from the "random and speculative scrutiny of the police." They did point out, however, that the police had common law authority to use sniffer dogs in appropriate circumstances, to investigate, for example, the potential presence of guns or explosives in the school. The Supreme Court reiterated the need for school authorities to maintain order and security in schools.

Summing up the impact of this latest Supreme Court ruling for school authorities the following should be emphasized:

- random warrantless police searches, especially those using "sniffer dogs" and used as a crime prevention investigation technique are unreasonable under the *Charter of Rights and Freedoms*;
- police searches are allowed in schools, but only where they are based on "reasonable suspicions;"
- school authorities, in carrying out their duties, are given more latitude in the matter of searches;

- students can expect some "privacy" in a school setting, but that expectation can be modified when circumstances make a search urgently necessary or reasonable;
- backpacks contain personal items and thus command a measure of privacy;
- any search must be done in a reasonable manner.

14.7 YOUTH CRIMINAL JUSTICE ACT

The *Youth Criminal Justice Act* (YCJA) is the legislation that governs the way in which youths are prosecuted under Canada's criminal justice system.° This act replaced the *Young Offenders Act* (YOA) in 2003 to govern the application of criminal and correctional law to youth 12 years old or older, but younger than 18 at the time of committing the offence (Section 2). Youth aged 14 to 17 may be tried and/or sentenced as adults under certain conditions. The *Youth Criminal Justice Act*, while not holding children to the same level of accountability as adults, recognizes both their responsibility for their actions and their legal rights and freedoms. Generally speaking, the *Youth Criminal Justice Act*, does not describe offences. Instead it provides procedures for dealing with federal offences committed by youth while requiring that these procedures and, more generally, the youth criminal justice system be separate from the system for adults. It places an emphasis on keeping youth out of court and out of custody. This is relevant to educators because of the focus on extra-judicial measures, rehabilitation and reintegration into their communities (and schools). Section 3(1)(b) of the *Youth Criminal Justice Act*—titled "General Workings of the *Youth Criminal Justice Act* - Declaration of Principle"—describes the underlying view as a separate youth justice system with special emphasis on rehabilitation and reintegration, proportionality and accountability consistent with youth's reduced maturity, enhanced procedural protections, and timely interventions and prompt action.

YOUTH CRIMINAL JUSTICE ACT, 2003

Key objectives of the *Youth Criminal Justice Act* include:°

retrieved May 2013 from http://www.justice.gc.ca/eng/cj-jp/yj-jj/ycja-lsjpa/back-hist.html

- Clear and coherent principles to improve decision-making in the youth justice system;
- More appropriate use of the courts by addressing less serious cases effectively outside the court process;
- Fairness in sentencing;
- Reduction in the high rate of youth incarceration;
- Effective reintegration of young persons;
- Clear distinction between serious violent offences and less serious offences.

The *Youth Criminal Justice Act* sets out a framework for using a range of measures other than youth court proceedings for responding to youth crime. These extra-judicial measures are particularly appropriate for responding to less serious youth crime in a timely and effective manner. They include:

- measures based on police discretion, such as warnings, cautions and referrals to community programs;
- cautions by crown attorneys; and
- extra-judicial sanctions, which are more formal extra-judicial measures (previously known as alternative measures under the *Young Offenders Act*).

Experiences have shown that measures outside the court process can provide effective responses to less serious youth crime. One of the key objectives of the *Youth Criminal Justice Act* is to increase the use of effective and timely non-court responses to less serious offences by youth. The *Youth Criminal Justice Act* provides that extra-judicial measures should be used for any offence, including more serious offences, if the measures would be adequate to hold the young person accountable for his or her offending behaviour and the use of the measures is consistent with the principles of the *Youth Criminal Justice Act* .°

retrieved May 2013 from http://www.collectionscanada.gc.ca/webarchives/20071127003903/http://www.justice.gc.ca/en/ps/yj/repository/3modules/01extjud/3010001a.html

Extra-judicial measures provide meaningful consequences. They also allow early intervention with young people and provide the opportunity for the broader community to play an in important role in developing community-based responses to youth crime. Increasing the use of non-court responses not only improves the response to less serious youth crime, it also enables the courts to focus on more serious cases. Most of the cases in currently addressed in youth court are nonviolent offences (theft under $5000 (e.g., shoplifting); possession of stolen property; failure to appear in court; and failure to comply with a disposition (e.g., breach of a condition of probation). By redirecting these cases to extra-judicial processes, it allows the court system to efficiently deal with the more serious cases and provides an appropriate path for rehabilitation and reintegration for the less serious offences.

The *Youth Criminal Justice Act* contains provisions that provide stronger legislative direction intended to:

- Increase the use of non-court measures for less serious cases;
- Reduce the use of youth courts for less serious cases;
- Enable the youth courts to focus on more serious cases;
- Provide support to police in their exercise of discretion;
- Re-orient the system's approach to non-court measures so that they are viewed as the normal, expected, and most appropriate response to less serious offending by youth.

Youth who are in trouble with the legal system may also exhibit at-risk characteristics at school. The profile of secure custody youth reveals clusters of risk factors:

- family lives in poverty and often have a high degree of dysfunction;
- extensive criminal record—particularly offences such as failing to comply with court orders;
- tremendous difficulties in school;
- little employment experience;
- friends are criminally inclined;
- 80% use intoxicants regularly;
- signs of self-marking and scarring on their bodies.

Therefore, the implementation of the YCJA encompasses:

a. where appropriate, the use of measures outside the court system to deal with youth crime;

b. increased focus on youth rehabilitation and reintegration and distinguishing between responses to youth who are chronic and serious violent offenders and those who commit less serious crime; and

c. monitoring of the new pressures created by the Act on youth justice resources, to determine where additional action needs to be taken.

As noted in the explanation of this piece of legislation,° the *Youth Criminal Justice Act* is an important part of the broader approach to addressing youth crime and improving the youth justice system in Canada. The combination of the legislative and non-legislative elements (e.g., increased federal funding for programs, crime prevention, public and professional education, partnerships with other sectors, and appropriate implementation) can achieve the objectives and thereby create a fairer and more effective youth justice system.

retrieved May 2013 from http://www.collectionscanada.gc.ca/webarchives/20071126234336/http://www.justice.gc.ca/en/ps/yj/repository/2overvw/2010001l.html

14.8 STUDENT HEALTH AND WELL-BEING

While parents are primarily responsible for the health and well-being of their children, schools often have to respond to emergency medical situations and other health-related issues with students. For a proper response, schools must be informed by parents and guardians about specific medical or health conditions of students. The statutory duty of school principals is to give assiduous attention to the health and comfort of the students.° Similarly, teachers have a duty to maintain a healthy physical, emotional and social learning environment.°

§ 265(1)(j) EA

§ 264(2.3) EA

14.8.1 Medical Officers of Health

§ 6(1) Health Protection and Promotion Act, 1990

§ 266(2.1) EA

§§ 265(1)(k), 286(1)(g) EA

§ 266(11) EA

For many years, school health nurses have played a vital part in the provision of support for student well-being. *Education Act* outlines the duties of school personnel in relation to cooperation with school nurses and/or medical officers. According to the *Health Protection and Promotion Act*,° health programs and services are provided in schools within the jurisdiction of the board of health. Upon request, the principal of a school must provide the required student information to the medical officer of health serving the area in which the school is located.° Medical officer of health are to be informed by the school board and school principal about the unsanitary condition of any part of the school buildings or premises or about existence of any communicable disease in the school.° Medical officers of health are also responsible for ensuring that students with communicable diseases are not present in school until all danger from exposure to contact with such person has passed.°

14.8.2 Provision of Health Support Services

Policy/Program Memorandum No. 81, "Provision of Health Support Services in School Settings"

§ 171(1)(25) EA

Schools often face the need to provide health support services to school-aged children that extend beyond educational services and are not included in the normal preventive health programs in placed through the boards of health to school children. According to PPM No. 81,° such health support services are jointly provided by the Ministries of Education, Health, and Community and Social Services. The Ministry of Health is responsible for Home Care Program, intensive physio-occupational and speech therapy, and for assisting school boards in the training and direction of school board staff performing certain other support services. The Ministry of Community and Social Services is responsible for ensuring the provision of health support services in children's residential care and treatment facilities. The school boards are responsible for the administration of oral medication where such medication has been prescribed for use during school hours. For physically disabled pupils, the school boards must provide such services as lifting and positioning, assistance with mobility, feeding and toiletting, and general maintenance exercises. Boards are also responsible for necessary speech remediation, correction, and rehabilitation programs. Specific guidelines in the *Education Act* also allow school boards to provide for surgical treatment of students (with parental consent) who suffer from minor physical defects that interfere with their proper education.°

14.8.3 Administration of Medication

Health Care Consent Act, 1996

As mentioned above, school board employees are responsible for administration of prescribed medication to students during the school day. This process is subject to the provisions of the *Health Care Consent Act*.° The consent, provided by the person capable of giving informed consent, implies that they school board employee can administer medication, but is not responsible for the treatment of the student. The informed consent can be given, according to the common law, by students who are 16 years of age or older. For students, younger than 12, parental consent is required. For students between 12 and 16 years of age, obtaining both parental and student consent is advisable. Board's guidelines may include other conditions for this process, such as the ease and safety of administering medication by a layperson or terms of the employee's collective agreement.

14.8.4 Sabrina's Law

Schools may also face life-threatening, emergency situations that will require administration of medication. Anaphylaxis as a serious allergic reaction is an example of such an emergency situation that requires immediate response and administration of epinephrine.

Sabrina's Law,° an act to protect anaphylactic pupils, came into force on January 1, 2006. It was triggered by the incident with Sabrina Shannon in 2003, a student with a severe dairy allergy who died at school after consuming food containing traces of cheese. This law ensures all school boards have policies or procedures in place to address anaphylaxis in schools, which includes: regular training for staff and others who are in direct contact with students on a regular basis; strategies to reduce the risk of exposure to anaphylactic causative agents; and a communication plan for sharing information with parents, students, and employees. The board's policy must also require every school principal to develop an individual plan for each student who has an anaphylactic allergy. This plan must include:

SABRINA'S LAW, 2005

- Details informing employees and others who are in direct contact with pupils on a regular basis of the type of allergy, monitoring and avoidance strategies and appropriate treatment;
- A readily accessible emergency procedure for the pupil, including emergency contact information; and,
- Storage for epinephrine auto-injectors (epi-pen), where necessary.

School principals must ensure that parents and students provide information about life-threatening allergies the student may have at the time of registration. They must maintain a file for each anaphylactic student relating to current treatment and including other relevant information.

The law provides guidelines for pre authorized administration of an epi-pen by school board employees if a school has up-to-date treatment information and the consent of the student and parent or guardian. School board employees may also administer an epi-pen if an employee has reason to believe that a student is experiencing an anaphylactic reaction. There is also a clause in this law that protects board employees from civil law actions for damages from anaphylactic interventions done in good faith or for any neglect or default in good faith in response to an anaphylactic reaction, unless the damages are the result of an employee's gross negligence.

14.9 HEALTHY SCHOOLS

§ 11(6)(e) EA

Active lifestyle and healthy school environment enhance students' learning and success, their social and emotional well-being, as well as help them reach their full potential. Research shows that children who eat a healthy diet are more ready to learn and more likely to be successful in school. Therefore, as outlined in the *Education Act*, school boards and schools are required to adopt and implement measures that promote the health of students.°

Healthy Schools: Foundations for a Healthy School, 2012, *retrieved May 2013 from http://www.edu.gov.on.ca/eng/healthyschools/foundations.html*

Foundations for a Healthy School, n.d., *retrieved May 2013 from http://www.edu.gov.on.ca/eng/healthyschools/foundations.pdf*

A number of coordinated efforts in Ontario (also known as Healthy Schools Plan) helped develop healthier learning environments and improve student achievement. These efforts are aligned with the Ministry of Education foundations for a healthy school.° A healthy school is the one that has quality instruction and programs, a healthy physical environment, a supportive social environment, and community partnerships. Within these broader foundations, a variety of foci guide healthy schools efforts in Ontario. These are: healthy eating; physical activity; bullying prevention; personal safety and injury prevention; substance use, addictions and related behaviours; healthy growth and development; and mental health.°

14.9.1 Healthy Eating

HEALTHY FOOD FOR HEALTHY SCHOOLS ACT, 2008

REGULATION 200/08, "TRANS FAT STANDARDS"

In an attempt to promote healthier eating, two significant pieces of legislation came into effect on September 1, 2008. The *Healthy Food for Healthy Schools Act*° outlined the power of the minister to establish policies and guidelines with respect to mandatory nutritional standards for food and beverages and for any ingredient contained in food and beverages provided on school premises or in connection with a school-related activity. The Trans Fat Regulation° required schools to drop trans fat from food and beverages sold on their premises, which included some baked goods, packaged snack food and deep fried food.

POLICY/PROGRAM MEMORANDUM NO. 150, "SCHOOL FOOD AND BEVERAGE POLICY"

Another important step in creating healthier eating in Ontario schools was the School Food and Beverage Policy (SFBP)° that came in effect in October, 2010, with school boards required to be in full compliance with the policy on September 1, 2011. It established nutrition standards for food and beverages sold in publicly funded elementary and secondary schools beginning in the 2011/2012 academic year, outlining strict guidelines for each food group (e.g., grains, fruits, and vegetables as well as 'mixed dishes') and miscellaneous items (e.g., condiments, dressings, gravies) to indicate the optimal amount of fat, sodium, and fibre that should be sold in schools. Food labels on each item were to be compared with the nutritional requirements outlined by the policy document to determine whether to "sell most (≥ 80%)," "sell less (≤ 20%)," or were "not permitted for sale." The nutrition standards align with the principles of healthy eating° and are intended to ensure that the food and beverages sold in schools contribute to students' healthy growth and development.

Eating Well with Canada's Food Guide, 2011, *retrieved May 2013 from http://www.hc-sc.gc.ca/fn-an/food-guide-aliment/index-eng.php*

The policy applies to all food and beverages sold on school premises for school purposes in all venues (e.g., cafeterias, vending machines, tuck shops/canteens) and programs (e.g., catered lunch programs), and at all events (e.g., bake sales, sporting events). The policy allows the school principal, in consultation with the school council, to designate up to ten days (or fewer, as determined by the school board) during the school year as special-event days on which food and beverages sold in schools would be exempt from the nutrition standards.

14.9.2 Daily Physical Activity

The absence of physical activity is detrimental for the proper growth and development of children and youth; it has become a serious health and social issue for children and youth in Ontario. According to PPM No. 138,° school boards must ensure that all elementary students, including students with special education needs, have a minimum of twenty minutes of sustained moderate to vigorous physical activity each school day during instructional time. Daily physical activity may include walking, active games, dance, aquatics, sports, and fitness and recreational activities (where facilities permit). This requirement has been included as an expectation in the elementary health and physical education curriculum.° The goal of daily physical activity is to enable all elementary students to improve or maintain their physical fitness and their overall health and wellness, and to enhance their learning opportunities. School boards are required to implement the policy, and ensure, together with principals, that appropriate action is taken to inform parents of their children's participation in these activities.

POLICY/PROGRAM MEMORANDUM NO. 138, "DAILY PHYSICAL ACTIVITY IN ELEMENTARY SCHOOLS, GRADES 1–8"

Ontario Elementary Health and Physical Education Curriculum, 2012, *retrieved May 2013 from http://www.edu.gov.on.ca/eng/curriculum/elementary/health.html*

14.9.3 Mental Health

According to the Children's Mental Health Ontario, one in 5 of children and youth under the age of 19 in Ontario has a mental health problem. This is the area of concern as almost 20% of students in an 'average' classroom may be dealing with some type of mental health problem that impedes their learning or behaviour. Among the possible consequences of untreated mental health problems are classroom disruption, bullying, poor academic achievement, and dropping out of school.

The most common mental health issues for children and youth are:° anxiety; Attention Deficit Disorder (ADD) or Attention-Deficit/Hyperactivity Disorder (AD/HD); depression; mood

Ontario Ministry of Children and Youth Services: Mental Health Services, 2011, *retrieved May 2013 from http://www.children.gov.on.ca/htdocs/English/topics/specialneeds/mentalhealth/index.aspx*

disorders; schizophrenia; and eating disorders. Early identification and intervention are conducive to improved school achievement and better health outcomes. Therefore, a Comprehensive Mental Health and Addictions Strategy has been developed in Ontario,° along with the three-year action plan, Moving on Mental Health, to ensure delivery of a coordinated, responsive system for children, youth and their families.°

Open Minds, Healthy Minds Ontario's Comprehensive Mental Health and Addictions Strategy, 2011, *retrieved May 2013 from http://www.health.gov.on.ca/en/common/ministry/publications/reports/mental_health2011/mentalhealth_rep2011.pdf*

Moving on Mental Health, n.d., *retrieved May 2013 from http://www.children.gov.on.ca/htdocs/english/documents/topics/specialneeds/mentalhealth/momh.pdf*

14.9.4 *Illegal Drug Use, Substance Abuse, and Addictions*

In November 2004, Health Canada produced the *Canadian Addictions Survey: A National Survey of Canadians' use of Alcohol and other Drugs – Prevalence of Use and Related Harms*.° The Canadian Center on Substance Abuse has also provided information respecting *Student/Adolescent Alcohol and Drug Use Statistics*.°

retrieved May 2013 from http://www.ccsa.ca/2004%20CCSA%20Documents/ccsa-004804-2004.pdf

retrieved May 2013 from http://www.ccsa.ca/Eng/Statistics/Canada/SAADUS/Pages/default.aspx

Drug abuse is commonly defined by health educators as:

- taking a lot of a drug at one time;
- taking a prescription drug without a prescription;
- taking a prescription or over-the-counter drug in a way it's not meant to be used;
- taking several drugs (including alcohol) at the same time;
- using drugs too often;
- using drugs for a long time.

And further that such abuse subject the user to the following risks:

- health problems;
- tolerance (having to take more of the drug to get the same effect);
- physical dependence (your body needs the drug just to feel normal);
- psychological dependence (you feel like you can't get by without the drug);
- overdoses, which can cause serious injury or even death;
- relationship problems with family and friends;
- problems at school or work;
- legal problems;
- money problems.

Substance Abuse in Children and Adolescents, 2007, *retrieved May 2013 from http://www.knowledge.offordcentre.com/images/stories/offord/pamphlets/SubstanceAbuse_en.pdf*

As reported by the Centre of Knowledge on Healthy Child Development,° teens and older children may use "legal" substances like tobacco, alcohol, glue, gasoline, diet pills, over-the-counter cold remedies, or prescription pain killers (like OxyContin). Some may go on to use illegal drugs like marijuana, LSD, cocaine, heroin, PCP, methamphetamine, or Ecstasy. According to the report, among students in grades 7 to 12, alcohol and tobacco are the most frequently used legal substances, while pot is the most commonly used illegal drug. Only 2% of children and teens are frequent users of other illegal drugs, such as stimulants like methamphetamine, hallucinogens (other than LSD or PCP), cocaine, or Ecstasy.

The report further posits that drug use and mental health problems seem to go together. Children and adolescents with AD/HD, Oppositional Defiant Disorders, or Conduct Disorder are more likely to use drugs or sniff gasoline or glue. Teens using substances may have depression or fear social situations. Some have post-traumatic stress disorder - a type of anxiety related to early history or current experience of physical or sexual abuse. Substance use is also frequently seen in adolescents with bulimia or with schizophrenia.

The Health Behaviour in School-aged Children (HBSC) study that captures health-related data from youth 11 to 15 years of age provides data about current situation (as of 2012) in Ontario schools.°

Health and Health-Related Behaviours among Young People: Ontario, 2013, *retrieved May 2013 from http://www.edu.gov.on.ca/eng/healthyschools/HBSCReportJan2013.pdf*

14.10 PERSONAL SAFETY AND INJURY PREVENTION

14.10.1 Occupational Health and Safety

Some of the goals of the Ministry of Labour's strategy, Safe At Work Ontario, are the improvement of the health and safety culture of workplaces, reduction of workplace injuries and illness, and lessening the burden on the health care system. According to the *Occupational Health and Safety Act*,° school boards (as employers) are to ensure the health and safety of workers. Employers are to provide information, instruction and supervision to workers to protect their health or safety; develop and review occupational health and safety policy; and establish an occupational health service for workers. On the other hand, every worker is to work in compliance with the health and safety provisions by taking reasonable care to protect his or her health and safety and the health and safety of others.

OCCUPATIONAL HEALTH AND SAFETY ACT, 1990

Each school board is required to have a central joint Occupational Health and Safety Committee, while school sites will have a school/site health and safety committees. Many school boards have established the policy of implementing a monthly safety inspection by a team of on-site teachers and administrators. The regular checks made by this team help identify potential hazards in their schools. These hazards may be as such as wet floors due to leaking windows, inadequate locks on a chemical storage room, ventilation issues, damaged floor tiles or dangling cords from computers that could be a tripping hazard. The occupational health and safety committees identify potential problems and monitor their repairs.

The School Gym – A Dangerous Place?

Over the years, school gyms have been the site of a significant number of unfortunate accidents and the source of a number of lawsuits relating to negligence.

In the Supreme Court of Canada decision in the case of Thornton et al. v. Board of School Trustees (Prince George, 1975) it was established that a physical education teacher owes a duty of care to his (or her) students higher than that of a careful parent. The Supreme Court then established four criteria to determine the appropriate standard of care within the context of instruction in physical education:

- Is the activity suitable to the age, mental and physical condition of the participant?
- Have the participants been progressively taught and coached to perform the activity properly and to avoid the dangers inherent in the activity?
- Is the equipment adequate and suitably arranged?
- Is the activity being supervised properly for the inherent danger involved?

In its findings in Myers et al. v. Peel County Board of Education (1981), the Supreme Court of Canada reiterated the idea that a physical education teacher, based on specialized expertise, owes a higher standard of care than that of a prudent parent. The court also reinforced the view that all methods available be used to ensure the safety of students and to prevent students from taking unnecessary risks. Failure to do so constitutes negligence.

Despite these precedents, injuries continue to occur in school gymnasia. In 1995, MM, a grade 11 student in Westlock, Alberta suffered a severe spinal injury and paralysis while attempting to execute a backward half somersault off a box horse. Using the criteria established by the Supreme Court in Thornton et al., the Alberta Court of Queen's Bench found that the teacher had failed to meet the "professional" standard of care, based on specialized expertise, demanded of a gymnastics teacher. The court found that the teacher's conduct was the direct cause of the student's injury (causation). It also found that since the activity was within a classroom environment, MM did not assume the risk of the activity (assumption of risk). Nor was she contributory negligent as she did not have the same knowledge or experience as her teacher (contributory negligence). Finally, the Court found that since the teacher was hired by the school board, it was liable for the teacher's negligence to the amount of $3.5 million (vicarious liability).

Education Law Reporter, 10(3), November 1998

14.10.2 Occupier's Liability

As property owners, school boards must ensure that appropriate safety measures are in place to prevent accidents resulting in damages and injuries to anyone in the school property or premises. The *Education Act* outlines the responsibilities of the school board to keep the school buildings and premises in proper repair and in proper sanitary condition, provide suitable furniture and equipment and keep it in proper repair, and protect the property of the board.° In addition to responsibilities about health and comfort of students, principals have the duty to care for the cleanliness, temperature and ventilation of the school teaching materials and other school property, as well as for the condition and appearance of the school buildings and grounds.

§ 170(1)(8) EA

Occupiers' liability is the branch of negligence law dealing with injuries caused by the condition of premises, or activities carried on at any place. An occupier may be any person in physical control of the premises; any person responsible for the control of any of the condition of the premises, the activities being carried on, or persons allowed to enter the premises. In accordance with the Occupiers' Liability Act, schools owe a duty to take such care as in all the circumstances of the case is reasonable to see that persons entering on the premises, and the property brought on the premises by those persons are reasonably safe while on the premises.° The duty is not an absolute requirement to act as an insurer of the safety of everyone. The phrase "in all the circumstances" and the word "reasonable" limit the duty. Occupiers' liability is a very important issue in schools. Teachers, because of their positions as occupiers and because their employers (school board) are owners of buildings, equipment, and grounds, are subject to the application of a common law standard of occupiers' liability.

§ 3(1) Occupational Health and Safety Act, 1990

There are several categories of entrants according to the occupiers' liability act. A compulsee is person who is required to enter and be compulsory present on the premises. An invitee is person who is invited to enter or remain on the premises for a commercial benefit to the possessor of premises, or for a purpose directly or indirectly connected with business dealings with the possessor. An invitation may be either express or implied. A licensee is a person who is invited to enter or remain on the premises for any purpose other than a business or commercial one with the express or implied permission of the owner or person in control of the premises. A social guest is considered to be a licensee, not an invitee. A trespasser is a person who goes upon the premises of another without an express or implied invitation, for his or her own purposes, and not in the performance of any duty to the owner. It is typically not necessary for a defendant to establish that the trespasser had unlawful intent in making such an entry.

These categories of entrants apply as follows in schools. Children, when they are in school, are a legal class of person called an invitee. (Sometimes, they are also viewed as compulsee, as they are required to attend school by law). Teachers as occupiers and their employers as owners owe the highest standard of care to the invitee. In a person's own home, the highest standard of care is owed to the invitee. Licensee are people who are on the property (without charge) by the expressed or implied permission of the occupier/owner (construction workers, contractors, service personnel for vending machines, etc.). Licensee, are owed a somewhat reduced duty of care, but must be warned of hidden dangers. Licensees are children on the school grounds before/after school hours or on weekends are in this class (unless school took responsibility on itself). Trespasser is owed no duty of care but does enjoy some rights. Occupiers/owners must not create deliberate danger, if they know or should know that the trespasser is present and must not create hidden dangers (traps) to forestall trespassers.

In deciding whether 'reasonable' care has been exercised, the courts will consider the likelihood of injury to others, the seriousness of the risk and the burden of avoiding the risk. The courts will expect school premises to be kept in a reasonably safe condition including grounds, equipment and buildings. According to the Ontario School Boards' Insurance exchange, claims are often made against school boards for injuries caused due to:

- grounds being in poor condition, e.g., potholes, ice and snow, pathways not maintained, etc.
- equipment in disrepair and lack of maintenance, e.g., guards broken on shop machines, lack of ground cover under playground equipment, broken glass in sandbox, etc.
- buildings in disrepair and lack of maintenance, e.g., parts of or attachments to buildings falling down, broken steps, improper or broken handrails, etc.

14.10.3 Negligence

Negligence is a common law concept defined as the failure to use reasonable care. Reduced to its simplest terms, negligence is doing something a reasonable person would not do, or not doing something a reasonable person would do. If a person under one's duty of care suffers injury or loss as a result of one's action or inaction, one may be held liable for damages. Most negligence suits related to schools arise from physical injuries which students suffer while under the teacher's supervision.

In order to find negligence in a civil law suit, four conditions must be present:

1. **Duty of Care.** It must be shown that the defendant had a "duty of care" toward the other person. The degree and nature of care required may vary according to the role or status of the defendant. In the case of teachers, the standard of care required toward students is usually cited as the standard of the careful and prudent parent of a large family. In other words, one is expected to do what a careful and prudent parent would do in the same circumstances. The Latin phrase *in loco parentis* is often used as a shorthand phrase for referring to this standard.
2. **Breach of Duty of Care.** It must be shown that the defendant breached the duty of care. In other words, with regard to students, it must be shown that you didn't do something that a careful and prudent parent would have done, or you did do something that a careful and prudent parent wouldn't have done.
3. **Loss or Damage.** It must be shown that the plaintiff has suffered actual loss or damage. (Note that "damage" is the legal term that includes physical injury, emotional distress, loss of income, etc.). In order the negligence case to be pursued, the loss or damage must not be minor but considerable or recognizable.
4. **Proximate Cause.** It must be shown that the breach of the duty of care was the immediate cause of the loss or damage. Even if the causality is present between the breach of duty of care and

Duty of Care

The duty of care owed to students is a well-established principle in law. Failure to meet that duty of care leaves teachers, administrators and board members liable to charges of negligence. To ensure an appropriate level of care and to avoid possible accusations of negligence, educators should ask themselves the following questions:

With Respect to Duty of Care

- Do I owe this student a duty of care in this context?
- Are there others who could foreseeably be injured as a result of my negligence in this context e.g., a student who drowns trying to rescue another student because of inadequate school supervision?
- Is this an activity during school hours and on school property?
- Is this a school sponsored activity off school property?
- Did I assume responsibility for this student when it was not necessarily required of me as when the gym was opened to students very early on cold mornings?
- Did I reasonably lead parents to believe that I would provide care for their children before and after the lunch hour?
- Did I make clear to parents, repeatedly when necessary, the limits of my scope of duty to their child during non-school hours?
- Did I, in my personal rather than in my professional capacity voluntarily assume a duty of care for this student so that my employer's insurance would not cover my potential liability for injury or damage in this context?
- Am I aware that the parent can not waive the student's right to bring an action for injuries sustained by the student?

Standard of Care

- Am I protected if I follow a reasonable professional standard of care, or am I bound by the prudent-parent standard of care?
- What factors, e.g., age of student, physical environment, nature of the activity, etc., should I consider when determining the standard of care I should adopt for this student in this context?
- What types of mishaps and injury are reasonably foreseeable in this context?
- What precisely would the prudent parent do in this context?
- What should I do to prevent the foreseeable mishaps and injury?

Breach of the Duty of Care

- Did I breach my duty of care?
- Is there anything I could do to prevent harm to students or to mitigate my potential liability e.g., ask for help or cut it short when I realize that I am not providing the safety necessary to students during an orienteering exercise?

Injury Sustained and Causation

- Was injury sustained?
- Was this injury or type of injury foreseeable?
- As a question of fact, was breach of my duty of care the direct cause of the injury?
- Alternatively, was the injury a reasonable consequence of the breach of my duty of care?
- If so, was breach of my duty of care the "proximate" cause of the injury or was it quite remote from the injury along a chain of events?
- Did the student or any other person contribute to this injury?
- Did the student voluntarily assume some or all of the physical and legal risk inherent in this activity?

Liability

- Is this activity a board approved or school sponsored activity?
- Is this activity within the scope of my duties as a teacher, school-aide, parent volunteer, etc?
- What are the limits of my board's insurance protection for me?
- If I am not insured for this activity am I personally insured against liability for damages that may arise from my involvement in it?

EduLaw, 6(2), October 1994

the student's injury, there needs to be a proof that the damage was not too remote a consequence of the negligence. Foreseeability implies that educators or school boards will be held liable if the damage was completely unforeseeable or occurred under unforeseeable circumstances.

Williams v. Eady (1893) 10 TLR 41

Thornton et al. v. Board of School Trustees of School District No. 57 (Prince George) et al., [1976] 5 WWR 240 (BCCA)

The British case of Williams v. Eady (1893)° established the principle that teachers in Canada must act as prudent parents. Two other Canadian school negligence cases established further guidelines. In the case of Thornton et al v. Board of School Trustees of School District No. 57 (Prince George) (1978),° the judge listed four tests for determining whether there was negligence, or breach of the duty of care, as follows.

- The activity must be suitable to the age and condition (mental and physical) of the student.
- The student must be progressively trained and coached to do the activity properly and avoid the danger.
- The equipment must be adequate and suitably arranged.
- The performance, having regard to its inherently dangerous nature, must be properly supervised.

The decision in the case of *Thornton et al.* has advanced the notion of the teacher as a "prudent expert." In this case the teacher was essentially expected to have "supraparental expertise" because the teacher was supervising gymnastics. Gymnastics is complex and has risk factors beyond conventional activities. If a teacher engages students in such activities (or is instructed by a principal to deliver such activities), it is reasonable to demand expertise consistent with the special nature of the activity.

Myers v. Peel County Board of Education, [1981] 2 SCR 21

In the case of Myers v. Peel County Board of Education (1981),° the court found that the standard of the careful and prudent parent must be qualified by several factors, as follows:

- The number of students being supervised at any given time;
- The nature of the exercise or activity;
- The age of the students;
- The students' degree of skill;
- The training that the students have received in connection with the activity;
- The nature and condition of the equipment in use;
- The competency and capacity of the students.

Teachers must exercise due diligence in activities that pose risk to students. Although it is particularly important in technology classes, due diligence applies to all teachers. Teachers must insure that they document that safety training was actually received by all students using a particular piece of equipment and that the equipment was maintained correctly the period of time that a given teacher has care and control over the safe operation of that equipment. Failure to provide safety training or failure to maintain equipment are just two serious examples of breach of the duty of care that can and do result in accidents and legal action.

14.10.4 Liability

Liability implies that a person is legally liable when they are financially and legally responsible for damages. Payment of damages usually resolves the liability. If a student under the educator's care is injured and a negligence suit results, it is likely that both the educator and the school board will be named as defendants. In other words, the board assumes liability on behalf of the employee for any damage or personal injury suffered by students during the school activities. The principle of vicarious liability implies that a school board may be held legally liable in tort law not only for its own actions or inactions, but also for those of its employees when they are acting within the course or scope of their employment. An activity may not have to be authorized by an employer for it to be considered as "within the course or scope" of the employee. Each case depends on its individual facts, but there must be a clear breach of the employee's authority by the employee before a school board would be held not liable for the employee's negligence. Therefore, the board should be aware of all activities being carried out in its name, and must ensure adequate liability insurance coverage; this is particularly important in the case of field trips and student club activities. Teachers should also be aware of the coverage provided by their employers' liability insurance.

In some cases, both the plaintiff and the defendant may be found negligent in varying degrees. That may be the case if the actions or inaction of the person who suffered the loss or injury are deemed to have contributed to the damages. This is called contributory negligence. The court will then decide who bears what portion of the responsibility according to the Ontario *Negligence Act*.° Then, when damages are calculated, they will be prorated according to degree of blame. For example, in the Myers case, the teacher and the school authorities were found 80% responsible, while the student was found 20% responsible.

NEGLIGENCE ACT, 1990

14.11 RISK IN LOCATIONS AND ACTIVITIES

In an attempt to provide rich, meaningful learning opportunities for students, educators must remember that the standard of care includes the duty to protect students from any reasonable risks of injury. Risk management is an important issue in certain spaces and activities that are inherently or potentially hazardous: technological education (auto shop, wood shop), laboratories for sciences (i.e., chemistry, physics), cooperative education or experiential learning work placements, playgrounds, gymnasia, and performing arts facilities are examples of potentially hazardous places and spaces. Some activities are inherently dangerous and therefore not allowed. For example, school boards may establish a policy to prohibit the throwing of snowballs during recess. Certain other activities may be hazardous if not effectively supervised; other activities require specific instruction on safety procedures and correct techniques, in addition to supervision, to ensure these procedures are correctly followed, e.g., physical education, science experiments, and practical arts (such as wood shop, welding, or cooking). It is essential that board and school personnel give due diligence by safeguarding students from inherently dangerous spaces or spaces that may increase their likelihood of harm, by prohibiting inherently dangerous activities, by providing sufficient supervision, and by maintaining and ensuring proper instruction. It should be emphasized that a special standard of care is required during physical activities, field trips, and some extracurricular activities.

14.11.1 Principles of Risk Management

Risk management is a systematic approach to preventing or reducing exposure to any type of hazard, loss, or damage. It is a multi-step process of awareness that involves:

1. Identify hazardous activities or situations.
2. Identify various risk management techniques (is it sufficiently dangerous to require complete avoidance, or can it safely managed).
3. Select and implement the appropriate technique.
4. Monitor the situation to determine if the appropriate action was taken and that the risk has indeed been managed successfully.

Numerous advisors to school personnel have suggested checklists or considerations that might be reviewed from time to time to ensure safety when planning and implementing student activities. Checklists of suggestions or considerations have evolved from case law involving student injuries arising from school activities and other sources as guides for school boards, administrators and teachers. Reviewing these guidelines will help ensure safety when planning, and implementing student programs and activities. For example, school boards and teachers are well advised to take into account several factors when considering whether or not a planned school activity is reasonable:

- the age of the students (e.g., physical size; developmental levels);
- the ability of the students (e.g., physical/mental limitations,

endurance);

- the number of students taking part in the activity (e.g., the supervisor-student ratio);
- the nature of the activity (e.g., foreseeable risks and hazards, collateral (incidental) hazards);
- the mode of transportation (e.g., walking, student transportation, volunteer vehicles);
- the supervision requirements (e.g., school personnel, volunteers, chaperones);
- the environmental factors (e.g., site location, layout, features).

A comprehensive source of risk-management resources and services° is available through the Ontario School Board Insurance Exchange (OSBIE), a school board owned, non-profit insurance program, aims to insure member school boards against losses, and to promote safe school practices. OSBIE has developed a number of recommended forms and checklists,° risk assessment toolkits, and risk management guidelines° and advisories on a variety of different issues affecting school and boards in Ontario from automobile coverage and cooperative education/experiential learning programs to school trips abroad and vandalism and arson prevention on school properties.°

retrieved May 2013 from http://www.osbie.on.ca

retrieved May 2013 from http://www.osbie.on.ca/risk-management/at-a-glance/forms-checklists.aspx

retrieved May 2013 from http://www.osbie.on.ca/risk-management/risk-assessment-toolkit/default.aspx

14.11.2 Student Travel

The *Education Act* states that a school board may provide transportation for pupils enrolled in schools operated by the board.° The school board and its employees are not responsible for the safety and care of students when they are traveling to and from school except if the transportation used by the student is under board control or if the transportation is associated with a board sanctioned activity that is part of the school program. If student transportation is provided, the responsibility of the board extends to the safe loading and unloading of students if a school bus is used. Students are accountable to school officials for their deportment while travelling on a school bus that is owned by a board or on a bus or school bus that is under contract to a board. School boards must have vehicle insurance coverage with respect to transportation services.

§ 190(1) EA

For those students who are walking to school, under the provisions of Highway Traffic Act, municipalities will maintain school crossings with a sign displayed by the school crossing guards.° Many schools participate in the School Safety Patrol Program, a joint partnership between the Canadian Automobile Association (CAA), the police, school boards, teachers, parents, and student volunteers,° that ensures children stay safe while travelling to and from school every day.

§ 176 Highway Traffic Act, 1990

retrieved May 2013 from http://www.caasco.com/Community-Action/School-Safety-Patrol.aspx

Sometimes, educators or volunteers use their own vehicles, or other private vehicles to transport students to sports or other activities away from the school. The use of personal vehicles to transport students to and from school activities must have proper licensing and insurance.

Generally school boards do (or should) have policies governing extended school sponsored travel such as overseas trips. School boards should check the travel advisories from the Department of Foreign Affairs and International Trade Canada before undertaking international school trips.

14.11.3 Field Trips

The responsibility of the board and its employees for the safety and care of students extends to any activity for which board permission is granted or can be assumed. Many of the school activities (whether on or off-site) are considered high-risk activities. Field trips, insomuch as they provide valuable learning experiences, potentially carry a high risk of injury and should be properly supervised by teachers and competent volunteers. Schools boards are held responsible if there are any losses or damages to students that occurred during the field trips even if it is organized by a third-party. For example, it may be that the board is responsible for the standard of care for students during overseas educational tours operated by a tour firm if the school's facilities have been used for tour advertisements, recruitment, and organization. In its exercise of due diligence, a school board needs to ensure that it has provided a risk appropriate standard of care for all sanctioned (or implicitly sanctioned) activities. The Ontario School Board Insurance Exchange (OSBIE) provides a comprehensive overview of field-trip risk management guidelines.°

retrieved May 2013 from http://www.osbie.on.ca/pdf/Field-Trip-Risk-Management-Guidelines.pdf

14.11.4 Informed Consents and Waivers

Schools or school boards have developed policies regarding informed consent forms or permission slips for student activities in their jurisdictions. An informed consent form or permission slip is intended to inform parents of an activity and request permission for their child to participate in that specific activity. Informed consent forms usually consist of at least three parts:

1. description of activity,
2. possible risks, and
3. statements for parental consent.

These are often mistakenly viewed as "releases" or "waivers" that purport, on grounds of the voluntary assumption of risk by the parent or student, to relieve the school of liability in the event of an accident. A waiver, as the relinquishment of a known right or claim for injury or damages between consenting parties, can only be enforceable under law if the two parties are legally capable of making such an agreement, and if the waiver fairly discloses the foreseeable dangers or hazards that exist. In Ontario, the case law suggests that waiver forms for persons under the age of 18 years are not recognized as being enforceable. Despite the fact that some legal exceptions exist with respect to their ability to enter into contracts (e.g. marriage, military service, etc.), persons under 18 are not deemed to be legally capable of entering into an agreement such as a waiver that would prejudice their future right to recover for an injury. Parents, guardians, principals or teachers also have no authority to waive such rights on behalf of a person under the age of 18 years. Parents cannot waive their children's rights, and a release signed by a child, because it is a contract that is not beneficial to the child, will not be enforced against the child.

Therefore, a parent's written authorization for a student's participation in a non-conventional activity only indicates that the activity is "reasonable" and does not lessen the school's obligation to provide adequate instruction, preparation, and supervision. A written consent form, even if it includes a "release of responsibility clause," does not purport to reduce the standard of care required of school personnel, i.e., it does not relieve the teacher and school board from liability for negligence resulting in injury to a student.

14.11.5 Safety Guidelines

Various activity advocate groups have established guidelines for policies and practices with respect to their activities areas. For example, the safety guidelines, developed by Ontario Physical and Health Education Association (OPHEA)° in partnership with other agencies, represent the minimum standards for risk management practice for school boards. They focus the attention of teachers, intramural supervisors and coaches on safe practices, in every activity, in order to minimize the risk of injury and damage. Divided into the Elementary and Secondary categories, the guidelines cover each of the three areas:

retrieved May 2013 from http://safety.ophea.net

- Curricular—physical education program;
- Interschool—competitive programs (practices and competitions);
- Intramurals—physical activity/recreation activities.

The guidelines apply to physical activities that occur on the school site or as part of a school sanctioned trip (i.e., day trip, overnight, out of province, or out of country), but they do not apply to free-play activities during recess and lunch. As these guidelines represent the minimum standards, schools boards are encouraged to raise the standards in their jurisdiction policies, but advised not to lower them.

14.12 VOLUNTEERS

The principal, under authority of the *Education Act*, may assign

§ 171(1)(4) EA

duties to voluntary assistants to serve without remuneration in respect of school activities.° Parents and others often volunteer to work in schools and the questions arise: What procedure should the school have in place for such volunteers? What is the liability of such volunteers and the board for volunteers' actions or inactions (negligent or intentional) which result in injury to a student?

S(C) (Next friend of) v. Boy Scouts of Canada, 2002 ABQB 152

R(GB) v. Hollett [1996], 30 CCLT (2d) 215 (NSCA)

Seeley v. Billows, 1995 CanLII 2510 (BCSC)

The school board may be vicariously liable for the negligent actions of volunteers who are considered in law as servants or employees of the board.° Further, school boards may be held to be negligent and hence liable for negligence in hiring or inadequately supervising the volunteer.° This matter has not yet been definitively resolved in Canada but we suggest that it is likely that liability would be found in such cases. In general, it is fair to say that a school board will be held vicariously liable for the negligence of a volunteer which is related to an authorized action and method of carrying out that action which is within the scope of the duties assigned to the volunteers.° It will not be a defence if the board merely has policies but no follow-through in supervision.

14.12.1 Volunteers & Intentional Harm

retrieved May 2013 from http://smhp.psych.ucla.edu/qf/volunteers.html and *http://volunteer.ca/volunteer/pdf/SafeSteps.pdf*

A volunteer who acts with intent to harm a student is both liable civilly and culpable criminally for that harm. Flowing from that act, the school board may be held vicariously liable in civil law if it board knew or ought to have known of the volunteer's proclivity to cause such harm. In particular, the issues of properly vetting, accepting, and supervising volunteers are crucial to school boards with respect to their liability for negligence and intentionally harmful actions by volunteers.°

In general five points should be considered in a board avoiding liability for the actions or inactions of volunteers which result in harm to students:

- will the volunteer have direct contact with students?
- will the contact be with primary, middle, or secondary students, or with special needs students?
- will the volunteer be primarily helping the teacher or the students themselves?
- will the volunteers have one-on-one contact or only contact with a group?
- will the volunteers be supervised all of the time, some of the time, or none of the time?

The answers to the above questions should help the school principal better define the risk involved with the use of volunteers at her or his school. However, having determined the risk, Volunteer Canada's Safe Steps Screening Program suggests the following:

- write a clear position description;
- establish a formal recruitment process;
- use an application form;
- conduct interviews;
- follow-up on references;
- request a police check;
- conduct orientation and training sessions;
- supervise and evaluate; and
- follow-up with the program participants.°

retrieved May 2013 from http://volunteer.ca/

The Ontario School Board Exchange Insurance (OSBIE) provides a helpful list to consider while recruiting volunteers to assist (not supervise or discipline students) in various school activities:°

retrieved May 2013 from http://osbie.on.ca/pdf/Field-Trip-Risk-Management-Guidelines.pdf

- Utilize a screening process for volunteers that includes interview screening and reference checks. For over-night excursions, or for activities that involve long-term interaction with students, criminal background checks (CPIC) are recommended.
- Define which activities are appropriate for volunteers to be involved in.
- Follow up or investigate any rumors of inappropriate behavior.
- Ensure volunteers are properly supervised by school staff.
- Ensure volunteer drivers have valid driver's license and automobile Liability insurance.
- Do not use volunteer drivers to operate passenger vans (9 + vans require special driver licenses).

14.13 CHILD ABUSE AND REPORTING

14.13.1 Duty to Report

The Ontario *Child and Family Services Act* (CFSA) recognizes that each person has a responsibility for the welfare of children and provides for the protection of children from abuse and neglect. Under section 72(1) of this Act, the public, including professionals or officials that work with children (e.g., teachers, school principals, and other educators), who have reasonable grounds to suspect that a child under their care is "in need of protection," are required to report both their suspicion and the grounds on which it is based to a Children's Aid Society (CAS). "Reasonable grounds" implies information that an average person, using normal and honest judgment, would need in order to decide to report. Section 72(1) of the Act defines the "child in

A Cautionary Tale for "Huggy Bears"

In November 1995, Robertson, a principal/teacher with 32 years experience, was charged with touching for a sexual purpose and with sexual assault under sections 151 and 271, respectively, of the *Criminal Code*. The charges were laid after a Grade 5 girl "M" told a teacher that the principal had touched her in a sexual manner; that he had touched and rubbed her knee, massaged her shoulder and back and kissed her on the forehead and cheek. "M" claimed that most of these actions took place in the principal's office, with the door closed, a practice always used by the principal when talking to students, parents and staff.

Robertson admitted touching "M" and other students on a regular basis, but never for a sexual purpose. He believed in close interaction and relationships with students, a caring attitude and a "hug-a-day" to enhance student self-esteem and thus promote better learning.

At trial, many teachers, students (past and present) and parents testified that Robertson was a warm, caring person, popular with students. They claimed that he was always "bubbly" and playful with students, who would often respond by grabbing and climbing onto him. He was described as an enthusiastic, hardworking teacher who related to people, children and adults alike, by touching them. All who testified said that they never saw Robertson do anything that would be considered inappropriate. The weight of the character evidence resulted in an acquittal for "huggy-bear" but the case raises a number of serious issues for individual teachers, school administrators and Boards of Education (From EdLaw, 7(6), February 1996).

Following are some common sense suggestions for teachers to avoid false allegations of sexual abuse:

- Know your students and developmental psychology well.
- Avoid closing your classroom door particularly when you are alone with a student
- Avoid keeping students in your classroom for long periods of time after dismissal

Love for children implies respect for their privacy. Show your love by listening to them, being verbally supportive and understanding and treating them fairly. Save physical demonstrations for caring and affection for when you are in public view of other students and teachers.

Beware of preadolescent and adolescent students who seem to find you attractive. Subdue the flattery. Cool the attention. Avoid and discourage teasing. Remember the danger of a lover spurned, real or imaginary.

Remember that the role of a teacher acting *in loco parentis* does not equate to the role of a parent. That doctrine places teachers in place of parents for the purpose of educating children and caring for them during school sponsored activity. It does not entitle teachers to the same degree of physical intimacy with students as is shared between children and their parents.

Many educators already use anecdotal assessment and reporting techniques. Use these techniques to further advantage. Make notes, in factual and objective terms, of any contentious matters that arise during the school day (e.g., "Jane received a D+ on her social studies assignment. She ran out of the room with tears in her eyes. Tried to talk to her about it at recess but she refused.")

Work cooperatively with colleagues of the opposite sex: buddy up; provide a gender alternative for the student who seems to need more attention; and develop co-ed administrative teams.

EduLaw, 2(9), May 1991.

need of protection" and explains the physical, sexual and emotional abuse, neglect, and risk of harm that need to be reported.

A person who has a duty to report is required to make the report directly to CAS and cannot rely on any other person to report on his or her behalf. A professional or official who has reasonable grounds and fails to report will be liable on conviction to a fine of not more than $1,000. (Please, note that in 2008, a private member's bill was passed that would see amendments to the Ontario *Child and Family Services Act* (CFSA) regarding tougher consequences for non-reporting. Under the proposed amendments, a professional or official who has reasonable grounds and fails to report will be liable on conviction to a fine of not more than 50,000 or to imprisonment for a term of not more than two years, or to both. However, since passing in 2008, these provisions have yet to be proclaimed into law).

14.13.2 Types of Child Abuse

According to the Ministry of Children and Youth Services,° there are four types of child abuse: physical, sexual, emotional, and neglect. Physical abuse happens when a parent or person in charge causes physical injury to a child, or fails to adequately supervise a child or if there is a pattern of neglect of the child. Sexual abuse happens when a parent or other person in charge sexually molests or uses a child for sexual purposes or knowingly fails to protect a child from sexual abuse. Emotional abuse occurs when a parent or other person in charge causes emotional harm or fails to protect a child from emotional harm that results from verbal abuse, mental abuse and psychological abuse. Neglect happens when a child's parent or other person in charge does not provide for a child's physical, developmental, emotional or psychological needs.

retrieved May 2013 from http://www.children.gov.on.ca/htdocs/English/topics/childrensaid/reportingabuse/recognisingabuse.aspx

14.13.3 Indicators of Child Abuse

The symptoms or indicators of abuse and neglect vary from case to case and the presence of any one indicator is not conclusive proof that a child has been abused. In most instances, child abuse will be exhibited in a number of physical and behavioural indicators. Ontario Association of Children's Aid Societies° provides a comprehensive list of injuries, physical and behavioural indicators of child abuse within the following categories: physical, sexual, emotional, neglect, abandonment/separation, and caregiver capacity.

retrieved May 2013 from http://www.oacas.org/childwelfare/signs.htm

14.13.4 Investigations

Child and Family Services Act, Ontario Regulation 206/00, "Procedures, Practices and Standards of Service for Child Protection Cases," and Child Protection Standards in Ontario° guide the process of responding to the report and investigation of case of abuse. When responding to a report that a child may be in need of protection, the child protection worker engages the reporting person to obtain a full and detailed report of the incident or condition that caused him or her to be concerned that a child may be in need of protection. The child protection worker completes an investigation to confirm that allegations of child abuse or neglect are either clearly verified or ruled out. The worker will

retrieved May 2013 from http://www.children.gov.on.ca/htdocs/english/documents/topics/childrensaid/childprotectionstandards.pdf make sure that there are no immediate safety threats and longer-term risk factors and that all reasonable efforts have been made to collect evidence.

14.14 SEXUAL ABUSE

§ 37(2)(c) CHILD AND FAMILY SERVICES ACT, 1990

§ 97(1) CHILD AND FAMILY SERVICES ACT, 1990

Sexual abuse is any sexual exploitation of a child by a person in charge of a child where the child is being used for a sexual purpose. In Ontario, child sexual abuse is defined in the child welfare legislation under two large categories: sexual molestation and sexual exploitation (including child pornography).° Abuse also implies a state or condition of being physically harmed.° Sexual molestation is the long-term forcing of undesired sexual behavior by one person upon another. Short-term, or infrequent, force accompanied by some form of sexual activity such as kissing, fondling, or sexual intercourse is called sexual assault. Sexual exploitation is the type of sexual abuse of children and youth through the exchange of sex or sexual acts for money, drugs, food, shelter, protection, or other basics of life.

14.14.1 Sexual Offense and the Criminal Code

The *Criminal Code* of Canada directly provides definitions for sexual offenses, where school-aged children are victims. The *Criminal Code* of Canada identifies a number of types of sexual abuse, including sexual interference; an invitation to sexually touch; sexual exploitation; parent or guardian procuring sexual activity from a child; householder permitting sexual activity; exposing genitals to a child; and incest. In section 151, the *Criminal Code* indicates that

§ 151 CRIMINAL CODE OF CANADA, 1985

> Every person who, for a sexual purpose, touches, directly or indirectly, with a part of the body or with an object, any part of the body of a person under the age of sixteen years is guilty of an indictable offence and is liable to imprisonment for a term not exceeding ten years or is guilty of an offence punishable on summary conviction. [Amended from the age of 14 as of May 1, 2008]°

Furthermore,

§ 152 CRIMINAL CODE OF CANADA, 1985

> Every person who, for a sexual purpose, invites, counsels or incites a person under the age of sixteen years to touch, directly or indirectly, with a part of the body or with an object, the body of any person, including the body of the person who so invites, counsels or incites and the body of the person under the age of fourteen years, is guilty of an indictable offence and is liable to imprisonment for a term not exceeding ten years or is guilty of an offence punishable on summary conviction. [Amended from the age of 14 as of May 1, 2008]°

The *Criminal Code* also states that

> every person who is in a position of trust or authority towards a young person or is a person with whom the young person is in a relationship of dependency and who (a) for a sexual purpose, touches directly or indirectly, with a part of the body or with an object, any part of the body of the person, or (b) for a sexual purpose, invites, counsels or incites a young person to touch, directly or indirectly, with a part of the body or with an object, the body of any person, including the body of the person who so invites, counsels or incites and the body of the young person [16 years of age or more but under 18 years of age°], is guilty of an indictable offence and is liable to imprisonment for a term not exceeding five years or is guilty of an offence punishable on summary conviction.°

§ 150.1 CRIMINAL CODE OF CANADA, 1985

§ 153 CRIMINAL CODE OF CANADA, 1985

In addition to federal criminal laws against child sexual abuse and exploitation, each province and territory has its own laws to protect children against abuse, exploitation and neglect. The Ontario's *Education Act*° obliges the school board to take prompt steps to ensure that the person, employed as a teacher or temporary teacher and who has been charged with or convicted of an offence under the *Criminal Code* involving sexual conduct and minors, or of any other offence under the *Criminal Code* that in the opinion of the board indicates that pupils may be at risk, performs no duties in the classroom, no duties in an extended day program and no duties involving contact with pupils, pending withdrawal of the charge, discharge following a preliminary inquiry, stay of the charge or acquittal.

§ 170.1(12.1) EA

14.14.2 Consent

Consent is defined by the *Criminal Code* of Canada as the "voluntary agreement of the complainant to engage in the sexual activity in question. The legal age to give consent to engage in sexual activity is 16 years (it was raised from 14 years on May 1, 2008 by the *Tackling Violent Crime Act)*. The age of consent for sexual activity that exploits a young person is 18, when it involves prostitution, pornography or occurs in a relationship of authority, trust or dependency (e.g., where there is involvement with a teacher, coach, or babysitter). Sexual activity can also be considered exploitative based on the nature and circumstances of the relationship, e.g., the young person's age, the age difference between the young person and their partner, how the relationship developed (quickly, secretly, or over the Internet) and how the partner may have controlled or influenced the young person.°

retrieved May 2013 from http://www.justice.gc.ca/eng/rp-pr/other-autre/clp/faq.html

Sexual activity without consent is always a crime and children under 12 are never considered able to consent to sexual activity. It is not a defense to sexual crimes for the accused to say that he or she believed the young person was older; the accused must have taken all reasonable steps to ascertain the correct age. It is recognized, however, that adolescents, as part of their development, may engage in exploration of a sexual nature. Therefore, the Criminal Code provides "close in age" or "peer group" exceptions where sexual activity is not a crime provided both adolescents give consent. In cases where the alleged victim is 12 or older, but under 14, the defense that the victim consented to the sexual activity can be raised by the accused and accepted by the court if the accused is less than two years older than the victim. In cases where the alleged victim is 14 or older, but under the age of 16,° the defense that the victim consented to the sexual activity can be raised by the accused if the accused is less than five years older than the victim. These defenses are not available if the accused is in a position of trust or authority or it the victim is in a relationship of dependency with the accused.°

§ 150.1 CRIMINAL CODE OF CANADA, 1985

Wells, M. (1990), *Canada's law on child sexual abuse: A handbook*. Ottawa, ON: Department of Justice Canada

§ 153 CRIMINAL CODE OF CANADA, 1985

The *Criminal Code* also protects 16 and 17 year olds against sexual exploitation, where there is sexual activity within a relationship of trust, authority, dependency or where there is other exploitation.° Consideration of a relationship to be exploitation of the 16 or 17 year olds depends upon the nature and circumstances of the relationship (e.g., the age of the young person, the age difference between the young person and their partner, how the relationship developed and how the partner may have controlled or influenced the young person). Finally, 16 and 17 year olds cannot consent to sexual activity that involves prostitution or pornography.

14.14.3 Other Sexual Offenses Related to Child Sexual Abuse

Sections of the *Criminal Code* noted below have been abbreviated to provide educators and other persons in a position of trust or authority over a young person with a general understanding of the crime discussed (for specific details, please, see the sections of the Code).

§ 163.1 CRIMINAL CODE OF CANADA, 1985

- **Child Pornography**° – Every person who makes, distributes, transmits, makes available, accesses, sells, advertises, exports/ imports or possesss child pornography is guilty of an indictable offence. Child pornography is broadly defined and includes materials that show someone engaged in explicit sexual activity who is, or seems to be, under the age of 18 years; or show a young person's sexual organ or area for a sexual purpose. Child pornography also includes written and audio material that encourages others to commit a sexual offence against a child, or is primarily a description of unlawful sexual activity with a child that is intended for a sexual purpose.

§ 170 CRIMINAL CODE OF CANADA, 1985

- **Parent or Guardian Procuring Sexual Activity of Child**° – Every parent or guardian of a child under 18 who prevails upon or induces a child to become involved in an illegal sexual activity with any person (other than the parent or guardian, in which case other sections such as incest are used) is guilty of an indictable offence.

§ 171 CRIMINAL CODE OF CANADA, 1985

- **Householder Permitting Sexual Activity**° – An owner or manager of a premises (house, place of business, or even a single room) who knowingly permits a child under 18 to be in or on the premises for the purpose of engaging in an illegal activity is guilty of an indictable offence.

- **Exposing Genitals to a Child°** – Every person who exposes his or her genitals to a child under 16 for a sexual purpose is guilty of a summary offence.

§ 173 Criminal Code of Canada, 1985

- **Vagrancy°** – Everyone who has been convicted of sexual assault, one of the sexual touching offenses, bestiality or exposure involving a child and is found loitering in or near a playground, school, public park or bathing area is guilty of a summary offence.

§ 179(1)(b) Criminal Code of Canada, 1985

- **Living Off the Avails of Child Prostitution°** – Every person who lives wholly or in part off the profits of prostitution of a child under 18 is guilty of an indictable offence.

§ 212(2) Criminal Code of Canada, 1985

- **Attempting to Obtain the Sexual Services of a Child°** – Every person who obtains, or attempts to obtain for consideration (payment with drugs, cash or by provision of clothes or shelter) the sexual services of a young person under 18 is guilty of an indictable offence.

§ 212(4) Criminal Code of Canada, 1985

- **Corrupting Children°** – Endangering the morals of children under 18 or rendering home an unfit place for a child is an indictable offence. Proceedings under this section can only be initiated by the police or crown prosecutor with permission of the provincial or territorial Attorney General. A child protection agency can initiate child protection proceedings without such permission.

§ 172 Criminal Code of Canada, 1985

- **Sexual Assault°** – Applying force to another person, directly or indirectly, without consent and under circumstances of a sexual nature can be either an indictable or summary offence.

§ 271 Criminal Code of Canada, 1985

- **Sexual Assault with a Weapon, Threats to a Third party or Causing Bodily Harm°** – Committing sexual assault while carrying, using or threatening to use a weapon, or threatening, or causing bodily harm or being party to an offence with someone else is an indictable offence.

§ 272 Criminal Code of Canada, 1985

- **Aggravated Sexual Assault°** – Wounding, maiming, disfiguring or endangering the life of a victim while committing a sexual assault is an indictable offence with a maximum penalty of life imprisonment.

§ 273 Criminal Code of Canada, 1985

14.14.4 Kids Help Phone

School administrators may choose to add Kids Help Phone° to their school handbooks and other resource for students. Kids Help Phone provides a website and telephone service where children and youth can go to get 24-hour; bilingual and anonymous phone counseling, referral and Internet service. Every day, professional counselors provide immediate, caring support to young people in urban and rural communities across the country. Its Board of Directors is composed of community members with a variety of experiences.

retrieved May 2013 from http://www.kidshelpphone.ca/Teens/Home.aspx

INDEX